W9-DFH-476

NICHOLAS BLACK ELK

24 March 2012

I read most this book in Santa Fe while in New Mexico seeing March Madness basketball in Albuquerque.

This was a follow-up to "Black Elk Speaks" some years back and reconciles Black Elk's native religion to his later in life work as a catechist — just further revelations from God with the arrival of Christianity to the belief based on the Sacred Pipe.

Jim Brown
Boulder, CO

Nicholas Black Elk

Medicine Man, Missionary, Mystic

By Michael F. Steltenkamp

UNIVERSITY OF OKLAHOMA PRESS : NORMAN

Also by Michael F. Steltenkamp
*The Sacred Vision: Native American Religion and Its
Practice Today* (Mahwah, N.J., 1983)

Black Elk: Holy Man of the Oglala (Norman, Okla., 1993)

Library of Congress Cataloging-in-Publication Data

Steltenkamp, Michael F.
Nicholas Black Elk : medicine man, missionary, mystic / by Michael F.
Steltenkamp.
    p. cm.
    Includes bibliographical references and index.
    ISBN 978-0-8061-4063-6 (hardcover : alk. paper)   1. Black Elk,
1863–1950.   2. Oglala Indians—Biography.   3. Shamans—Great
Plains—Biography.   4. Missionaries—Great Plains—Biography.
5. Mystics—Great Plains—Biography.   6. Oglala Indians—Religion.
I. Title.
    E99.O3B539 2009
    978.004'9752440092—dc22
    [B]
                                                        2009000551

The paper in this book meets the guidelines for permanence and
durability of the Committee on Production Guidelines for Book
Longevity of the Council on Library Resources, Inc. ∞

1 2 3 4 5 6 7 8 9 10

To all who quest for Black Elk's good red road

Contents

Illustrations

Figures

Maps

Preface

Nebraska's gifted poet and author John Neihardt (1881–1973) met an Oglala Sioux elder and produced what he called the man's life story in 1932. Neihardt never could have imagined his work would become as immensely popular as it has. Since that time, many people from around the world have read *Black Elk Speaks*.

Referred to as a "bible of all tribes," the book is the best-known literary portrait of American Indian life (V. Deloria 2000, xiii). In it, Neihardt detailed the extended reminiscence of a wise, but discouraged, "holy-man." American professor of religious studies Joel W. Martin concluded that Black Elk's "romantic autobiography" had become "the preferred text of scholars and teachers." Being "the most influential book ever published on American Indian religion," it further served as a "canonical text for the study of religion" as a whole (Martin 2005).

Consisting largely of first-person accounts, *Black Elk Speaks* poetically communicates images of a nomadic life and virgin landscape that no longer exist. It portrays the heart-wrenching decline of a people who were forced to contend with massive social disruption brought by settlers to the West. An emotionally moving biography, it tells of destroyed tipis, extinguished campfires, slaughtered buffalo, and slain relatives. At the book's conclusion, the reservation system is in place and Black Elk laments the loss of his people's way of life.

Black Elk Speaks became the focus of seminars and conferences and appeared regularly on college syllabi. Especially riveting for readers was an often-quoted account of horror: a description of the Wounded Knee killing field of December 1890. The bloody snow left by this tragic event symbolized the end of a people's "beautiful dream." At the book's conclusion, the holy-man dejectedly confesses that he had "done nothing" to make the dream come true (J. Neihardt 1961, 279).

Neihardt portrays Black Elk going to Harney Peak in the Black Hills one last time in the hope of getting some sense of affirmation, saying that a rainfall will signify the supernatural assurance Black Elk seeks during this period of drought. The final scene is moving as a light rain begins to fall—its life-giving essence the descent of a sacred blessing. This concluding narrative is probably the book's most familiar passage and is unrelenting in its sympathy-eliciting depiction of Black Elk's pitiable state.

The holy-man was, however, not as dispirited or infirm as readers were led to believe. He lived another nineteen years after praying in the feeble voice attributed to him. Not until decades later did readers learn that Black Elk never offered the prayer that Neihardt described. The words were, rather, what Neihardt thought the holy-man *might* have uttered.

Joseph Epes Brown (1920–2000) reinforced Neihardt's image of the Lakota patriarch in *The Sacred Pipe: Black Elk's Account of the Seven Rites of the Oglala Sioux*. More focused than the life story, this later book presented the holy-man's recollection of certain ceremonies that were once a vital part of the Oglala Sioux religious world. Like its predecessor, *The Sacred Pipe* portrayed Black Elk as a special man who witnessed his people's religion vanish along with most everything else he held dear.

Black Elk's literary representation became important for the role it played on a cultural stage far removed from the holy-man's boyhood era. Portrayed as a religious philosopher, defeated warrior, wilderness ascetic, saddened elder, and Native ecologist, he crystallized into one person the different stereotypes related to Indian people of the pre- and post-reservation era. Both books experienced a rebirth in the 1970s and moved many people to reevaluate their worldview and way of life.

Neihardt and Brown presented a man whose early years were freedom-filled and satisfying. Presumably, Black Elk's twentieth-century life was stagnant by comparison, since neither book reported any information related to that period. This portrayal made the holy-man a symbol of all disenfranchised Indians and an American version of oppressed peoples worldwide.

Although they drew only a small audience when first published, *Black Elk Speaks* and *The Sacred Pipe* later generated widespread interest. Social unrest of the 1960s and 1970s moved many people to tap the wisdom contained within other cultural traditions. Tribal religions especially appealed to those who were in the forefront of a nascent environmental movement. Western culture, by contrast, was the benefactor of war, Agent Orange, broken nuclear reactors, pesticides, global warming, and other environment-killing initiatives. Many people were motivated to find a religious understanding of the universe that might render the planet more habitable. It seemed, Brown suggested in his 1971 preface, that Black Elk's worldview was where this understanding might reside.

Other Black Elk Literature

The early literature about Black Elk became popular enough that anthropologist William Powers titled an article (1990) "When Black Elk Speaks, Everybody Listens!" The one-time warrior-turned-philosopher enchanted a growing audience as Neihardt's work appeared in thirteen languages. By the year 2000, anthropologist Raymond Bucko could provide a bibliography for *The Black Elk Reader* that cited several hundred works associated with the man and his culture.

Black Elk had achieved revered status, but doubt had been raised concerning the reliability of *Black Elk Speaks*. Sally McCluskey's 1972 article pointedly stated in its title that "Black Elk Speaks: And So Does John Neihardt." Neihardt buttressed her assertion since he replaced the words "as told to" in his original title with the qualifier "as told through" (the author) in the 1961 edition.

Educators expressed concern about the extent to which *Black Elk Speaks* was used in high school and college courses. They questioned whether education was being served when students left classrooms with only the partial sense of Indian identity that the book's author conveyed (Arnold 1999). Black Elk strode from a hunter-gatherer existence into the nuclear age, but Neihardt and Brown only addressed the early period of his life.

Paul Steinmetz's *Pipe, Bible and Peyote* (1990) revealed that Neihardt and Brown did not show how significant a role Christianity played in Black Elk's thought. Raymond J. DeMallie's *The Sixth Grandfather* (1984) then corroborated Steinmetz's finding. Its primary contribution was an examination of Neihardt's stenographic notes. The work included more than a hundred pages of interview material that Neihardt collected when visiting Black Elk in 1944.

In 2008, *Black Elk Speaks* made national news when the director of the University of Nebraska Press assumed a new position at the State University of New York Press (Jaschik 2008). Nebraska had published the book for close to fifty years, but the Neihardt estate also severed ties with Nebraska, and joined SUNY Press and gave it publication rights. SUNY's edition featured a review of the literature on Black Elk and a new commentary by DeMallie (he concluded that Black Elk's life will remain a fertile topic). Since this version of Neihardt's classic indicates where *Black Elk Speaks* diverges from the poet's field notes, it should be considered the premier edition, eclipsing all others.

Contributing to the Black Elk Literature

I became acquainted with *Black Elk Speaks* and *The Sacred Pipe* while in college, and these books fanned my growing interest in Native cultures. They also stoked a desire to find Indian wisdom keepers who could reveal to me the ways that afforded them access to the sacred, or supernatural entity, whom Black Elk referred to as Wakan Tanka. Although raised a Catholic, I was moved to quest within the world of Indian religious practice. Black Elk's image cast appeal, so I visited Pine Ridge (the holy-man's reservation) and accepted a teaching position at the Red Cloud Indian School.

Before assuming the role, I undertook studies in American Indian culture. My goal was to develop a greater understanding of Indian ways so that I would be culturally sensitive to the students in my care. Arriving at Indiana University to begin grad school, I learned that Joseph Epes Brown was a visiting professor that year within the Religious Studies Department.

I enrolled in his course, Religious Traditions of the North American Indians, and had many conversations with him about Black Elk, Indian religion, and culture. His inscription in my copy of *The Sacred Pipe* was a source of inspiration. He wrote, referencing a ritual described in the book, "To my good friend and student, Mike, who is walking the good red road, and who will help his students to catch the Sacred Ball."

Once among the Sioux, I wanted to learn firsthand the religious wisdom they preserved from their old tradition. Before arriving at Pine Ridge, I had fantasized images of buffalo, battles, ancient elders, and sacred rites. Now that I was among Black Elk's people, those images gave way to school busses, classes, sporting events, young Lakota faces, and a plethora of other responsibilities related to dormitory life and teaching.

Although I wanted a sabbatical among Sioux elders, I was absorbed with the role of high school teacher. I introduced into the curriculum a two-semester, required course entitled Native American Studies, and it was within this context that the esteemed Lakota spiritual leader Frank Fools Crow, nephew of Black Elk, addressed my students. I also managed to meet and converse with Black Elk's son, Ben. Unfortunately, he died a short time later, but I felt privileged to be part of the choir at his funeral.

Weeks after Ben died, I broke from the classroom to breathe in the spring air. Joining an elderly woman on a bench in front of the school, I introduced myself and offered her a cigarette. Unexpectedly, intending only to take a short break, I there met Lucy Looks Twice, Black Elk's only surviving child. She consented to my request for a visit, and weeks later I again was seated with her. This time we were outside a log cabin that was once home to her famous father.

At some point in their relationship with Black Elk, Neihardt and Brown sensed they were part of a much grander project than they initially had devised. Given my accidental encounter with Brown and Lucy, I, too, wondered if something providential was at play. Meeting Lucy could have been considered a chance occurrence, but meeting Brown was just as unplanned—i.e., of all the universities I could have attended, I unknowingly chose the one at which he taught. These events were significant moments in my religious quest, and I was reminded of the observation that coincidence is God's way of remaining anonymous. Whatever the reason for why these events occurred the way they did, they led me to a deeper understanding of Black Elk and the spirituality that he internalized.

Although Neihardt's daughter Hilda (1916–2004) would later characterize me as a "writer" who visited Lucy one summer, the facts were otherwise (H. Neihardt 1995). I was someone Lucy came to call *takoja* (grandchild) until her death five years later in 1978. Our many visits and much correspondence during that period helped produce *Black Elk: Holy Man of the Oglala* (1993). It included Lucy's account of the religious legacy Black Elk bequeathed to his family and the reservation community as a whole. However, the content of her account was not what I had expected to hear or what I had planned to record.

Lucy, the only daughter born to Black Elk in two marriages, informed me that the books on her father were an incomplete portrait of his life and thought. They did not address what she considered to be the most important part of his life! Lucy surprised me when she reported that her father established strong ties with the Jesuit missionaries and that many Lakota from his generation became active lay missionaries themselves. In saying what she did, Lucy echoed what a priest reported when eulogizing her brother. The priest recalled Ben telling him that he would someday write "the last chapter of" *Black Elk Speaks*, and that it would address his father's work as a Catholic catechist. Ben reportedly said that this was "the most important chapter" of his father's life (Steinmetz 1990).

Lucy was disappointed to hear people repudiate this history and was vocal in stating how her father's stereotypical representation only as a medicine man conflicted with her memories of family life. Along with elders and extended family members, she told of her father's close relationship with priests, his dedicated work as a "catechist," his powerful preaching on scriptural passages, and his zealous devotion to the rosary prayers and Mass. I was more interested in, and wanted to learn about, ancient rites, buffalo hunts, traditional Lakota lifeways, and cavalry skirmishes. However, Lucy said that he rarely spoke about these things since his work for the church absorbed his attention and was all-important and time-consuming. Because she wanted people to know about his life as a catechist, I became the biographer for his life in the twentieth century.

Black Elk: Holy Man of the Oglala became a kind of appendix to Neihardt's book—the final chapter that Ben referred to, and that Lucy also hoped would be written. It brought into the discussion family members and friends of Black Elk who witnessed, and participated in, many of the events and concerns that composed his life. Ultimately, readers learned that most of Black Elk's story went unreported by Neihardt and Brown.

Holy Man also brought to the fore Black Elk's extensive involvement in church work. It showed how this otherwise stereotypically presented Plains Indian medicine man assumed a Christian identity, and how this was the religious legacy for which he was most remembered within his reservation community. When appended to *Black Elk Speaks* (combined with *The Sixth Grandfather*) and *The Sacred Pipe*, *Holy Man* became a companion volume that completed a trilogy of portraits.

It was after learning of Black Elk's fuller story that I became a Jesuit priest. Because authorial bias had been raised as a concern relative to Black Elk material, I anticipated readers of *Holy Man* possibly assuming that the priesthood colored my thinking or unduly influenced what I reported about Black Elk's life and thought. I wanted to avoid this pitfall, so I strove to make certain that the defining voices of his biography were Lakota. His daughter entrusted me with the task of making his full story known, so I read to Lucy my account of what she provided. I was satisfied that my mission was accomplished when she bestowed her blessing upon the transcript, and also upon me, her takoja.

I originally had set out to discover and benefit from knowledge of the Sacred that Lakota tradition preserved. En route to this goal, I unexpectedly learned about Black Elk's life, which previously had not been fully told. As it turned out, instead of me projecting a bias onto Black Elk's experience, I simply recounted what was reported to me by those who knew him best. In the end, it was not I who colored his portrait, but rather the holy-man's example that influenced my vocational decision.

Black Elk in Historical Perspective

Black Elk's life has been an important source of information to his people, historians, anthropologists, and the reading public at large because it sheds light on the pre- and post-reservation period. His story is neither just about the old days nor the modern era. Born when his people hunted buffalo and dwelled in tipis, Black Elk also traveled throughout the United States and Europe.

Raised a horseman, he lived to ride in cars and on a motorcycle. The man who had taken scalps as a youth later greeted young Lakota soldiers returning from a war that included carnage wrought by A-bombs. As a result, his life is an intimate glimpse, or microcosm, of what transpired among his people during very different eras.

Religious Questing

Black Elk's religious practice, however, has drawn most attention and stirred most debate. When readers learned of his Christian identity, a growing body of literature addressed to what extent his involvement in the church was sincere and enduring. If he was a devout Catholic for some period of time, perhaps he reverted to a pre-Christian practice at the end of his life. These concerns stoked scholarly interest in matters of sociology, but other readers were drawn to Black Elk because they associated his religious grounding with what enabled him to survive. He offered a lifeline to those who sought the strength of conviction he seemed to possess.

This focus on Black Elk's religion resonated with an observation made by John Collier, a former commissioner of Indian Affairs (whose book Brown used in classes he taught). Collier claimed that Indians had "what the world has lost." Presumably, within people like Black Elk was something that Collier said "the world must have again, lest it die" (Collier 1947, 7). It was this religious strength the holy-man embodied that seemed to account for his more general appeal.

Black Elk became a provocative topic since he represented a variety of Native identities—dejected traditionalist, ecological prophet, wise shaman, pious Christian, oppressed Native—all of which seemed plausible depending on which commentary one read. Writers extolled these identities in books and articles. Over time, readers sought to personalize practices or internalize sentiments that arose from the sphere they thought he occupied.

The chapters that follow distill into one volume what is known of the special elder whose life has been instrumental in guiding others. The pages condense primary works on Black Elk, include material not published elsewhere (or that is difficult to find), and flesh out historical events and topics that may be vague for some readers. For the first time, a full portrait of Black Elk's life is accessible in one volume. The note on sources section at the end of the text indicates literature that served as a resource, which can be consulted for more in-depth coverage. Black Elk quotations (and those of his daughter, Lucy) in this book come from the primary sources of Brown, DeMallie, John Neihardt, and Steltenkamp.

All of what Black Elk spoke remains a compelling story, not just for academics or people on Black Elk's reservation, but for people of all backgrounds and at all points of the compass. By publishing this biography, the University of Oklahoma Press has produced a volume that might motivate the uninitiated to rediscover the primary works. New readers can now benefit from learning about the rich cultural tradition of the Lakota and one of their special representatives, Nicholas Black Elk, a medicine man, missionary, and mystic holy-man of the Oglala.

Acknowledgments

In shepherding this manuscript to completion, I am indebted to editors Alessandra J. Tamulevich and Emily Jerman of the University of Oklahoma Press and the Jesuit community of Loyola University in Chicago. Revisions benefitted from the counsel of Jesuits Raymond Bucko, Guy Consalmagno, Carl Starkloff, and Paul Steinmetz. Research assistance also was provided by Steve Alexander; James Ashton, Ph.D.; Daniel Caron; Dominic DeFilippis, Ph.D.; William Emerson; Thomas Foley; Mark Gabel, Ph.D.; Bruce Howard; Karl Markus Kreis, Ph.D.; Daniel Molter; and Mark Swiger. Special thanks are in order for Mark Thiel of Marquette University and Trappists Jean-Yves Ricordeau and Armand Veilleux of Scourmont Abbey in France.

Editorial assistance was provided by Janet Boyle; Margie Cooke; Damien Costello; Angela Martin; MaryAnn Sonntag; and Charles J. Steltenkamp, Ph.D. Special thanks also go to Minnie Carey and her daughter, Sarah McIlvaine. Minnie was the last surviving child of a Little Bighorn participant (trooper Henry Mechling). As elderly children of the event's Lakota participants had done, Minnie put a human face on that page in history.

Most of all, I am grateful to Black Elk's daughter, Lucy Looks Twice; George Looks Twice; Pat Red Elk; and friends of the holyman whose warmth and wisdom indelibly branded my mind and heart.

NICHOLAS BLACK ELK

CHAPTER 1

Cultural Background

For many years, the only known photograph of Lakota spiritual leader Nicholas Black Elk was one that appeared in *The Sacred Pipe* (1953). Joseph Epes Brown, the book's author, took the photograph two years before the holy-man's death in 1950. It showed an elderly patriarch, garbed in nineteenth-century Indian buckskin, holding the stem of a two-foot-long smoking pipe. With a short haircut and receding hairline, Black Elk reflectively stared into the camera. His was a visage that immediately told of one who had seen much suffering and no doubt had much to say about what he had witnessed. Brown's photograph stereotyped Black Elk as a wisdom keeper of very advanced age and as a grandfather figure to a twentieth-century reservation.

John Neihardt took many photographs when he interviewed Black Elk in 1931, but he allowed readers only to imagine the holy-man's appearance. No shots were included in his 1932 book, *Black Elk Speaks*, until a half century after its initial publication. *Black Elk Speaks* was subtitled a "life story," but it was actually a partial biography with embellished details. It told the story of a much younger man—who grew up in a tipi on the plains, who hunted buffalo and scalped enemies—than was pictured in Brown's photograph.

In not covering Black Elk's life after 1890, Neihardt did not report everything that the holy-man said during his interview. Black Elk also discussed aspects of his people's history and culture. This context, and much more that he shared, is key to understanding the boy who became the venerated elder of Brown's well-known photograph.

The Sioux

By the mid-1800s, "Sioux" had been the popular term applied to Black Elk's people, but they called themselves Lakota, which was the preferred term as the twentieth century came to an end.[1] These people made up an Indian culture popularly described as a buffalo-hunting, tipi-dwelling warrior society. In the twentieth century, motion pictures often portrayed the Lakota fighting the cavalry, attacking wagon trains, and being the scourge of settlers moving west. Contrasting with these images, Black Elk and his story—as told by Neihardt and Brown—put a human face on the Lakota people and, to some extent, remythologized their identity. Neihardt and Brown tapped the pulse of a person whose humanity came to life for readers.

Black Elk's western Lakota were related to other branches of their nation whose dialects and economies differed slightly. At the time of his birth in the 1860s, his people occupied territory that stretched from Minnesota to Montana, and included North and South Dakota, Wyoming, and Nebraska. One set of relatives was the Dakota, who lived northeast of the Lakota. Another branch was the Nakota, who occupied land between these two groups. (In older collections, "Dakota" often is used, inaccurately, when identifying photographs of people from all of these divisions.)

Over time, and without negative connotation, the people all began referring to themselves by the generic name, Sioux. They also used the terms "Lakota," "Nakota," and "Dakota." These were names for their regional dialects and were associated with a word meaning "ally." Since explorers often first learned of tribal groups from enemies who fought them, the newcomers labeled these groups with the "foreign" names that their enemies bestowed. Only in the late twentieth century have Indian nations reclaimed the names that originally identified their people (e.g., just as the western "Sioux" prefer now to speak of themselves as "Lakota," the "Chippewa" call themselves "Anishnabé," the "Crow" are "Apsáalooke," and the "Navajo" are "Diné," etc.).

When referring to the settlers who encroached upon the Sioux, Neihardt introduced readers to a word he transcribed as "wasichu" (wah-she'-chew). This was the Lakota term long applied to white people, but it did not refer to color. Black Elk translated the word for Neihardt to mean simply that "they are many." The holy-man also said that the term formerly referred "to buffalo in very large numbers" (DeMallie 1984a, 151). Other etymologies make the word's origin difficult to ascertain—not unlike the origins of the Lakota themselves.

Origins

As with all Native peoples in North America, the Lakota genesis is shrouded in a distant past. One oral tradition tells of a subterranean existence, from which the people eventually emerged through Wind Cave in the Black Hills of South Dakota. Their leader sacrificed his life on their behalf by being transformed into a buffalo. Henceforward, this special four-legged creature played a central role in the Lakota's life.

Black Elk told Neihardt that all Indian nations came from an ocean to the south. According to the holy-man, one group, led by High Hollow Horn, went east. Another, led by Slow Buffalo, traveled to the west, and the group that eventually became the Lakota moved north. Contrary to what researchers have concluded, Black Elk believed "the Sioux were the first Indians" and that, originally, "everyone talked Sioux" (DeMallie 1984a, 333). Over time, he claimed, different languages developed after this exodus from the south.

Anthropologists have looked elsewhere for a Lakota origin. While it was once thought that the people's occupation of the plains was an ancient one, the consensus of scholars now points to a woodland beginning.

The Nation as a Whole

Woodland groups often referred to their affiliation with one another by the term "council fires," and Black Elk's people employed this same term.[2] Representing an ethnic identity more than a political alliance, the phrase "Seven Council Fires" referred to four groups of Dakota—the Wahpekute (Shooters among Leaves), Mdewakantonwan (Spirit Lake People), Wahpetonwan (Dwellers among Leaves), and Sisitonwan (People of the Swamp); two Nakota groups—the Ihanktonwan (Campers at the End) and Ihankton-wanna (Little Campers at the End); and a seventh group, the Teton Lakota, who were Black Elk's people. The Seven Council Fires, however, was not an inflexible construct, since the Assiniboines (Cook with Stones) associated, relative-like, as a Nakota-speaking people. This three-part division—Dakota, Nakota, Lakota—describes a kind of national portrait of Black Elk's people that is not mentioned in the earliest accounts that simply distinguished between eastern and western Sioux.

Like the nation's grouping into council fires, the Lakota also consisted of seven groups, with Black Elk belonging to the Oglala (Scatter Their Own) division. Located in southwestern South Dakota, the Oglala reservation, Pine Ridge, is the second largest in the United States. It was officially created out of the Great Sioux Reservation in 1889, along with the Standing Rock, Cheyenne River, Rosebud, and Lower Brule reservations. The Oglala's Lakota neighbors to the east on the Rosebud Reservation are the Sicangu peoples, who were formerly referred to in literature by their French name Brulé, meaning "burnt thigh people."

Also Lakota, the Hunkpapa (Entrance), Miniconju (Planters by the Water), and Oohenunpa (Two Kettles) peoples occupy reservations elsewhere. A sixth set of Lakota, the Sihasapa, is referred to in literature as the Black Feet, but this group should not be confused with the Blackfoot tribe of Montana and Alberta, Canada. The seventh group of Lakota is the Itazipacola. As with the Sicangu, the Itazipacola are often known by their French name, Sans Arc, which means "no bows." Each of these groups consists of smaller social units, or bands, which, in turn, include extended families.

Tradition and Innovation

Historically, Lakota lifeways fostered independence and creative self-expression that benefited the community. Thus, each person could make a special contribution to the nation's self-preservation. Repeatedly surfacing in Black Elk's life, however, is the hard fact that tradition to people in one era was considered innovation to those in an earlier period. This has been true for cultures everywhere, and the Lakota experience was no exception.

During their exodus from the woodlands to the plains—which ethnohistorians conclude took place in the early to mid-eighteenth century—the people confronted new challenges that required adaptation based on expedience instead of reliance on tradition alone (the best-selling 1979 novel *Hanta Yo* strove to tell this story and stirred as much interest as it did controversy when turned into a 1984 made-for-television movie). Especially when confronting a wholly different culture in the historic period, standards from the past were not always helpful. Consequently, innovative behavior was a necessity. However, camp police kept people in check by commanding strict obedience, sometimes brutally, when on the move. At other times, noncoercive leadership reinforced one's sense of independence.

While the stereotype is otherwise, the period before contact with settlers was not stress-free or timeless for Plains Indian cultures. Rather, these groups, which arose in the relatively recent past, faced many challenges (Lehmer 1977, 25–43). According to Black Elk, the quest for food was a constant in the world of his youth. Dogs were second to buffalo as a source of meat and also served as the people's traditional "beast of burden,"[3] carrying belongings from one campsite to the next. Even in less stressful times, the Lakota quest for food was a challenging one.

Eating took place twice a day, in the morning and evening. Black Elk once remarked, "I never heard anyone say it was time to eat at noon" (DeMallie 1984a, 386). When visiting another family, people would usually be fed there, and such sharing was the earmark of a virtuous host. The Lakota never presumed they would find sustenance, so prayers of gratitude always preceded eating. Joseph Epes Brown recounted watching Black Elk observe this custom at an unlikely diner in Denver. The holy-man's praying drew the respectful attention of everyone present.

Adaptation was necessary for survival, and this strategy of adjusting to one's circumstances is what people like Black Elk preserved. As the Lakota adapted to different circumstances in order to survive, their lifeways changed over time, not only in terms of shifting their home from the woodlands to the plains but also in terms of warrior traditions and dependence on dogs and later horses. Black Elk's life later revealed that Lakota theological discourse did the same.

Lakota Lifeways

The serious business of group survival was probably the origin of a warrior tradition that became a way of life in the 1700s as the nation gained a foothold on the plains. Black Elk admitted, "We did not fight for our lands" (DeMallie 1984a, 314). Rather, he said, "enemies" were people "whose language we did not understand" (friends of the Lakota—the Cheyenne and Arapaho—were an exception to this rule).

"Counting coup" on opponents became a normative expectation that all men of fighting age eagerly sought to meet. It consisted of touching an enemy in battle or after he had been slain. Shooting someone from a distance was honorable, but Black Elk told Neihardt that another Lakota should have the second honor of touching the fallen foe. Still another should do the scalping. Contrary to popular belief, archaeological evidence shows scalping to have been a custom in Native North America prior to European contact, although there has been advocacy for seeing scalping as a European import and not a tradition.

Several works have called attention to and reinforced the idea of the warrior lifestyle that historically defined the Lakota world and brought status to individuals. Royal B. Hassrick's seminal work describing Lakota culture, *The Sioux: Life and Customs of a Warrior Society*, is a rich ethnography that describes how the people lived. However, this book's title might leave readers with the false impression that these high-plains folk preferred militancy to living in peace. Another classic study, *Warriors Without Weapons*, argued on behalf of a debatable thesis: namely, since men were no longer able to conduct raids in the twentieth century as they had in the past, they lost a premier life pursuit that previously had brought them honor.

By stressing the people's traditional "militancy," these studies conveyed an impression that the Lakota were somehow genetically bellicose or prone to desiring warfare as a way of life. As a result, Black Elk's people were misrepresented, not just in popular culture but in academic works, as an inherently hostile nation. In reality, war exploits brought prestige to an individual but were part of a larger survival strategy. Overall, the warrior tradition was a preemptive lifestyle that arose for the purpose of self-preservation.

Neihardt and Brown purposely chose to de-emphasize this aspect of the culture. By doing so, they provided the compelling worldview of a people whose warmth and wisdom were far more transparent than their desire to fight. The writers' portrayal of the Lakota was quite different from the one-dimensional warrior stereotype that arose in the late nineteenth century.

Dogs, Horses, and the Origin of Warfare

While not historically accurate in every detail, Black Elk's folk history rightly showed that Lakota lifeways changed over time. Without elaboration from Neihardt, Black Elk associated the warpath with Indian peoples who originally migrated westward. He said that these people became numerous and quarrelsome, and he attributed warfare to his people's acquisition of horses from the Cheyenne. Horses contributed to key changes in his people's way of life.

Indian nations did not have horses in prehistoric times. The Spanish introduced them to the Southwest before Black Elk's people eventually acquired them. They replaced dogs—which Black Elk told Neihardt originated as wolf pups domesticated by a legendary figure known as Moves Walking—as the people's beast of burden. With lodge poles attached to their backs (a device known as the "travois"), horses could drag larger burdens. Far more powerful than the dog (*sunka*), the horse had unequalled speed and utility. It earned the name *sunka-wakan*. *Wakan* usually translates as "sacred," but implies mystery, awe, and wonder. By 1680, Lakota culture accommodated this "sacred dog" to such an extent that the people came to rely on it for hunting and transportation. "Wakan" was also added to the Lakota word for "water" (*mni*) when liquor was introduced to the people. It became "*mni-wakan*" or "sacred water" because it produced behaviors and visions that were out of the ordinary and difficult to explain (Steltenkamp 2005).

The Buffalo in Lakota Culture

Although horses were crucial to the Lakota for hunting, no animal they hunted was so key to their shifting way of life when they moved to the plains as the buffalo. Coming onto the plains introduced the Lakota to vast herds of bison, and Black Elk told Neihardt that the "Thunder-beings" (thunder and lightning) gave the "two-leggeds" (humans) the right to hunt "four-leggeds" (animals with four legs). A man named Red Thunder won a race with all the four-leggeds and received a bow and arrow with which his people could hunt. Had the outcome been different, buffalo would have had the right to hunt and eat people![4]

Black Elk said that Red Thunder performed his exploits at a time when the four-leggeds were not wild, so hunting was much easier. Red Thunder made a wooden arrow, and his first kill was a beaver. He had a vision that showed him an arrow with a stone point on it, so he applied flint to the arrow and with it killed a deer. Letting the sun dry the deer meat, he produced the first jerky (DeMallie 1984a, 309).

Red Thunder's people then began hunting buffalo, and ever since that long-ago time, this creature and the Lakota have been inseparable. It is not surprising that when the term "vanishing American" came to be applied to all Native peoples at the end of the nineteenth century, the buffalo shared the same unwanted distinction. The animal's existence paralleled theirs.

The Sacred

Just as buffalo underscored the Lakota's entire way of life on the plains, so did the people's understanding of "the Sacred." Both coursed through every aspect of their existence. Throughout Black

Elk material, the phrase "Wakan Tanka" appears in translation as "Great Spirit." Monotheism, or the belief in one all-powerful deity, is associated with its usage (the Algonquian phrase "Kitchi Manitou" similarly appears in literature in reference to beliefs of peoples of the Great Lakes).

Many people assume that the words Wakan Tanka are a traditional Lakota reference to an all-powerful creator figure, interchangeable with "god," "Great Spirit," or "the Creator." Ethnohistorians have argued that this monotheistic conception of deity arose in the historic period. Previously, however, when *wakan* (sacred, the mysterious) was combined with *tanka* (great), the phrase referred to the totality of the spirit world, its incomprehensibility, and its mysterious, wondrous power. Over time, however, Lakota prayers that were in English simply came to invoke the Great Spirit, which connoted monotheism. Black Elk's spirituality reflects this shift.

Implicitly in Neihardt and explicitly in Brown, the notion of a monotheistic deity was identified as the Lakota cultural tradition. However, Raymond J. DeMallie observed that *"Wakan Tanka* traditionally was a collective concept, embodying various *wakan* beings in many different aspects" (DeMallie 1984a, 81). It was during the historic period that Wakan Tanka was transformed into an all-powerful, personalized creator figure. Neihardt's material from his interview referenced Black Elk using the terms "Great Spirit," "Mysterious One" and "One Above" as synonymous with Wakan Tanka. In his work with the holy-man, Joseph Epes Brown understood that the prayerful invocation of Tunkashila Wakan Tanka (Grandfather, Great Spirit) was "identical to the Christian god" (Brown 1953, 5n). Part of Black Elk's legacy is the now widespread association of Wakan Tanka with one god.

In Lakota culture, individuals humbly petitioned the mysterious, awesome reality that their tradition long ago named Wakan Tanka. This reverential phrase referred to the inexplicable mystery that sustained all creation. Use of the term "supernatural" to explain this mystery is tenuous because wakan realities were so evident in the natural order. No neat separation existed between religion and the rest of Lakota daily life.

Daily Life and Spirituality

From the historic period into the present, Lakota daily life struck a balance between perspectives based on the individual and the community. The people gathered in large numbers only during special times in the summer season. At the everyday level of interaction, family members composed camp life, and Black Elk's worldview was formed within this setting. However, these groups were interdependent and strove to create familial ties throughout the Lakota universe.

Organizational belonging also fostered a sense of relatedness. People joined what researchers have referred to as "sodalities" or "societies," and these organizations were based on gender, age, common interest, or a specialization of some kind (e.g., handicraft maker, dancer, warrior, healer, etc.). Participation in these organizations produced camaraderie between members that was often expressed in kinship terms.

Lakota relationships were not always based on genetics, but people were required to behave as if they were. Black Elk's generation commonly referred to male age-mates as brothers or cousins, and elders by kin terms such as uncle, aunt, grandmother, and grandfather. "Making relatives," or establishing kinship relations, was even a sacred ceremony that made relatives of people who were not related by blood or marriage. Militancy, marriage, and all modes of subsistence ultimately had the common goal of realizing a prayerful phrase often quoted from the Black Elk literature. Behavior was oriented so that "the people may live" (Brown 1953, 137). One's larger community was one's larger family, and this fostered an affective bonding and esprit de corps that made self-defense a familial, or a more intimately communal, undertaking.

This communitarian focus was reflected in and central to the holy-man's adult spirituality. It was not, however, the primary theme found in earlier Lakota prayer traditions. Physician James R. Walker's turn-of-the-century interviews with Lakota people noted that the more common emphases in prayers were on acquiring personal power and success in war. By the time Brown interviewed Black Elk in 1947 and 1948, the holy-man innovatively had integrated or associated social concern for his nation's strength with the individual's quest for merit.

This connection between the two is evident when considering the Lakota's prayerful utterance *mitak oyasin*. Although absent from the Black Elk literature, it became commonly employed in the late twentieth century. Translated literally as "all my relatives," the phrase's focus seems narrow, concentrated solely on the petitioner's kin. However, "all are relatives," a more universal variation of the literal translation, is also said in ritual contexts. In this latter form, Black Elk's sense of kinship with all people—an adaptation of his own as time passed—might well have inspired this usage, given his influence on late twentieth-century practitioners.

CHAPTER 2

Childhood

In midsummer of 1866, Black Elk's mother went into labor along a Wyoming riverbank. Her son's birth was then recorded in the minds and hearts of his people, and nowhere else. The exact date and year of his entry into the world would be debated in the century to come.

Traditionally, the Lakota kept numerical track of years with notched sticks, which were in the possession of male elders. However, few of these sticks have been preserved. The people also recorded events through oral tradition and a device known as the "winter count." Winter counts, many of which still exist, consist of pictographs that were sketched on buffalo hides by historian-like members of the community. The Lakota phrase for these *waniyetu wowapi* (winters they draw or winter depictions) derives from *waniyetu yawapi*, meaning "winters they count."

Winter counts recorded one significant event that occurred each year. They served as a memory aid for recalling what happened to the people over long periods of time. A winter count year covered two calendar years because it extended from one winter—one first snow—to the next. Neihardt cited a winter count that said Black Elk was born in a year when "four Crows were killed" (De-Mallie 1984a, 101).

Black Elk's mother told him that he was born on the Little Powder River in Wyoming in what she said was "the moon when the chokecherries are ripe." Black Elk named the months for Neihardt, although variations of these names exist.⑮

Lakota months

January	Moon of frost in the tipi
February	Moon of the dark red calf
March	Moon of the snow-blind
April	Moon of red grass appearing
May	Moon when the ponies shed
June	Moon of the blooming turnip
July	Moon of red cherries
August	Moon of black cherries
September	Moon of the black calf
October	Moon of changing seasons
November	Moon of falling leaves
December	Moon of popping trees

Based on his mother's account, Black Elk was born in July, the moon of red cherries or ripe chokecherries.

Birth Discrepancies

Both the year and month of Black Elk's birth have been matters of debate. According to Neihardt's notes, Black Elk was seventy-two years old in 1931, but the poet's book reported that the holy-man was born in 1863 (thus he would have been sixty-eight and not seventy-two). This 1863 birth year is in accord with the Pine Ridge census of 1900, which recorded that Black Elk was thirty-seven years old. However, Joseph Epes Brown said the holy-man was born in 1862.

Meanwhile, Black Elk's gravestone reports his birth year as 1858, while historian David Humphreys Miller suggested an even earlier year (1957, 185). Bud Duhamel—a Rapid City, South Dakota, businessman and friend of Black Elk—understood his birth year to be later than all the others (1866), which is in agreement with what the holy-man's daughter, Lucy, believed. Addressing the matter with her father in 1950, the summer he died, she concluded he was eighty-four years of age. Similarly, the archives at Holy Rosary Mission on the Pine Ridge Reservation indicate 1865 as his birth year.

Despite records suggesting Black Elk was born in the 1850s or 1860s, religion and mythology scholar Joseph Campbell said Black Elk was "over ninety" years of age in 1931.② Campbell's assumption is understandable because Neihardt and Brown made it *seem* Black Elk's wisdom was from a time beyond memory. A very advanced age could be equated with his owning knowledge that was lost to the modern era. Dating problems are also compounded by Neihardt's stenographic notes that record Black Elk remembering events that would have occurred when he was an infant or very young child. He claimed to recall the Wagon Box Fight between the Lakota and U.S. Army that took place on August 2, 1867, and the death of a man named Hump in 1870. Perhaps he learned about these events from others.

To further complicate matters, while Black Elk's physical birth occurred in July, Neihardt thought that the holy-man was born in December (the moon of popping trees). However, Neihardt was not aware of the theology, or religious piety, that lay behind Black Elk's claim of being born then. Early Christian converts would say they were "reborn" at their baptism, and Black Elk said the same thing about himself. The holy-man was baptized a Catholic on December 6, 1904, and ever after used this as the month and day of his birth. Assuming a new name because of this significant event, he was henceforward known as Nicholas William Black Elk. "Nicholas" was chosen because December 6 was the feast day of Saint Nicholas, the real person behind the legend of Santa Claus. After Black Elk's baptism, people addressed him as "Nick." This was the name they used when referring to him throughout his life, and years after his death.

Red Cloud's War

While the Civil War occupied everyone's attention in the East around the time of Black Elk's birth, the intrusion of numerous Americans upon Indian land in the West created friction throughout the plains. The reason for this was obvious to the Jesuit priest-explorer and nineteenth-century frontier figure Pierre DeSmet (1801–73). He told Washington that the Lakota felt violated because of the "incessant provocations and injustices on the part of the whites."⁵ He further observed, "When the savages raise the hatchet to go on the warpath, it is because they are pushed to the limit of endurance, and then the blows that they deal are hard, cruel and terrible. . . . It is always true that if the savages sin against the whites it is because the whites have greatly sinned against them" (Killoren 1994).

These were the prevailing thoughts and behaviors when Black Elk was born within Big Road's Oglala band somewhere on the Little Powder River in present-day Wyoming. In this region, military posts (Forts Philip Kearny, Reno, and C. F. Smith) situated along the Bozeman Trail saw wagon trains bring waves of miners and immigrants into Lakota country. DeSmet noted that travelers sullied the landscape by leaving refuse in their wake. The arrival of these people made Black Elk's father "an inveterate hater of the encroaching whites," according to historian Eli Ricker's interview of part-Lakota interpreter William Garnett. The holy-man's father "possessed the same type of spirit as Crazy Horse" (1840–77), with whose father he was a cousin (Jensen 2005, 60).

Responding to the encroachment, Red Cloud (1822–1909), a Lakota, became prominent at this time for his effort to rid his people's territory of the Americans and their military. During a December 21, 1866, incident in Montana that history books call the Fetterman Massacre and Lakota oral tradition refers to as the Battle of the Hundred Slain—probably the most significant incident in Red Cloud's War (1866–68)—Black Elk's father was wounded in the leg and became "a partial cripple for life" (Jensen 2005, 60). The resistance Red Cloud led ultimately made Washington withdraw from the region. Only after troops abandoned the forts did Red Cloud and others sign the Fort Laramie Treaty on November 6, 1868. This stressful period served as the social incubator of Black Elk's infancy and early childhood. The conflicts spawned at the time created a legacy of strife that later generations inherited.

Provisions of the Fort Laramie Treaty required all the Lakota bands to occupy "the Great Sioux Reservation." This large tract of land included the state of South Dakota that was west of the Missouri River and what eventually became Boyd County, Nebraska. Lakota bands also could continue to hunt in the Powder River region of Wyoming. This region was declared "unceded" territory along with the Sand Hills and panhandle of Nebraska. Compensation for what the Lakota relinquished in terms of land area later became a source of dispute. The treaty said that the Lakota would receive clothing, schools, food, and enough provisions to meet their needs over a four-year period. Washington claimed that this was the length of time it would take them to become self-sufficient by means of agriculture and ranching. However, the area eventually assigned to Black Elk's people had few buffalo (upon which they traditionally relied), relatively little game, and was practically not arable.

Critical of those who took advantage of Indians, Pine Ridge agent Col. H. D. Gallagher tellingly addressed the issue of land cessions that resulted from the treaty in 1890. While Indian agents often are charged with having a penchant for self-aggrandizement and being insensitive toward their wards, Gallagher did not match this stereotype. In his final report before he was replaced by a political appointee (whose tenure in the role was disastrous), Gallagher wrote:

> I am well aware that [dealing justly with Indians] is objected to by land speculators and others who have no sympathy for the Indians, who think it no crime to do them the greatest wrong, and would be willing to see the last one of them perish if such a thing could be turned into profit by them. But is it right that the government should be influenced by such men in its dealings with these people? I hope for humanity's sake that the time is not far distant when the interest of the Indian will be considered of paramount importance to the wishes of any unscrupulous politician or professional land-grabber. (Gallagher 1890, 53)

Gallagher also condemned the too common occurrence of provisions arriving at the agency in less quantity than promised.

When the General Allotment Act (also called the Dawes Act) of 1887 further reduced the size of the Lakota homeland in 1889, groups of Black Elk's people were made to locate on scattered reservation parcels that lay within the immense territory they once occupied. The Lakota had accepted the firearms, ammunition, knives, axes, blankets, food, and other goods that were offered to them by governmental negotiators, but they did not understand that the treaty would require them to forfeit living in Nebraska and Wyoming. Only when pressure was exerted on the Lakota to move toward the Missouri River to the east did they learn otherwise.

Many delegates to the treaty council later claimed that the conditions were not explained to them. It was their understanding that the treaty simply reestablished peace and trade. Ceding all of this territory, especially the Black Hills, was inconceivable. A century later, in 1980, Washington decided in favor of Lakota descendants and offered a financial settlement for the loss of their land. The settlement eventually was rejected, and the different Lakota groups instead asked that the Black Hills be returned to them. The issue continued to smolder in litigation, having been forged during Black Elk's childhood.

Black Elk's Family

Young Black Elk knew that his name was on his father's side for at least three generations before his birth. He did not know his great-grandfather, and all that he knew of his grandfather is that he was killed by the Pawnee. These men and Black Elk's father all went by the Black Elk name and were known to be healers. The holy-man's maternal grandmother was Plenty Eagle Feathers, while Neihardt referred to Black Elk's mother as "White Cow Sees." The holy-man's daughter understood this name as perhaps her grandmother's childhood name because "Leggings Down" was the name she carried as a woman. (Neihardt might have avoided using "Leggings Down" because it would have been suggestive and distracting.) The Holy Rosary Mission archives reported that "Mary" Leggings Down was born in 1844.

The only known photograph of Black Elk's mother, Mary Leggings Down, depicts her tending her granddaughter Lucy circa 1909. Steltenkamp collection.

Black Elk's mother was married for a while to Good Thunder, a brother of Black Elk's father. This arrangement was probably an example of what anthropologists refer to as the "levirate" rule. This "rule," found globally, refers to the social obligation of a man to "marry"—the equivalent of supporting and caring for—the wife of his deceased brother, even if he already has a wife (or wives).

Black Elk also had an older brother, Runs In The Center. Years after his brother's death, Black Elk honored his memory. Family members recalled seeing him go to a hill near his cabin and pray in emotional remembrance of his sibling. Black Elk only made passing reference to Runs In The Center during interviews, but his late-in-life prayer revealed a bond that apparently was strong.

Black Elk also was close to his mother's father, Keeps His Tipi, a beloved grandfather who gave him a bow and arrows. Armed this way, he undertook his first hunt and proudly brought home a slain frog. *Black Elk Speaks* reported that this deed prompted the young hunter to cry, but it was actually on another occasion that tears flowed. Black Elk was hunting antelope with his father and the senior Black Elk somehow managed to kill four of the animals with just two shots. Only a young boy at the time, Black Elk ate the kidneys and liver while his father butchered the animals. After getting his fill, the young Black Elk was overcome with regret that they had killed the antelope and asked his father to make a prayerful offering on their behalf. Taught to address prayer to "Grandfather, Great Spirit," Black Elk learned at a young age that when taking the life of another creature, he should ask "Tunkashila, Wakan Tanka" to bless his people with abundant life.

This perspective flowed throughout the young Lakota's daily activities. When fishing, Black Elk and his playmates would kiss the fish they caught. In throwing smaller ones back in the water, they hoped their kindness would inspire the little fish to "tell the bigger fish to come along" (DeMallie 1984a, 156). Not always sensitive to their fellow creatures, boys threw stones at birds. However, Black Elk did not want to participate in this play because he was coming to realize that "we should be like relatives to all animals." He did, however, admit to shooting at squirrels that were "hard to hit" (DeMallie 1984a, 158).

Rough play ultimately defined growing up as a Lakota boy.[4] Young boys would play a game that pitted one group against the other. The object was for one group to charge the other on horseback, and the participants would then wrestle each other until one of them fell to the ground. Playing naked one day, Black Elk was thrown from his horse and landed in the center of a cactus!

Boys aspired to being a warrior since dying in battle was the "greatest thing an Indian [could] do" (DeMallie 1984a, 323). As little children, they were given a knife, rope, and bow with arrows. Mastery of their use was the cultural ideal. Young girls, by contrast, played a game comparable to bowling. It entailed rolling a stone at a stick that was about two inches in length. This game was intended to teach them patience (since they repeatedly missed the target). Girls learned that accomplishing life goals often would require the virtue of patience.

Despite times of rugged play, Black Elk's childhood had its lighter moments. Pranks also had their place. Black Elk cited one of them when recalling his childhood experience with a certain man, Watanye. Young boys would try to make this man laugh because he had severely chapped lips. They would perform some humorous stunt, and he would put a hand on his mouth to prevent hurtful movement.

Fishing one day with Watanye, Black Elk threw his spear into the stream, lost his footing, and accompanied the spear into the water. This unplanned plunge made Watanye double over in laughter despite the pain it brought to his lips. From that time on, Watanye would have to hold his mouth when seeing Black Elk. Remembering the incident would instantly make him start to laugh.

For all the lighter moments during Black Elk's early childhood, both he and Lakota winter counts also reported clashes with, and the killing of, many enemies during the period. Bloody encounters with the Shoshones, Pawnees, and Flatheads were regular occurrences when the holy-man was a young boy. An engagement with the Flatheads in 1871 left a special impression on him. He reported that his people killed sixty-six Flatheads and that these people were "pitiful and cried to stop fighting" (DeMallie 1984a, 337). This being a boyhood memory might account for why it was remembered as a larger-than-life reality—other Lakota sources said that the number of enemy slain was half of what Black Elk recalled. Curiously, in the holy-man's recounting of Lakota victories in Neihardt's notes, Black Elk does not appear to lament humans killing one another. He seems upbeat and tolerant of slaughters that saw his people gain the upper hand.

Childhood Visions

Beside clashes with enemies, the ebb and flow of daily life also included experiences that not only colored Black Elk's childhood but also his later years. Upon first riding a horse at the age of five, he had a vision that lasted about twenty minutes (the word for vision and dream is the same in Lakota). He said that a kingbird, or flycatcher, told him that two men were approaching and that they were descending from out of a cloud in the north. Each was holding a spear and singing the words "a sacred voice is calling you" (DeMallie 1984a, 109).⁵They departed in the west, appearing as geese. After this experience, when Black Elk heard another vision-voice beckon him, he would disregard it—so much had the early vision frightened him.

Then, when he was between eight and ten years old, he had another mysterious vision or dream. Black Elk later recounted this vision to Neihardt, and it was steeped in images common to the nineteenth-century Lakota world. As such, its meaning has been as elusive for readers of *Black Elk Speaks* as it was for Black Elk. Still, many have interpreted the material as prophetic about Black Elk's life and the future of his people. It cast enough appeal for an editor to dedicate his anthology of "Essays on Native American Religion" to "Black Elk's vision." Other writers similarly cited the vision and paid tribute to it.⁶

As with all of what the holy-man told Neihardt, the vision that appears in *Black Elk Speaks* was filtered through a lifetime of experience, Black Elk's interpreter and son Ben, Neihardt's artful skill as a writer, and his daughter Enid's shorthand. Given this production format and that the boyhood vision took place a half century earlier when Black Elk was a child, the original experience can only be more or less appreciated.⁷

CHAPTER 3

The Vision

Like the account in the book of Revelation with which it is sometimes compared, Black Elk's vision is not engaging for everyone. Its detailed images take the reader into a dreamworld that could just as well be dismissed as the delusion of a sickly boy. The abridged version that follows relates the main episodes of the vision-dream that Black Elk said he experienced about the year 1874 when he was around eight years old. His full account of the vision is detailed in Raymond J. DeMallie's *The Sixth Grandfather* (1984), which contains the stenographic notes, or transcript, of Neihardt's interview with Black Elk.

It was on the Little Bighorn River, perhaps in August, that Black Elk heard a voice calling. One day, just after his people had killed a hundred or more Pawnee, he collapsed, and his legs, arms, and face became swollen. His vision began as he saw the two men from the cloud of his first vision and he exited a tipi and ascended on a cloud in pursuit of them.

In the clouds, the men showed him a bay horse, which said, "My life history you shall see" (DeMallie 1984a, 114). Black Elk then looked to the west and saw twelve black horses with swallows flying above them. To the north he saw twelve white horses with geese above them. Eagles flew above twelve sorrels in the east, and in the south he saw twelve buckskin horses with hawks flying above them (proceeding from west to north, east, and then south is a ritual pattern among the Lakota).

The bay horse said it would take Black Elk to a council of the grandfathers. The forty-eight other horses lined up twelve abreast in four lines. Neihardt's notes reported Black Elk saying that "millions" of other horses then filled the sky in all directions (DeMallie 1984a, 115). Since this figure was not traditional among the Lakota, the holy-man, his son, or Neihardt used a colloquial English word that conveyed the assembly was too numerous to count. Leading the column of forty-eight, Black Elk and the bay horse then saw the large herd transformed into animals of all kinds departing in the cardinal directions.

Under a rainbow gate were six grandfathers, and Black Elk stood in front of them as the forty-eight horses returned to the quarters from whence they had come. A grandfather invited Black Elk to enter the gate, and the horses cheered as he did so. The first grandfather represented the west and encouraged him by saying "be not afraid" (DeMallie 1984a, 116).

This quote of Luke 1:13, unreferenced in the stenographic notes of Neihardt's transcript, is like other biblical material that appears in the vision account. It might reflect wording that the vision actually contained but more likely indicates the holy-man's familiarity with and use of the Bible later in life, before he met Neihardt. The biblical reference is a reminder that the holy-man's narrative was of a boyhood experience that occurred more than five decades earlier and that probably became laced with a lifetime of reflection.

Continuing his account, Black Elk said that the first grandfather gave him a cup of water because he was to become a powerful healer with it. He also received a bow and arrows because he would be a great warrior. Running toward the west, the first grandfather turned into an emaciated black horse.

A second grandfather who represented the north then gave Black Elk an herb, which he used to restore the black horse to health. Black Elk's connection to horses as an adult might have been partly linked to this detail in his vision. He was again told that he would be a great healer and that he would "create a nation" (DeMallie 1984a, 117) by bringing children back to life. This scene in the vision is probably an after-the-fact allusion to infant and child baptisms that he performed or witnessed as an adult. These rituals represent a spiritual rebirth according to the Christian theology he later adopted. The second grandfather then ran toward the north and turned into a white goose. There, the white horses turned into white geese and the black horses became the sound of thunder (Thunder-beings).

The third grandfather of the east then showed Black Elk the morning star with two men flying beneath it. This grandfather held a pipe that had a live, spotted eagle on its stem. This, too, assured Black Elk that he would be a great healer. The grandfather pointed to a red man who changed into a buffalo. Running toward the east, this buffalo glanced at the horses in that direction and they also transformed into buffalo.

The fourth grandfather of the south told Black Elk to behold a stick he carried. It sprouted at the top and had birds singing in it. This would be a cane for both him and his people, upon which they could lean. Black Elk was then shown a good and sacred red road that ran from north to south. From it, he was assured he would receive good things. He was also shown a black road of fear that ran from east to west. From it, he would get the power to destroy. The grandfather then moved to the south where he became an elk, and all the buckskin horses were likewise transformed into elks.

The fifth grandfather represented Wakan Tanka. He turned into a spotted eagle and told Black Elk that the fowls of the universe would help him, and that he would have the power to destroy enemies.

The sixth grandfather was very old and had white hair. He empowered Black Elk to return to earth and help his people, who the grandfather said would suffer hardship.

Following this grandfather out the rainbow gate, Black Elk mounted the bay horse. Then the sixth grandfather, holding a spear, was transformed into a young man Black Elk recognized as himself. The man then appeared as a young boy.

Black Elk carried the gifts he had received within the rainbow gate. As he rode with the formation of black, white, sorrel, and buckskin horses, he carried a cup of water, bow and arrows, wind, an herb, and a pipe. He headed a column of twelve riders down a road of ruin. A man in flames and dust emerged out of the water at the fork of the Missouri River, and he destroyed all kinds of creatures. This man was identified as Black Elk's enemy.

From the west, north, east, and south, riders attacked the man, but he repelled them all. At last, Black Elk attacked this man, now painted blue, with his cup of water and a spear (his bow and arrows had transformed into this weapon). All creation cheered Black Elk as he thrust his lightning spear into the man, who turned into a turtle. The other horsemen came and counted coup on the dead enemy, and all who had been dead came back to life.

Black Elk came down to earth, was taken to his village, and was given a sprouting stick. With it and the pipe, he understood he would help people walk the red road. At the village, he saw many people dying and was frightened. It was here that he learned he was to become a holy-man.

The people cheered his arrival, and he was instructed to give the sacred pipe and sprouting stick to them. These gifts would help them walk the red road and live in peace. He was also told to give them the herb and the wind.

Then, a spirit of the west presented him with more items: a hoop (a sign that he would be a leader of the people and be responsible for their prosperity), a wooden cup of water, a bow, and arrows. The water was to be a great source of power for him to bring life to the people. He had acquired it when he killed the spirit-man in flames at the Missouri River. The bow and arrows would help him and his people be victorious.

In recalling the next part of his vision, Black Elk referred to "ascents" (DeMallie 1984a, 125) of his people and creation, but the meaning of this word (and other references in the vision) is not clear. Some readers have associated an "ascent" with a generation, and many have since tried to identify which generation paralleled Black Elk's description of it. Parenthetical explanations within the stenographic notes in *The Sixth Grandfather* leave this interpretation debatable.

Black Elk then had a vision of his people in the past when they and all creatures experienced bliss, but the second generation became fearful. The third generation would see everyone living for himself or herself, and the fourth generation would see terrible times. Despite this bleak forecast, Black Elk himself was assured that his power would help the people.

He looked down on the blighted multitude and saw a man painted red and holding a lance. This man walked to the center of the nation, rolled on the ground, and turned into a buffalo as he came to a standing position. The buffalo then rolled on the ground and turned into an herb as the people and horses emerged with new life. A spirit wind blew over everyone and all that was dead came back to life.

Black Elk saw a flowering stick at the center of the nation's hoop, and all kinds of singing birds surrounded it. The people were rejoicing, and women were making a tremolo (an approbation that consists of a wavering, high-pitched sound). Men said to look at the stick. From it, the Lakota would multiply, and the stick would "take care of the people" (DeMallie 1984a, 129).

Black Elk's lifelong friend then appeared within the vision. Neihardt referred to this man as "One Side," a name Black Elk claimed to have bestowed on his friend because his hair was cut on one side in one of his visions. It was also a warrior hairstyle of the period, and Black Elk's daughter, Lucy, said that One Side was actually a man named "Kills Enemy." She said he sometimes went by "One Side" later in life because he wore a hat tilted in one direction. Otherwise, everyone always knew him as Kills Enemy. Neihardt probably called him One Side because he avoided references associated with warfare and killing in *Black Elk Speaks*.

In the vision, One Side mirrored Black Elk by carrying a cup of water, bow, and arrow. Three others on horseback joined them as they confronted an enemy amidst the sound of thunder and flash of lightning. As the people cheered, Black Elk slew a dog, one side of which was colored black and the other white.

The holy-man was next instructed to wave an herb over an emaciated horse, and it transformed into a beautiful stallion. It snorted lightning and dashed, neighing, to the west, north, east, and south where "millions" of other horses appeared prancing and dancing. The western grandfather entrusted them all to Black Elk.

The stallion sang, and all created things danced to the music of his song. The horse assured the holy-man that he would have the power to make the earth happy. All creatures joyfully returned home, and Black Elk saw that all the people enjoyed a blissful state in a bountiful land.

The holy-man was then taken to the "center of the earth" with the sixteen riders from the four directions, and he saw two men with wings (DeMallie 1984a, 134). Black Elk was told to depend on these creatures who, in his later years, he would refer to as angels. The winged men gave him an herb that he was instructed to drop to the earth where it proceeded to grow and blossom. He was shown what was good and not good for people. Some were rejoicing in the north and east while sickness beset others in the south and west.

Before returning to the six grandfathers, Black Elk saw a man in flames who had horns and lightning flashes over his body. People near the man, whose depiction seems a conventional representation of the devil in Christian art, were sad and moaning. The man transformed into a gopher (an animal the Lakota associated with war) and then an herb that would be deadly if touched.

Later in life, Black Elk called this herb the "soldier weed," and said that it could be found in the Black Hills. Claiming to be the only one to know about this herb, he said that its appearance was that of a "little tree with crinkly leaves, reddish in color" (DeMallie 1984a, 136). Had he been old enough to use the herb, Black Elk said that he could have killed many enemies with it. The plant is difficult to identify based on Black Elk's description, so perhaps he *was* the only person who knew about it. However, two candidates for the herb could be poison dogwood (*Cornus sericea)* or smooth sumac *(Rhus glabra)*.

Black Elk then described the appearance of four riders on bay, sorrel, gray, and white horses. The bay rider wore a buffalo headdress that was alive, with the buffalo's eyes and nostrils flaring and its horns filled with all kinds of animals. The other riders were clad in comparable regalia (the meanings of which were not noted in the transcript), and they charged as smoke ascended and the sound of guns could be heard along with that of horses screaming, dogs yelping, and women and children wailing.

While triumph in war would have made him a successful chief, Black Elk reflected that this elevated status was not preferable to the simple life he was destined to embrace. He saw war occurring everywhere. Four riders turned into black-tailed deer with wounds on their sides. They faced the herb, and a black-horned man changed himself into a gopher, then an herb, and finally a skeleton. During this time, Black Elk received the power to destroy with the herb. He breathed lightning. His body was painted red and his joints black. White stripes also decorated his joints.

Then, after receiving the power of the goose from the western grandfather, Black Elk joined all the grandfathers who, with all creation, enthusiastically greeted and cheered him. The west spirit gave him a cup of water, and in it, Black Elk saw buffalo. His nation would become strong and happy by drinking from this cup.

Recalling that he was shown "millions of faces" in his vision (DeMallie 1984a, 138), Black Elk told Neihardt that this was prophetic. Throughout life, he established friendships with many diverse people. The multitude in the vision was happy that he took the cup.

The northern grandfather put butterfly cocoons on each of Black Elk's wrists. All winged and walking creatures had given him their power as his people were in travail. Presented another cup of water, he saw a distressed man who was painted blue within it. The man carried a bow and arrow, and Black Elk was told to drink the cup's contents.

The confusing conclusion of Black Elk's account of the vision to Neihardt reported that this blue spirit-man was a fish, and that Black Elk received great power from this experience. The holy-man said that he was able to make this blue man appear and swim in the cup for healing ceremonies he later conducted. His comment parallels an experience common to the initiation ritual that Lakota underwent when becoming medicine men. These practitioners commonly reported that the ritual included their gazing into a bowl, or cup, of water and seeing a person appear. In light of this cultural convention, Black Elk's report of the "blue man" swimming in a cup should not be regarded as extraordinary. He and others might have found it consistent with their own ceremonialism when later witnessing Christian missionaries use a sacred cup within Communion services (i.e., the resurrected Christ present in their cup; Black Elk having the "blue man" in his).

Getting closer to earth as he interacted with each grandfather, Black Elk next met the eastern spirit. It showed him a cup of water containing the morning star, from which he acquired wisdom. Told to return to earth, the holy-man received a cup from the fourth grandfather who also gave a curing song to him. The fifth grandfather had a cup that represented Wakan Tanka, and it had a dancing spotted eagle in it. This creature would provide Black Elk with spiritual insight.

The sixth grandfather then showed him a cup that was filled with small people. Black Elk was told that he would walk among these needy people. Upon closer examination of the sixth grandfather, the holy-man again recognized that the man was himself. He then learned that this twelve-day experience of happiness was now coming to an end. Outside the rainbow tipi, riders and all kinds of creatures were in the four quarters, and all were rejoicing and happy.

The grandfathers then took their places in the different directions, and the rainbow set in the east. A spotted eagle instructed Black Elk to look back, where he saw Pikes Peak. He found himself on earth, alone, walking toward his village and to his family's lodge. Once inside, he looked down on himself lying there as a sick child.

It was then that Black Elk came to consciousness. According to his boyhood friend, Standing Bear, the experience lasted twelve days. Whirlwind Chaser, the medicine man who doctored Black Elk, acquired prestige for bringing him back from near death. The medicine man told the boy's parents that their son had a sacred duty to perform and that he could see the power of lightning throughout the boy's body. However, Black Elk knew his vision was what had made him well, and he was sad that his parents were unaware of the profound journey he had taken.

Black Elk's father reportedly said that after his son was cured, he was "not the boy he used to be" (DeMallie 1984a, 144). Spending time alone, the contemplative young man did not wish to socialize with family members as he previously had done. He only spoke with his mother's father, Keeps His Tipi (elsewhere referred to as Refuse To Go), and behaved more like a man than the child that he was.

Long as it is, this description of Black Elk's vision is just a summary of what he reported to Neihardt. Neihardt's publisher wanted the vision to be placed as an appendix to the text of *Black Elk Speaks*, but Neihardt made it the cornerstone of his book. By focusing on this childhood event, the poet proceeded to show that the holy-man spent a lifetime trying to understand and fulfill the vision. However, by doing so, readers were left to conclude that this one experience preoccupied Black Elk. Instead, his visions were cumulative, and the holy-man's religious quest was lifelong. It was not limited to one inspiration he acquired as a youth.

Black Elk's experience was like that of others within Lakota tradition. Beginning early in life, one would seek or somehow find supernatural guidance and build upon the revelations received. It is not surprising, then, that the boyhood vision is absent from Joseph Epes Brown's *The Sacred Pipe*. Religious questing was just that, a journey that did not linger solely at one point.

CHAPTER 4

Little Bighorn

In late June of 1876, young Black Elk was part of a large camp that peacefully stretched about three miles along the Little Bighorn River. A half-mile wide in places, the camp was the largest he had ever seen, and included many Cheyenne, some visiting Gros Ventre families, and five Arapaho men. They had fought General Crook at the battle of the Rosebud a week earlier (June 17), and these people had no desire to engage the U.S. Army again. They leisurely attended to caring for the wounded from the previous battle, friendly visiting, and participating in religious ceremonies. Despite being at war, no one expected the arrival of an enemy force on this hot, dry, and tranquil day. So they were caught off guard June 25, on what was for most of the camp a sleepy afternoon. Many were still dozing when the U.S. cavalry attacked.[1]

Black Elk's participation in and memory of the event that followed and went down in history as the Battle of the Little Bighorn can best be understood within the battle's broader context. His and others' accounts of the battle of the Greasy Grass, as the Lakota came to call the engagement, simply told of a people's spirited response to an opponent who attacked their families. At the time of the charge, they did not even know who was leading the force they faced.

The Lakota's Opponent

Years before he took his men on their ill-fated mission against the Lakota, a few years before Black Elk was born, George Armstrong Custer (1839–76) became the youngest major general in U.S. Army history at age twenty-three. After the Civil War, it was customary for battlefield commissions to revert to a lower rank, and his returned to that of lieutenant colonel. Assigned to the newly formed Seventh Cavalry in 1866, he served with it for ten years. Then, in 1876, he led his troops in a final battle that became known as "Custer's Last Stand."

Called "Long Hair" by the Lakota (although his hair was cut short just before this final campaign), Custer had gained a reputation for fighting Indians. He intended to score a big victory when he found a large Indian camp at the Little Bighorn in what is now Montana. Instead, his failure that June spawned numerous studies that chronicled what "actually" occurred and why the attack, which resulted in the annihilation of his men, was unsuccessful. Popular opinion has tended to chide Custer for poor judgment. However, late twentieth-century scholarship found that his plan was neither foolhardy nor doomed from the start by his facing a superior force. Historian Robert Utley's droll conclusion (2001, 194) summarized a century of debate when he noted that "the Army lost largely because the Indians won."

"General" Custer became a larger-than-life figure whose memory endured because of, and long after, Little Bighorn. The event also stoked interest in Black Elk's culture. However, contrary to the folklore that arose after the event, Black Elk's people did not attack Custer, did not know the commander was even near, and did not learn until much later that it was Custer they had defeated.

The Battle of the Greasy Grass

After discovering the Lakota camp, Custer ignored the advice of his Apsáalooke (Crow) scouts who said it was too large to engage. Instead, since the terrain of the region was similar, he employed a strategy that he had used eight years earlier against a peaceful Cheyenne camp on the Washita River in present-day Oklahoma (however, contrary to popular opinion, fanned in part by Custer's inaccurate report, Indian casualties were relatively few at Washita). He divided his regiment into three battalions that would attack from different directions, and he expected to see the inhabitants of the Indian camp flee—a valid expectation since Indian custom was to retreat in order to protect women, children, and elders.

Shortly after noon on June 25, 1876, Custer led one battalion, Maj. Marcus A. Reno led another, and Capt. Frederick W. Benteen commandeered the third. What then took place within a large field of battle has stirred unending controversy. Contrary to popular opinion, there was no en masse engagement that raged for any length of time. Except for one suicidal attack, Lakota marksmen fired from a distance and followed the Plains Indians custom of gaining an advantage by hiding in the landscape and shooting from a protected area. Army soldiers who fled were easily felled since pursuit of them was, for their pursuers, "like hunting buffalo" (Michno 1997). Custer learned too late that the strategy he had used at Washita would not work here. According to the most popular mythology, the "boy general" was the last to fall on what became known as "Custer Hill." However, since Custer's command perished, the exact plan of attack, and precisely where or when he died, is unknown.

According to one Indian account, the battle lasted "as long as it takes a hungry man to eat a meal" (Kifaru 1992)—a reference that likely refers to a given person's participation (Black Elk's, for example). Reevaluations set the battle's duration between one-and-a-half to three hours (Utley 1972). Since it lasted this long, a formal inquiry later sought to learn why Reno did not attempt to help his commanding officer (he said he was pinned down and could not take the risk).

Black Elk and other Lakota did not think of the large camp in numerical terms. As a result, battle participants could not provide reliable figures on the number of Indians taking part. Later scholarly estimates held that a thousand lodges were home to between four thousand and ten thousand people. Benteen initially thought

Indian fighters numbered between fifteen hundred and eighteen hundred, but by 1879 he increased that figure to nine thousand. Evaluations suggest his first tally was more accurate than the second one.[2]

Those who died with Custer included some civilians. Combined with others under Reno and Benteen, about 262 on the army's side were killed that day. Indian losses were thought to be less than one hundred. Neither toll represents the most losses suffered by either side during the Indian wars.[3] However, news of Custer's defeat reached the East just when it was preparing to celebrate the nation's centennial. The gruesome death of Gettysburg's hero touched a nerve that made the event a national tragedy.

Black Elk at Little Bighorn

Decades after the battle, Black Elk reported to family members and interested others that his heart pounded excitedly when he rushed to give his older brother, Runs In The Center, two pistols that would be helpful against the oncoming soldiers. Young Black Elk, who was about ten years old, was proud of his brother and the other men who rushed out to face the attacking cavalry. He joined their effort by letting fly a few arrows at one of the troopers hiding behind some bushes. Even before Little Bighorn, he had been exposed to battle. He had accompanied Lakota and Cheyenne men who attacked a wagon train headed for the Black Hills. The boy had clung to his pony, circled the wagons, and managed to avoid being hit by the incoming bullets.

At Little Bighorn, Black Elk heard the agonizing sounds of wounded ponies, horses, and men. Engraved in his memory was blood flowing from the mortal wounds of soldiers and Indians alike. He walked among dead bodies that lay strewn across the hills and could not understand why the blue-coated soldiers had attacked his people.

After the shooting stopped, Black Elk joined his age-mates on the battlefield. He sent arrows into soldiers who lay dead or dying until the arrows made the men look like porcupines with their quills showing. The young warrior even scalped one man who had not yet died. The soldier ground his teeth in agony, so Black Elk ended the man's misery with a bullet. He then proudly presented the scalp to his mother (and she proudly accepted it).

The future holy-man took another scalp from a dead trooper and gave it to a younger companion as a trophy. Shortly after, he could no longer stomach the stench of death and gunpowder, and he left the battlefield. Just a youth, Black Elk was "happy" that he had helped save his people this day (DeMallie 1984a, 194). Their victory was a decisive one, and he had made a contribution.

As for Custer, his mortal wounds at the battle consisted of a bullet wound to the left temple and chest.[4] Since the Lakota did not know it was Custer's command they were fighting, they did not single out his body for the conventional treatment it received: a postmortem gash on the thigh and some genital mutilation. Their grisly treatment of dead soldiers was not reserved for army enemies alone. Had Little Bighorn been fought with any Lakota foe, corpses would have been treated in the same ritual fashion. Black Elk recalled what befell an Apsáalooke who tried, but failed, to steal horses from a Lakota camp one night. The would-be thief was shot, killed, scalped, and butchered such that his torso was used for target practice. It was thought that bodily disfigurement would accompany a person into the afterlife, so the dead person would be less of a threat should another encounter take place there.

In later years after the Battle of the Little Bighorn, Black Elk recalled seeing pieces of paper money blow across the plains that bloody afternoon. However, when scavenging the battlefield, his people did not bother to pick up the currency since no one knew what it was. With self-deprecating humor, Black Elk later regretted not collecting the strange pieces of paper that seemed to float in every direction.

Periodically, as time passed, reunions took place at the battlefield, but Black Elk did not attend them. These occasions brought Indian and army opponents together, and participants would exchange their memories of the event. Despite the emotional toll the battle exacted on him, trooper Henry Mechling (a Medal of Honor recipient) professed a friendship with Sitting Bull years after the event. By contrast, Black Elk's sentiment toward the soldiers remained one of distrust. As might be expected of participants in any war, former combatants harbored different opinions of one another.

Today, a Black Elk quotation—"know the power that is peace"—greets visitors at the Little Bighorn Battlefield National Monument Welcome Center in Montana. It appears in Lakota and English on an outside wall in raised lettering. Even though Black Elk's role at the 1876 battle of the Greasy Grass was that of a child, a vast amount of literature invokes his perspective on the much-debated conflict. His association with Little Bighorn placed his name alongside the names of others who became legendary after the event. Their place within American history is secure in connection with this battle that continues to intrigue students of history and culture.

The Aftermath of Little Bighorn

When Black Elk's family broke camp after the battle, they headed toward the Bighorn Mountains. In describing their flight, Black Elk sketched for Neihardt a telling portrait of his emergence into manhood. Hours earlier, the warrior-youth had fired his pistol at a soldier's forehead and scalped two enemies. Come nightfall, as the people set forth on an escape route, childhood returned when his mother told him to sit with others his age in a travois.

According to Black Elk, boys reached manhood at twelve or thirteen years of age, and he appears to have been on the cusp of that stage. Although a battle participant who took scalps, he was still assigned the responsibilities associated with childhood. His duty was to tend the family's puppies and make sure that they remained with him in the travois during the journey.

The chaos of Little Bighorn preceded Black Elk's people resuming an almost tranquil lifestyle that was not to endure much longer. Black Elk matter-of-factly recalled that after the battle, his family members made their way to Wood Louse Creek at the base of the Bighorn Mountains and hunted buffalo. They then joined Crazy Horse's band.

Crazy Horse

Crazy Horse, Black Elk's second cousin, attracted a significant following during this period. He and Sitting Bull were chief among the "hostiles" pursued by the U.S. Army. In a business-as-usual fashion, these people moved within the region hunting buffalo, fighting the Apsáalooke and taking Indian scalps, all the while being pursued by the army. After Col. Ranald S. Mackenzie destroyed their village on November 25, 1876, Dull Knife's Cheyenne found a safe haven with their Lakota friends and joined Crazy Horse in skirmishing the army (they later took up residence at Pine Ridge). Black Elk recalled this period as one of famine.

In early May of 1877, Sitting Bull (circa 1831–90) found temporary refuge in Canada and Black Elk's family members made their way to Fort Robinson, Nebraska. Crazy Horse's people (numbering between nine hundred and eleven hundred) joined them on May 6, 1877. As the summer months passed, rumors of Crazy Horse being a flight risk were bothersome enough that the army decided to arrest him. Expecting a council and not confinement, Crazy Horse willingly went by escort to a stockade. Upon entering, he realized where he was and turned to leave but was stopped by Little Big Man. A scout at this time for the army, Little Big Man was an Oglala with whom Crazy Horse had feuded earlier in life. As they scuffled, an infantryman held his bayonet in a forward, ready position. The conflicting accounts of eyewitnesses state that Crazy Horse either fell into the bayonet while struggling to escape, that the soldier lunged the blade into him, or that both these actions occurred.[5] The Lakota leader's wound was mortal, and he died a few hours later on September 5, 1877.

According to Neihardt's notes, Black Elk (or his translator) referred to Crazy Horse as "the last big chief" (DeMallie 1984a, 322).[6] No photographs of him are known to exist but one of another person with the same name circulates and periodically elicits discussion. Biographical details for Crazy Horse have been based on interviews with army personnel who fought him in the 1860s and 1870s and the memory of elderly Lakota like Black Elk who were interviewed decades after his death.

Black Elk told Neihardt that Crazy Horse's disposition was never "excited" but always measured. He recalled him as "sociable in the tipi, but at war he was not at all sociable" (DeMallie 1984a, 203). In 1930, Eleanor Hinman collected information on Crazy Horse from those who knew him, but she interpreted Black Elk's response as uncooperative, noting, "He felt he ought to be paid for telling us the biography of Crazy Horse (he suggested a rate of two cents a word) and that it would require about two weeks" (Paul 1998, 184). Hinman's interpreter told her that Crazy Horse's relatives had a history of silence when asked to speak of him. However, upon seeing Black Elk, Hinman said, "For just that fraction of a second I saw . . . Crazy Horse reflected in his cousin's face."

Known as both "Light Hair" and "Curly" in his youth, Crazy Horse was "slightly below medium size" and his weight "was not above 140 pounds" (Jensen 2005). However, he became larger than life in memories of him. Both Crazy Horse and Black Elk remain at the forefront of mythic leaders who continue to stir the imagination of people familiar with the myth-laden history of American Indians (Grimes 2000). Revered as a visionary like his second cousin, Crazy Horse came to symbolize a free spirit who defied constraints. His biographer, Mari Sandoz, referred to him as a "strange man" whose idiosyncrasies did not diminish the esteem accorded him by his people. Although it also is said that some were jealous of the Native leader, a Lakota biographer, Joseph Marshall (2004), reflected that when people remember Crazy Horse, they say his name as if it were a prayer.

Life after Crazy Horse

After Crazy Horse's death, Washington ordered the Lakota to move close to the Missouri River. In the fall of 1878, many Oglala bands moved to the Pine Ridge region and the Sicangu to the Rosebud region of what was then the Great Sioux Reservation. The parcels on which they settled eventually became isolated tracts within southwestern South Dakota designated as the Rosebud and Pine Ridge Reservations. En route to this area, Black Elk's family chose instead to do as Sitting Bull had done and flee to Canada. Since conditions were not good there, they returned to American soil (Montana's Fort Peck agency) in 1880. Sitting Bull's people returned south as well a year later on July 20, 1881. Accompanied by thirty-five families (187 people), Sitting Bull surrendered at Fort Buford, Dakota Territory.

For the period between Little Bighorn and his people's surrender, Black Elk spent his boyhood in Montana and Canada subsisting on buffalo and performing daily household chores while elders fought the Apsáalooke. One of his responsibilities was to help his father with the horses and hunting. It was the custom at this time for a young man and his father to go in search of game.

Black Elk remembered the winter of 1880 as one of hunger that brought death to his people's horses. Everyone wanted to leave Canada and return south, and this harsh time engraved memories on Black Elk that he would never forget. During this cold spell, while he was hunting with his father, they met up with another group of hunters. With the weather below zero, they came upon a herd of buffalo. Despite blizzard conditions, the young men and the two older men got five head of buffalo. It took them two days staying where they were to do the butchering.

One night, after retiring into the warmth of their lodge, Black Elk and his father heard a man singing his "death song." He was approaching the camp as he sang. Finally, he reached their tipi and called out: "Friend, are you awake? I have my son here with me but I don't know if he is still alive."

Black Elk, his father, and the others in the hunting party hurried outside, and took the boy down from the horse. He was in a pack and was still breathing, so they pulled him into their tipi and rubbed him with snow. Soon, he opened his eyes and said he was hungry, so they fed him. When they looked outside to tell the boy's father of his son's recovery, they found that he had fallen off his horse and died of exposure.

Experiences like this were difficult enough without Black Elk's family having to cope with Blackfoot Indians who stalked them. As a result, he and his family struggled back to Poplar, Montana,

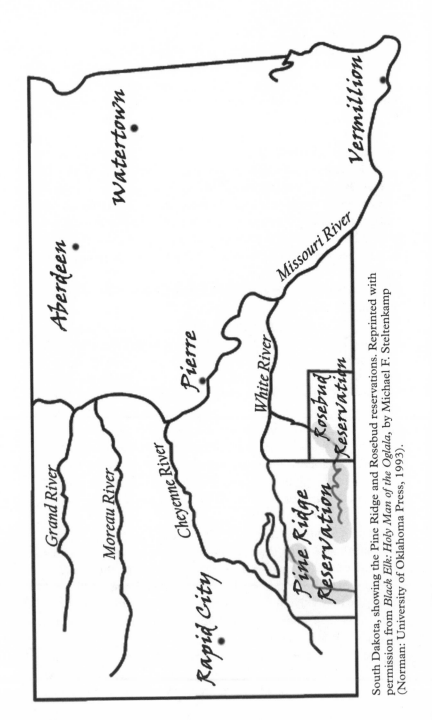

South Dakota, showing the Pine Ridge and Rosebud reservations. Reprinted with permission from *Black Elk: Holy Man of the Oglala*, by Michael F. Steltenkamp (Norman: University of Oklahoma Press, 1993).

where they found refuge with the Assiniboine in the Fort Peck region. Unfortunately, their traditional enemies lurked everywhere, and the Assiniboine were reluctant hosts. Coping with the climate and starvation in a hostile environment, Black Elk's people sought refuge at Fort Keogh, Montana, in 1880. There the army confiscated the people's firearms and allowed them to retain two horses each and enough tipis for shelter.

Just before going to Fort Keogh, Black Elk desired to "count coup" on an opponent—a wish that was only natural. His people were stalked like prey, and survival depended upon the emergence of new warriors to fill the ranks. Black Elk's desire was so strong that he misidentified a group of Lakota as foes and rushed forward to "count coup" on them! Later in life, he could laugh at this experience because he knew that wanting to count coup was the understandable dream of young boys. (His inability to identify another Indian as friend or foe is not as peculiar as it sounds. At Little Bighorn, a Cheyenne killed a Lakota ally whom he mistook for an Apsáalooke scout working for the army.)

During this same period, Black Elk witnessed an event of nature that left a lasting impression. With elders on a hunt, he came upon three male buffalo challenging a large bull that was alone with a cow. One by one, the males butted heads with the bull, and one by one, they died. When the hunting party drew close, the lone bull also fell—mortally wounded by his encounter with the other three. An older man decided that they should not butcher the four bulls since these creatures had "murdered" each other. With moral principle overriding pragmatism, the hunting party then slew and butchered the female.

Since Black Elk said that the "worst thing to an Indian is murder" (DeMallie 1984a, 391), the men were clearly not indifferent to what the "buffalo people" had done to one another. The Lakota word for murderer (*ti wicakte*) is rich with connotation and reveals why this act was considered abhorrent. Meaning "he kills their home" (DeMallie 1984a, 394), the term could refer both to the killing of a body that "housed" a person's spirit and the killing of someone upon whom others relied (for providing a "home").

Emerging into manhood at this time, Black Elk's religious vocation was gaining substance. These flight-or-fight years took an emotional toll on an understandably insecure youth. However, from fighting to fleeing and the near starvation and ultimate surrender of his people, he was able to view his coming of age through spiritual lenses.

CHAPTER 5

Medicine Man

While *Black Elk Speaks* was subtitled "the life-story of a holy-man of the Oglala Sioux," from a Lakota perspective it actually reported incidents in the life of a medicine man, or *pejuta wichasha*. This term referred to doctors within and outside the Lakota world (the English phrase was derived from the French word meaning "doctor," *le médicin*).[1] The Lakota term for "holy-man" (*wichasha wakan*) could include healers but properly referred to elders whose venerable presence drew upon a lifetime of practical and mystical experiences.

John Neihardt's book, however, addressed the period during which Black Elk technically served as a medicine man. As Black Elk advanced in years, his identity expanded. Only by the time Neihardt visited in 1931 had Black Elk earned the multifaceted designation of holy-man or *wichasha wakan* (also used for the priests with whom he worked). However, by the late twentieth century, these technical distinctions were not of particular importance since "medicine man" had become the standard reference to people involved with any form of traditional healing or religious practice.

One could also be a medicine woman (*pejuta we'yan*), and Black Elk actually made reference to "women medicine men" (DeMallie 1984a, 379). These women, he said, specialized in treating babies who cried more than usual. Gender-neutral terms like "pipe carrier" or "medicine person" eventually eclipsed the distinction between "medicine man" and "holy-man."

Black Elk's path toward becoming a medicine man may have originated in his visions of early childhood, but a ceremony that took place when he was a teenager revealed and solidified his calling.

Black Elk Becomes a Medicine Man

In his mid-teens, Black Elk became increasingly fearful of what the Lakota called "Thunder-beings." These were wakan powers of the west symbolized as "thunder and lightning, horses, dogs, swallows, butterflies, and dragonflies" (DeMallie 1984a, 99). Restlessness and anxiety about these beings haunted him to such an extent that his parents enlisted the assistance of Black Road, a respected medicine man. Perhaps, they thought, Black Road could cure their son or in some way help him make sense of the anxiety he was experiencing. Although never cited as the source of his fear, the thunderlike sound of guns in battle might have been what had traumatized Black Elk since infancy. His fear finally required attention in 1881 when the family was camped three miles from Fort Keogh on the Tongue River in Montana. Black Road diagnosed the youth's symptoms and suggested performance of the horse dance as a cure. It would be therapeutic, but it would also help the boy fulfill his vision to become a contributing member of Lakota society.

In a specially painted tipi at the center of the camp, Black Elk taught the songs he had learned in his vision to Black Road and the aged Bear Sings. They were to chant them during the ritual. The occasion required Black Elk's parents to bring four black, four sorrel, four buckskin, and four white horses along with a bay horse for their son. He then performed the customary purification rite in a sweathouse with Black Road and Bear Sings.

Four young women also participated in the horse dance. One carried a flowering stick; one carried a pipe; one carried a bow, arrow, and cup of water; and one carried an herb. Twelve riders, blowing on eagle-bone whistles, accompanied them. These riders wore black masks over their faces and were naked except for eagle feathers on their heads.②

Lightning streaks and a star were painted on some of the riders, who were otherwise painted all black. Some others were painted white with red streaks. Yet others were painted red and had black streaks on their arms, while others appeared yellow with black streaks in this elaborate, colorful, and solemn ritual. The horses were also painted, and six elderly men accompanied the riders while singing songs throughout the ceremony.

Black Elk was painted entirely in red and wore a black mask and a feather across his forehead. Seated on his bay horse, over a spotted eagle design drawn on it, he thought that horses, near and far, appreciated the sacredness and power of what was at play. The Thunder-beings, too, seemed to be attentive to all that was occurring. Toward the end of this very exacting observance, people hastened to tie down their belongings throughout the village in fear of a terrible storm that threatened. This storm reflected the presence of the Thunder-beings.

Young women, old men, and riders gathered in the tipi. Within its center was a circle wherein was etched a north-south red road and an east-west black road. Other ritual items were placed at the cardinal points of this circle. Painting his forearms black, Black Elk eventually exited the tipi and followed the other participants. Everyone performed precise roles that must have required a choreographer of some sort, but Black Elk made no mention of such a person.

Riders painted black faced west and sang. Riders painted white sang facing the north, those painted red toward the east, and those yellow to the south. Young women then followed and likewise faced the south. At last, Black Elk saw the entire village assembled on horseback to acknowledge and benefit from the sacredness of the occasion. He then mounted his bay horse.

Facing west, Black Elk said that he saw a cloud that contained a rainbow tipi with six grandfathers extending their hands toward him. In the north was a man painted white whose right hand was likewise extended to him. Black Elk prayed that the power he now received through this ritual would be used on behalf

Red Feather, with a rosary around his neck, smokes his pipe with Father Buechel, who smokes his own. Courtesy of Marquette University Catholic Indian Mission Archives.

of his people. The procession continued and came to a conclusion with the people rejoicing, hail pelting down a short distance from the village, and thunder clapping. The universe itself seemed to be in a state of joyous excitement.

Black Road's counsel that the dance should be performed was apparently redemptive. Black Elk was elated—as if on a cloud himself. Everyone was pleased with what had taken place, and Black Elk claimed that many of the community's sick were healed. To him, the horses even appeared to be healthier than they were prior to the ceremony. His fear of the Thunder-beings vanished, and he felt that the four-leggeds even seemed to regard him with deepened respect.

Lavished with gifts from the community, Black Elk was now recognized as a medicine man. The ceremony both alleviated his anxiety and commissioned him as a healer. Whereas he had earlier felt uncomfortable in the presence of senior healers, he now felt composed. Moreover, these elders wanted to speak with him. Compassion for his people welled up within the young Black Elk as he felt the presence of what he understood to be a "little blue man" within his body who gave him power (DeMallie 1984a, 225). He also claimed to have received the power of little whirlwinds that were attached, cocoon-like, to his forearms. They enabled him to provide "a good wind" to those who were sick. He, like other medicine men, also received the power to find herbs for curing (DeMallie 1984a, 225).

Black Elk's account of his experience puts flesh on the skeletal description of how one became a medicine man that Red Feather (the younger brother of Crazy Horse's first wife) gave Father Buechel. In reporting how medical practitioners acquired membership in the different healing societies, Red Feather simply said that a particular type of dream or vision would reveal the type of medical specialty a person would practice. One would be initiated into a particular society based on dreaming of a bear, horse, eagle, wolf, or other animal.

The Context of His New Vocation

Black Elk described this profound experience as taking place in his mid-teens. However, more was at play than what was included in his extended account to Neihardt. Behind the obvious of the detailed reminiscence is quiet evidence of a family and community that profoundly valued one of their members.

Black Elk's parents were concerned enough about their son that they sought a healing specialist for his malady. Sparing no expense, they made sure that he received the best treatment available. If the guns of war had played a role in producing his fear, their sound was transformed into the voice of Thunder-beings (i.e., the clap of thunder) that he believed called him into a life of service.

The communal support that was an essential part of Lakota life became a significant source of affirmation for Black Elk. The people's ceremonial and festive blessing descended upon him as the community "ordained" into service one of its own. This rite of passage not only helped heal a cherished member of society but the expression on the people's faces also poignantly suggested to Black Elk that their survival was dependent upon his new vocation. Knowing that his people needed him helped Black Elk face the challenges that followed.

In July of 1881, the young medicine man and his people were taken to a Missouri River steamboat and transported to Fort Yates. Remaining there until September, Black Elk walked to Pine Ridge over the course of seven days (the government had taken everyone's ponies). There he could be with his fellow Oglala. Upon arrival, he needed to perform another ceremony since no one at Pine Ridge knew of the power he had received. Black Elk did not explain why, but he thought that the community had to acknowledge his status. Apparently, without its blessing, he could not bestow his. He therefore underwent the ritual he described for Brown known as the *hanbleciya*, the "crying for a vision."

Under the direction of Few Tails, a medicine man, Black Elk again entered the sweathouse. He was then placed on a specially selected hill over which sage was strewn. Alone on this sacred site, he sought guidance from the spirit world.

A spotted eagle soared overhead and a chicken hawk hovered nearby. A black swallow flew above him, and he began to cry in remembering relatives and friends who were no longer part of his life. As weeping butterflies fluttered above him, he said a spotted eagle told him that they were his people and that they were in great need. A chicken hawk then told him to listen to his grandfathers when they came.

Two men approached, cheered from the clouds, he said. These men chased a dog, killed it, and one of them lofted high the dog's head on an arrow he was carrying. The dog's head then turned into a man's head. The other man shot an arrow into the dog's heart, and it became a man's heart. A thunderstorm arose with rain and hail pelting down everywhere except within the sacred area occupied by Black Elk.

Although such lamenting experiences could last longer, Few Tails removed the young Black Elk from the hill in the morning.

Older men awaited them in a sweathouse, and they expressed interest in learning what had been revealed to the youth. After telling them what he saw, he received their affirmation in words that made a lasting impression. They said Black Elk was being called to greatness and encouraged him to begin using his gift to "help mankind" (DeMallie 1984a, 231). He had earlier understood his power was to be exercised in a more restricted sense—to his nation only (130). Now the elders were suggesting a more universal orientation. They told him that very few had ever received the inspiration to reach out to humanity as a whole.

The counsel of these men profoundly imparted a sense of mission that was to be an abiding one throughout Black Elk's life. When recounting this experience for Neihardt, he summarized it by quoting the Christian gospel's observation on discipleship. He said that "many are called but few are chosen."[3]

Practitioners like Black Elk often made connections like this between Lakota religious tradition and the tenets of Christianity they gradually came to learn. However, while some saw continuity between the two traditions, others avoided affiliation with Christian practice. By the end of the twentieth century, the trend was for the number of medicine men to proliferate, with many (if not most) having little involvement with a Christian church. Regardless of their perspective on Christianity, medicine people might pray with a pipe at a high school graduation, funeral, installation of tribal officers, traditional ceremony, or alone on a hill, away from distraction, seeking guidance.

Black Elk's Yuwipi Ritual

Besides performing an herbal medical practice that extended from the early 1880s to 1904, Black Elk also performed the "*yuwipi*" ceremony. This ritualism falls within a complex of Lakota ceremonies known as *lowanpi*, or "sings," and may or may not include healing (W. Powers 1982). Generally, yuwipi is associated with a benevolent function, such as healing, as in Black Elk's case. However, specialists could also call upon evil spirits to inflict harm on individuals. Good or bad spirits might make their presence known by means of sparkling flashes, water droplets splashed on participants, or animal sounds. Black Elk's ceremony included the voices of women in particular. Specialists in yuwipi, forms of which are found throughout North America, conduct their ritual within the completely darkened setting of someone's home and are bound within a quilt wrapped tightly by rope during the ceremony.

At the end of a ceremony, the yuwipi man would be free of his bonds (the spirit helpers were said to be responsible for his release). Joseph Epes Brown referred to this aspect of the practitioner's art as "ceremonial magic" (Brown 2007, 110). Not everyone in attendance knew that he or she was actually witnessing or experiencing sleight of hand, ventriloquism, and someone anonymously functioning as the practitioner's assistant. During his yuwipi ceremony, Black Elk likewise had the help of an assistant whose role in helping orchestrate effects was secret. This accomplice was his lifelong, trustworthy friend Kills Enemy.

Black Elk told his daughter that he was adept in his practice of yuwipi when active as a medicine man. Like other practitioners conducting the ritual, he knew there were few, if any, skeptics in attendance. However, he came to oppose practices that made people think that the Sacred could be manipulated. He described the role he played as "just like a magician trying to fool" people (Steltenkamp 1993, 26). He was not comfortable taking part in an intentionally deceptive practice that made people believe the supernatural was unexplainably manifesting itself, and so abandoned the practice.

For Black Elk, if the *lowanpi* tradition had value, it was not in convincing people that spirits accounted for strange and varied sounds or a practitioner escaping a rope's knots. The value and purpose of ritual was, rather, to evoke an awareness of the Sacred's presence (Brown 1953, 64n5). A powerfully symbolic experience, yuwipi-like rituals could show that the wakan, the mysterious and sacred, was at work within a ceremonial context of people expressing need.

With Buffalo Bill in Europe

About five years later, a still-young Black Elk ventured into a very different world of experience. This was the Wild West Show of

Black Elk, as he appeared in the Buffalo Bill Cody show, circa 1888. Courtesy of Pete's Buffalo Saloon & Trading Post.

William F. "Buffalo Bill" Cody (1846–1917). Black Elk agreed to work for two years at twenty-five dollars per month. Since baptism within the Episcopal Church was a formality required of all who joined the show, he also agreed to be baptized.

In the middle of November 1886, Black Elk joined about one hundred Lakota who departed from Rushville, Nebraska, on a train headed for New York. His were pragmatic reasons for undertaking the journey: "I wanted to see the great water, the great world and the ways of the white men; this is why I wanted to go." He told Neihardt that if he learned "the white man's ways were better" than his people's, he wanted to see his people adopt those ways (DeMallie 1984a, 245).

En route east, the train stopped at Omaha and Chicago. The group performed at Madison Square Garden on November 24, 1886, and concluded its run there on February 22, 1887.

Black Elk later admitted to living the life of a "common man" during this period and not fulfilling his life's mission. His confession defined a lifestyle that simply saw him move from one experience to the other without much purposeful reflection or direction. Although he contemplated returning home, friends persuaded him to accompany the show to England. The entourage included 133 Indians, who left the United States on the steamship *State of Nebraska* on March 31, 1887. Black Elk's companions were Strong Talk, Red Shirt, and Dreaming Bear.

Although many Indians wanted to join the traveling shows, Agent H. D. Gallagher at Pine Ridge did not hold this form of entertainment in high regard. He submitted a critical report in 1890 that sought to close access to the shows. Referring to them, he wrote: "The record of suffering, demoralization, and death among the Indians traveling with shows, for one year, would fill a volume" (Gallagher 1890, 51). The agent's resistance had little effect on the practice. Indians continued to appear in the shows for many years.

The trans-Atlantic trip was bittersweet for those who made the journey. It introduced them to high adventure and sights they never imagined. But it also made them sick and fearful, and Black Elk thought the boat would at some point come to the edge of the ocean and fall off. He saw what was probably a whale, which he described as a "big black thing" (DeMallie 1984a, 248), and compared the large waves to mountains. When a severe storm made the crew distribute life preservers, many of the Lakota began to sing their death songs.

Buffalo Bill's Wild West Show performed in London from May 9 to October 31, 1887. A command performance was given for Queen Victoria on May 11, and Black Elk said that he was among only five who were chosen to participate on this occasion. Perhaps humorously feigning pride, he reported that show officials selected him because he was one of "the best looking types" of Indians and one of "the best dancers" (DeMallie 1984a, 249).

Queen Victoria, whom Black Elk called "Grandmother England," was impressed by what she saw. A popular but apparently fictional account later circulated about her bowing to the American flag on this occasion. However, she did shake hands with Black Elk and the other Indians who were lined up according to height. Black Elk said that she did not shake hands with the non-Indian performers, and he recalled this event as a "most happy time" (DeMallie 1984a, 251).

The queen told everyone how handsome she thought they were and that she did not think they should be placed on display as "beasts" were (DeMallie 1984a, 250). Perhaps her observation was actually a reflection offered by Black Elk, or his son, years later. It seems out of place since the queen then proceeded to invite the cast of the show to perform again at Windsor Castle on June 20, instead of promising not to display them. Seeing the queen's jewel-studded crown and shiny dress, and the ornate silver and gold harnesses on her horse-drawn carriage, Black Elk thought "she looked like a fire coming" (251). At least four kings and twenty members of European royal families attended the event, signifying its importance.

When the queen parted, her subjects bowed in honor to her, but she bowed to the assembled Indians. Returning the honor, the Indians raised a tremolo for her and sang. It was just as memorable and happy an occasion for Black Elk as it was for the royalty.

Buffalo Bill took his show to Birmingham and Manchester, and then sailed from London to New York on May 6, 1888. However, Black Elk said that he and three friends "got lost" and did not remain with Buffalo Bill after their command performance for the queen (DeMallie 1984a, 251). Unable to speak English, they wandered around London until they were arrested by police as possible suspects in a crime that would later be associated with Jack the Ripper. An interpreter verified that they were not involved in the incident and suggested they connect with a smaller show that was comparable to Buffalo Bill's.

Black Elk told Neihardt that "there was nothing there but Omahas" (DeMallie 1984a, 251). He was referring to members of the Omaha Indian nation traveling with this company. Still, he and his companions joined the "Mexican Joe" Shelley Show because the pay of thirty dollars a month was more than what Buffalo Bill had provided. Traveling through France, Germany, and Italy, young Black Elk eventually beheld Mount Vesuvius where he learned about the destruction of Pompeii. Feeling homesick, he wanted and was encouraged to return home. Before doing so, he found comfort in Paris where, he said, "lots of white friends" welcomed him (252).

Black Elk's time in Europe was not limited solely to performing in the shows. Besides sightseeing, he also met and romanced a young woman. Neihardt's notes suggest Black Elk may have confused London with Paris, so some researchers think the woman might have been English. Black Elk's daughter, however, thought otherwise.

Apart from a briefly detailed recollection of the woman, Neihardt's notes reveal nothing about how she and Black Elk met or sustained the relationship. Black Elk did not report how they managed conversation or what helped him establish rapport with her family. Before leaving the young woman in the spring of 1889, he told her that he thought their relationship was strong. He asked her to follow him as soon as she could, but this never took place.

While playing the role of showman in Europe, Black Elk also was on a quest to learn all he could about "the white man's ways" (DeMallie 1984a, 245). He was especially interested in learning about the Christianity he saw practiced in Europe. He remarked in letters home how impressed he was to see so many people attending religious services at cathedrals.

European piety left a lasting and favorable impression that Black Elk reported to Neihardt and described while still overseas. His letters from Europe (1886–89) reveal an interest in religion that was lifelong:

I live remembering God. . . . [T]he show runs day and
night . . . but all along I live remembering God so he en-
ables me to do it all. . . . I know the white man's customs
well. One custom is very good. Whoever believes in God
will find good ways.

. . . Of the white man's many customs, only his faith,
the white man's beliefs about God's will, and how they act
according to it, I wanted to understand. . . . So Lakota people, trust in God! Now all along I trust in God. (De-
Mallie 1984a, 8–10)

Curious about Christianity before having much exposure to it
within the reservation setting, Black Elk expressed in another letter the desire to see where Jesus was killed.

This early exposure to Christian practice in Europe was formative. Overseas, Black Elk was able to evaluate the religion objec-
tively, as an outsider "looking in." This contrasted with the
experience of Pine Ridge residents who, like it or not, *had* to accept
the presence of religious and secular newcomers.

Envisioning a Return Home

Black Elk's departure from Europe came about through a peculiar experience that took place one morning when he sat down
for breakfast. He was "all slicked up" (i.e., clean and well-dressed),
he later told John Neihardt, when he suddenly fell off his chair, unconscious (DeMallie 1984a, 252).[5] A doctor pronounced him
dead, so the family he was staying with ordered a casket, but then
Black Elk awakened. While he was seemingly dead to his hosts,
Black Elk was alive within an entirely different world of experience.
He said that he felt as if he were on a cloud that carried him across
the ocean until it hovered above his mother's tipi. From that high
position, he saw relatives mourning his death! This is when he
snapped back into consciousness.

The week after this experience, Black Elk boarded a White Star
Line ship and made the eight-day voyage to New York. He took a
train from there to Chicago, then on to Omaha, and finally

Rushville, Nebraska, where he found a ride to Pine Ridge. Arriving home in 1889, he found his mother's tipi pitched just as it had been in his dream. The people who greeted him were also the ones he saw from on top of his cloud. Black Elk regarded this experience as extraordinary, but his dreaming of home, perhaps in delirium, seems as unremarkable as his home appearing just as he left it. Nonetheless, he and others considered the dream a wakan, or sacred, visionary experience.

In the year after this out-of-body experience, Black Elk again was swept into another realm of consciousness. This time, as an active participant in the ghost dance religion, he fainted and had a vision of someone he understood to be the Son of God, the *wanikiye* (savior). As had occurred during his boyhood vision, this experience also communicated to him a strong sense of mission or religious leadership. However, Black Elk's heart would soon be broken and his confidence shaken in a spirit world that had earlier so powerfully conveyed supernatural affirmation.

CHAPTER 6

Ghost Dance

When Black Elk returned from Europe in 1889, many Plains Indian peoples were being attracted to a religious movement known as the ghost dance. Treaty obligations had not been met, and this federal miscarriage combined with crop failures, drought, disease, and death to produce suffering on a large scale. In the fall of 1890, Indian agent H. D. Gallagher accurately described the mood of Pine Ridge when he wrote, "There has been gradually growing among them a feeling of indifference to the future, which I attribute to an entire loss of faith in the promises of the Government" (Gallagher 1890, 49).

Losing faith in the government gave way to finding it in a Nevada Paiute named Wovoka, known also as Jack Wilson. While old traditions still held sway during this period, the new doctrine contained overt Christian themes that the people found appealing. This nuanced theological milieu profoundly affected Black Elk's generation. When Gallagher was replaced as agent by the political appointee Daniel Royer, conditions were ripe for what some journalists called "the messiah craze."[1]

The Lakota had some exposure to Christian teaching, but their version of the ghost dance added claims that became a source of conflict with mainstream tenets. Key among them was that the Son of God would return again, but only for Indian people. Adherents maintained that God's son knew that Indian people would treat him in a manner he deserved and not kill him as the whites had done many years earlier. Sometimes Wovoka himself was identified as the *wanikiye* (savior).

Short Bull and his brother-in-law, Kicking Bear, were the dance's primary advocates at Pine Ridge and Rosebud. Bringing word of the ghost dance to Pine Ridge in the spring of 1890, the year after Black Elk returned, they said that the wanikiye would restore all that was lost and rekindle the people's spirit. The savior also would raise to life the Indian dead, return the vanished buffalo, and make the earth swallow up all non-Indians, along with Indians who did not accept the dance.

However, by the end of the year, a mass grave of ghost dancers would instead give silent witness to what happened on the reservation at Wounded Knee, an iconic name that came to symbolize the suffering endured by Indian people since 1492. Almost a century later, the name continued to resonate. *Bury My Heart at Wounded Knee* became a 1970 best seller (and 2007 award-winning made-for-television movie), its title drawn from the Stephen Vincent Benét poem "American Names." Both the poem and the book referred to the 1890 event that saw many Lakota die in confrontation with the U.S. Army.

Texts that survey Indian history often conclude with this event, and *Black Elk Speaks* is quoted probably more than any other source in references to it—words attributed to the holy-man conclude *Bury My Heart*. His reflections represent an "end of the trail" worldview that became attached to him and Native people as a whole. Because of this association, Wounded Knee and the religious practices that preceded it merit special attention.

Black Elk's Ghost Dance Participation

Black Elk worked as a store clerk upon his return from Europe in 1889, and his father died in the fall of that year. Lucy said that her grandfather's body was placed on a scaffold, which was a customary committal for the deceased when they were not placed in tree limbs or buried. Neihardt noted that the elder Black Elk was "buried," but this might have been a shorthand way of saying that the family took care of funeral arrangements.

Black Elk remained in mourning as the dance gained adherents over the months that followed. Like others who similarly lost loved ones at this time, he was dispirited. Many Lakota were, however, buoyed by the hope they acquired in visions while dancing and this drew Black Elk's attention.

Going into a trance state was common for ghost dance participants like Black Elk. For prolonged periods, they would hold hands, move to the left, sway back and forth with eyes closed, and dream of the messiah's new day. Falling to the ground, the dancers eventually emerged from the trance as others asked what vision they saw or what revelation they received.

Father John Jutz, the Jesuit superior at Pine Ridge, described a ghost dance he witnessed there in October of 1890, and it parallels an account Black Elk provided. Jutz wrote: "The leader of the dance . . . loudly spoke several words that were repeated by everyone. Thereupon all of the dancers turned their faces southward, raised both of their hands . . . and sang at the top of their voices. . . . This singing lasted for about 2 or 3 minutes; then they all turned to face the holy tree and firmly interlocked their hands" (Kreis 2007).

Jutz then reported that everyone stood calmly and close together. They gradually started moving around in a circle en masse, with their eyes closed or staring at the ground. The pace quickened as everyone sang to a dance that included much hand and foot movement.

After about twenty minutes, people began to stagger, moan, and roll their eyes. Other dancers tried to support them, but to no avail. Falling within or outside the circle, people flailed their arms, rolled in the dust, and scraped the ground, seizure-like, until completely spent. Jutz said that it took about thirty minutes for these dancers to recover from what appeared to be an unconscious state.

This continued for about ninety minutes until everyone paused for rest—only to resume the dance in another two hours. According to Jutz, the dancers' unconscious condition was a state of dying, "and the medicine men told them that in this state they would see the Messiah and their deceased parents and friends, and that those who died in this way would be especially sanctified." The priest also noted that dancers were clothed in war regalia, and protective shirts that the medicine men said would deflect bullets (Kreis 2007, 158–60).

These "ghost shirts" had religious insignia painted on them, and believers thought their protective power was indeed a blessing. The savior had taken pity on their condition and provided them with a new defense, or so it seemed (Wovoka later denied making this assertion).

Contrary to what is sometimes claimed, Black Elk was not the shirt's originator. He did, however, possess one of the garments and designed them for others (he painted images on shirts that he saw in a vision). While the idea of protective shirts may have been adopted from a Mormon initiation practice (which included vesting in a religious garment considered to be invulnerable), American anthropologist James Mooney learned that inspiration for the shirt usage came from a vision of a Lakota woman, Return From Scout's wife.

The shirt worn by Black Elk had a spotted eagle painted on the back and a star on the left shoulder. From there, a rainbow extended across his chest and to his right hip. Another rainbow was sketched around the neck like a necklace with a star at the bottom. He also attached eagle feathers to the shoulders, elbows, and openings at the wrists of the garment. Over the entire shirt were red streaks representing lightning.

Although Neihardt parenthetically noted that "Black Elk was considered the chief . . . [and] most important ghost dancer," his name does not appear in any of the standard histories (DeMallie 1984a, 266). Of the sixty-six men whom Indian police considered "prime leaders" in the movement, Black Elk's name is number sixty-five.[3] Nonetheless, Neihardt's account of the holy-man's experience prompted a Hollywood film director to visit Pine Ridge in the 1970s. He had read *Bury My Heart at Wounded Knee* and *Black Elk Speaks* and concluded that the Lakota could be filmed still dancing as Wovoka had instructed. Eight decades too late, the director returned to Los Angeles without the footage he sought.

Biblical Themes within the Dance Visions of Black Elk and Others

In early December of 1890, the much-respected Jutz went on a peacekeeping mission with Jack Red Cloud (ghost-dancing son of the elder statesman-warrior, Red Cloud) into a Badlands refuge known as "the Stronghold." Taking refuge there were many dancers who were prepared to fight the army, but Jutz persuaded them to return to the agency headquarters at Pine Ridge. This prevented what could have been a larger death toll than was to occur a few weeks later. Ecstatic religious experience like that of the ghost dancers is a global phenomenon found in many religious traditions and is protected under the freedom of religion in the U.S. Bill of Rights. However, its appearance in the ghost dance elicited little tolerance from the U.S. government or general public at the time.[4]

Black Elk's dance vision, however, resonated with Christian scripture. He fell to the ground in what could be variously described as a delusional, mystical, or rapturous state of mind. In that condition he met "12 men" who assured him that he also would meet the "two-legged chief" (DeMallie 1984a, 263).

At the center of a circled village, he saw the tree of his boyhood vision "in full bloom" and against this tree he "saw a man standing with outstretched arms." This figure addressed Black Elk, saying: "All earthly beings that grow belong to me. My Father has said this. You must say this." According to Black Elk, the figure "was a nice-looking man." "All around him there was light," he said. "It seemed as though there were wounds in the palms of his hands" (DeMallie 1984a, 263).

Since Black Elk became familiar with Christian teaching while in Europe, these images are not surprising. His ghost dance vision drew upon the European experience and religious ideas that were circulating among his people at the time. Hence, the twelve men were the disciples, or followers, of the "two-legged chief" (the Christ). As Christian doctrine taught, this son of the "Father" was given power over "all earthly beings" (DeMallie 1984a, 263).[5]

Black Elk's vision was of a crucified wanikiye (the man standing against a tree with arms outstretched and wounds in his hands).

However, this savior was now in a glorified state, i.e., light surrounded him and his body "changed into all colors and . . . was very beautiful" (DeMallie 1984a, 263). DeMallie suggested this vision paralleled the Transfiguration story of the synoptic Gospels, in which the Christ's face shone radiantly and his clothing gleamed white (263n).

The experience was potent enough to stir within Black Elk an expanded sense of mission during the ghost dance period. At first, the dance vision was enigmatic and difficult to understand. As time passed, he understood Jesus to be the "chief" who could make the tree of his childhood vision reach "full bloom." The wanikiye spoke through this vision and personally enjoined him to preach the gospel when he told Black Elk, "You must say this."

Many dancers reported comparable themes in their visions. Kicking Bear, for example, claimed to have a vision in which he met a longhaired man who bore the wounds of crucifixion. This sacred individual told the dance's chief protagonist that he was aware of what the Lakota were enduring and that he would come to their rescue. The people accepted Kicking Bear's teaching as a new "way of prayer" that would help them (a "way of prayer" referred both to the praying one did and the religious tradition one practiced).

When asked in the 1930s why he wore his hair long in two loose hanks, the much-respected, often-quoted, and long-lived Iron Hail, a survivor of the impending violence who was also known as Dewey Beard, replied, "Because our savior, Jesus Christ, is always pictured that way" (Miller 1971). This hairstyle was part of the theological legacy passed down by wisdom keepers like Kicking Bear, Wovoka, and others of the ghost dance period.

Wovoka's teachings gained additional credibility when troops arrived in Lakota country on November 19, 1890. This occurred because Washington thought a show of force could prevent an uprising that some observers said the ghost dance would spawn. Instead of discouraging the ghost dance, however, an expanded military presence had the opposite effect. While it frightened the population, it also suggested that the soldiers were summoned to prevent the prophecies from being fulfilled! Unfortunately, these elements conspired to make a hope-filled dream become the nightmare of Wounded Knee.

Black Elk's role in that nightmare occurred after the initial engagement between the military and ghost dancers, and it was this role that Neihardt chronicled. Accurate in describing the carnage, Black Elk's story was also an interpretive account. Probably the most-quoted narrative of the much-disputed event, the holy-man's perspective requires further comment since Neihardt's book did not reveal how the holy-man eventually internalized the experience.

The Confrontation at Wounded Knee in 1890

Since the Office of Indian Affairs had banned ghost dancing, and since Big Foot's band of Minneconjou ghost dancers was absent from its reservation without proper authorization, the dancers were ordered to be arrested by five hundred soldiers of the Seventh Cavalry. Big Foot's people had traveled to Pine Ridge from the Cheyenne River Reservation and had been joined by some Hunkpapa Lakota from the Standing Rock Reservation. They sought refuge among the Oglala after fleeing the reservation in the wake of Sitting Bull's killing by Indian police there on December 15. Big Foot's people said that they came to Pine Ridge because they were fearful of action the army might take against them. Not having the same sense of alarm as Big Foot's band, most of the population at Cheyenne River and Standing Rock remained at home. If more people had followed Big Foot's lead, a greater tragedy could have unfolded.

Big Foot was a tired and sickly leader who agreed to have his people be escorted to Pine Ridge when stopped by Maj. Samuel M. Whitside near Wounded Knee Creek on Sunday December 28, 1890. Whitside supplied him with a private hospital tent and gave tents to others in need. Artillery was placed on what eventually became a cemetery hill that overlooked the camp.

Indians and cavalry spent the night in close proximity to one another, and soldiers were pleased that Big Foot's surrender occurred without incident. James Asay, a local trader, provided a small amount of liquor to officers (not the enlisted men), and the soldier

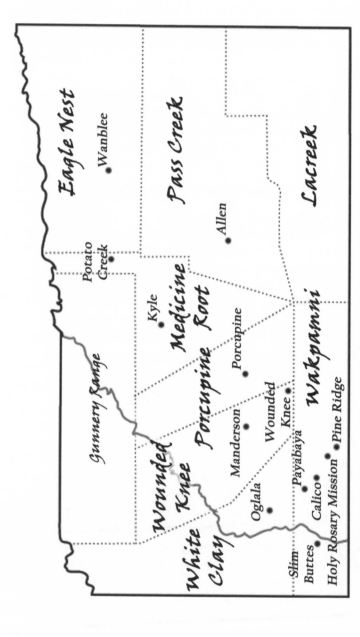

Pine Ridge Reservation, with districts and villages. Reprinted with permission from *Black Elk: Holy Man of the Oglala*, by Michael F. Steltenkamp (Norman: University of Oklahoma Press, 1993).

camp was in bed early. Indians reported that they were restless and afraid during the night.

Shortly after 8 A.M. on December 29, Col. James W. Forsyth took charge, and he asked the Lakota men to separate from the women and children. In what was later evaluated as a tactical blunder, his troops intermingled with Indians at the site since no hostility was expected. Forsyth told Big Foot to have his people turn over their arms, but this request garnered only a few old pieces (the number of weapons varies in accounts). When told that his people were not cooperating, Big Foot insisted that they had surrendered their firearms.

Forsyth then ordered soldiers to conduct a search-and-seizure operation. Some of Big Foot's people were cooperative and some were not. At one point, diehard dancers resisted and raised their twelve-shot Winchesters that had been hidden under blankets they carried.

Did the infirm Big Foot know that some arms were not surrendered? Was he lying to Forsyth, who knew some dancers had repeating rifles? These are unanswerable questions that only contribute to the controversy. Later Lakota accounts charged that Big Foot's men were defenseless and so scrambled to retrieve their confiscated weapons. Maybe some of the Lakota surrendered guns and some did not.

Leading up to the violence, nerves were frayed by the behavior of what might positively be described as a "devout" medicine man named Yellow Bird. By contrast, his actions and words also could be understood as the behavior of a ghost dancing "fanatic." Blowing an eagle-bone whistle as he danced, Yellow Bird chanted a song that part Santee Dakota interpreter Philip Wells translated: "Do not be afraid! Let your hearts be strong to meet what is before you! There are lots of soldiers and they have lots of bullets, but the prairie is large and the bullets will not go toward you, but over the large prairies. . . . As you saw me throw up the dust and it floated away, so will the bullets float harmlessly away over the prairie" (Utley 1963, 210).[6] One scholar argued that Yellow Bird's chant was intended to calm Big Foot's people by assuring them of protection (Ostler 2002, 343). Wells, however, sensed something more sinister was at play—imminent armed resistance, backed by the dancers' belief that the protective shirts would be effective.

Accounts differ in detail but agree that tension was in the air. Since some among Big Foot's people thought their shirts would make them invulnerable, a contentious attitude was no doubt present to some degree at the time of surrender. Others in the band, however, simply wanted to end the whole affair and return home. Not everyone thought alike.

A deaf Minneconjou variously identified as Black Fox or Black Coyote (the latter being correct) resisted the soldiers who came to take his rifle. Turning Hawk described this person as "a young man of very bad influence and a nobody" (Utley 1963, 212). He discharged his weapon skyward (one account says a soldier was shot), and its report triggered gunfire that might have come from the soldiers or the Indians. Who fired the first volley will likely never be resolved. Most reports say that a group of warriors drew rifles from under their blankets and fired at the troops in front of them. According to some Lakota survivors, it was the army that immediately sent a volley at Indians across from them when the first shot was fired. The ensuing chaos saw men, women, and children flee, fall dead, or suffer serious wounds. Smoke from gunfire quickly filled the field, and survivors on both sides said that it was difficult to see anything in the confusion.

Black Elk recalled two casualties of the encounter when Neihardt interviewed him in 1944. The holy-man was describing how his people understood instances of feeble-mindedness when it surfaced in former times. These persons, he said, were never dangerous, and one such soul was named Bear Fool. Since he was not present when the exchange of gunfire took place, Black Elk learned of Bear Fool's experience from others.

Camped at Wounded Knee when gunfire erupted, Bear Fool was perched on a wagon. When he saw someone get shot (presumably a soldier), he would shout, "They got another—woo woo." In doing this, he stood to "cheer," and then was shot and killed (DeMallie 1984a, 395). Black Elk added that Bear Fool's grandmother also died at this time, not from a bullet, but from what Black Elk said was a "heart attack" (not a clinical diagnosis, but his way of reporting the shock and fear she must have experienced).

Bear Fool and his grandmother were like many others who watched the proceedings from their camp behind the soldiers. Historian Robert Utley concluded that Indians opened fire and that "every shot that missed a soldier plowed into the village, where women and children scrambled in terrified confusion to get out of the way" (Utley 1963, 213). Troops returned deadly fire immediately as both sides were in a "kill or be killed" confrontation. Each side might well have taken casualties from their own "friendly fire."

Black Elk at Wounded Knee

The sound of Hotchkiss guns could be heard from far away, and this drew Black Elk from Pine Ridge. Perhaps he associated this sound with the voice of Thunder-beings calling him as they had in the past. He came upon the scene, and chaos reigned. The bodies of men, women, and children, dead or dying, were strewn about the ravine, and wounded others needed immediate attention.

Black Elk told Neihardt that he charged soldiers and that their bullets bounced off him. He also claimed that his power made the soldiers run from him in slow motion. The stenographic record of this experience portrays Black Elk depicting himself as an inspired warrior who made a frightened enemy flee his unarmed attack—he carried only a bow. He said that supernatural protection accompanied him, but the mythical quality of his account raises suspicion as to its factual content.

No other source corroborates the type of encounter Black Elk described. Neihardt's notes read as if they are one continuous commentary coming from the holy-man, but perhaps they include the contribution of others. His portrayal could thus be an embellishment or a composite of several accounts. Other sources report that about one hundred fifty men from Pine Ridge deployed themselves around the site and sporadically fired at troops. However, Utley (1963) concluded that "the fresh force of warriors had no intention of challenging the soldiers."

Whatever his role on the field of battle, Black Elk saw the carnage and did all he could to remove people to safety. He returned to Pine Ridge at night and found his mother and others fearing for their lives. The next day he went with a friend, He Crow, to Holy Rosary Mission.

Located four miles north of the town of Pine Ridge and built by the Jesuits in 1888 while Black Elk was in Europe, Holy Rosary was also known as the Drexel Mission or Red Cloud Mission. In the days after Wounded Knee, some Cheyenne immigrants wanted to burn the mission but were prevented from doing so through the intervention of Red Cloud and others. Most Lakota considered the mission home to "black robes," whom they believed to be trustworthy mediators. Interpreter Philip Wells said that the Lakota agreed that the mission "would be treated as sacred, and that all that was therein would receive protection and be exempt from danger" (Jensen 2005, 162).

In the hills behind the mission, Forsyth's command came under fire on December 30, 1890. Newspapers informed readers that the clash saw Maj. Guy V. Henry's Ninth Cavalry buffalo soldiers save the Seventh Cavalry from suffering another Little Bighorn. However, this version of the event, while popular, was not accurate. Both sides reported a few casualties, but the incident amounted to the exchange of gunfire that could have, but did not, become more deadly.

It was Henry's heralded African American cavalry unit that discouraged further engagement with Forsyth's command. Black Elk referred to these buffalo soldiers as "black white men," but this understanding was not his alone. When the Alcan Highway was constructed through Canada to Alaska in the 1940s, a Canadian Native echoed the holy-man's perception when he recalled "the first white man I ever saw was black."[7]

Black Elk was at this clash by the mission and recalled not trusting his vision. He thought he would have remained bulletproof had he kept charging the soldiers with his hands up and imitating the sound of geese traveling north in the spring. Their sound was one of triumph since it announced that winter's challenges had been overcome. In not making this sound, Black Elk said that his

fear and doubt caused him to receive a bullet wound in the ab-
domen. When this occurred, a friend by the name of Protector con-
vinced him to withdraw and get medical treatment.

Taking refuge with others in the Stronghold, Black Elk recovered from his wound with the help of Old Hollow Horn, a "bear
medicine man" or specialist adept in treating wounds and fractures.
On January 3, 1891, Black Elk captured five horses in a skirmish,
later giving a couple to two men who were on foot. The next day
he wanted to kill soldiers but was restrained from doing so by his
three companions, Kills Enemy, Poor Buffalo, and Brave Heart.
Neihardt reported this restraint Black Elk exercised but an in-law
of Black Elk's later claimed that the holy-man admitted to shooting a soldier during this period.

Returning to the Stronghold, Black Elk invoked the power of
his vision and assured those there that they would be protected. He
wanted to resume battle exploits but it was then that Red Cloud
and Young Man Afraid of His Horses came from Pine Ridge and
persuaded the "hostiles" to return to the agency. On January 14,
1891, the surrender took place. Black Elk was part of the caravan
that either walked, rode horseback, or returned in wagons through
two lines of soldiers who presented arms. He said that officers
"saluted" them (DeMallie 1984a, 282) as they passed by (presumably a respectful gesture).

Aftermath

After the fighting and surrender, both sides had to deal with the
deaths that had resulted. Although the official report listed twenty-
eight army personnel killed and thirty-four wounded that day, a
later report said that about fifty coffins were needed for soldier fa-
talities (Ames 1933). The Lakota toll was much higher, and estimates at the time ranged between two hundred (the army figure),
two hundred fifty (Mooney), and three hundred (General Miles,
Dewey Beard, and Pipe-on-Head). Some also died in the days after the engagement. Utley said that twenty to thirty others should
be added to the 153 known dead. However, when the casualties are
seen only as figures, these different tolls conceal that each tally

represents the treasured lives lost of men, women, or children within a community that was not large.

A private company was hired to bury the Lakota dead, and charges were levied decades later that some were buried alive. Witnesses of the interment made no such observation, while members of the burial party reported being distressed by their task because so many women and children were involved. Interred at the battlefield's mass grave on January 3, 1891, were eighty-four men, forty-four women, and eighteen children. In 1902, a stone memorial was placed on the grave etched with the names of forty-five persons who were buried there. Located at a major crossroads of the reservation, this site has been a permanent reminder to Black Elk's people of a literally indescribable horror that occurred there.

CHAPTER 7

Wounded Knee Legacy

Wounded Knee took place in 1890, and its painful memory became an oral tradition that expanded with the passage of time. In the twentieth century, the repercussions of the event bled into art and American pop culture that often drew on Black Elk material. By invoking the holy-man's memory of this tragic event, commentators called attention to one of Indian history's worst chapters. However, what readers accepted as Black Elk's reminiscence was actually John Neihardt's poetic interpretation of how the holy-man must have felt. As a result, Neihardt's rendering and the event itself—and their twentieth-century pop culture representations—call for clarification.

From the Dakota community, renowned artist Oscar Howe contributed to Wounded Knee's legacy in 1960 with a work titled "Wounded Knee Massacre." The painting grimly captured a stereotype associated with the event that partly arose from its depiction in *Black Elk Speaks*. Howe sketched soldiers shooting Big Foot's unarmed people.

Hollywood reinforced this theme of wanton slaughter in the 1970s by producing a series of films that generated a cult following. The main character, Billy Jack, was portrayed as an Indian Green Beret Vietnam veteran who seemed to be a kind of contemporary Black Elk (religious mentor, one with nature, wise counselor, ecologist, etc.). One scene showed Billy witness his

fellow soldiers massacre a village of innocent people, and this paralleled an incident—the My Lai massacre—then in the news.
Army personnel perpetrated the same heinous act against Viet-
namese peasants, and Wounded Knee, for many people, was considered the event's precedent.

Along with films of lesser note, another film popular in Indian
country, *Little Big Man,* like the Billy Jack series, liberally drew from
Black Elk material. Apart from its lead Indian character sounding
like Black Elk's persona in *Black Elk Speaks,* and apart from depicting events such as the Battle of the Little Bighorn, the film's last
scene paralleled the well-known conclusion of Neihardt's book that
portrayed Black Elk praying on Harney Peak in the Black Hills. In
his Academy Award–winning performance, Indian actor Chief
Dan George seemed the cinematic embodiment of the aged holy-
man. Susan Forsyth's book *Representing the Massacre of American Indians at Wounded Knee, 1890–2000* reveals other portrayals of the
event in addition to these.

Indian activism in the 1970s prompted many artists, directors,
and historians to present versions of what had happened to Native
peoples since 1492, and some of their accounts remain in conflict.
As for Wounded Knee, modern attempts to look at the event with
a new perspective do not always ring true with the accounts of those
who, like Black Elk, were there. In the meantime, Black Elk was cast
in *Black Elk Speaks* as a person bound by the experience of
Wounded Knee when his life illustrated that his dream for his people, and all people, was much greater than that.

Conflicting Accounts of What Happened

Accounts of what transpired at Wounded Knee are often difficult to reconcile with one another. Inflammatory journalism of the
period charged that the event served as the Seventh Cavalry's revenge for Custer's defeat. However, interviews with the military and
Lakota testimony in 1891 did not raise this specter. Another ac-
cusation was that the U.S. Army troops were intoxicated when the
conflict broke out, but this was not noted by Indian or non-Indian
participants at the time.

Disagreement lingers over which side fired the first volley, how events unfolded, who fired the last shot, and what acts of intentional cruelty, if any, took place. Black Elk heard that it was Yellow Bird who discharged his rifle while wrestling with a soldier. Mooney agreed with him, but most accounts say it was someone else. One person thought he heard Forsyth give the order to "fire," while someone near the colonel said that he heard no such command. Father Craft, a Catholic priest who was present, understood that Big Foot died from a single wound to the neck, while another account reported his body was bullet-riddled.

The time line for what occurred is more or less known, but even it has been debated. Black Elk's daughter understood that her father was at Wounded Knee "after it was over" (Steltenkamp 1993, 27). However, Neihardt reports Black Elk saying "the battle started at about 10 o'clock" and "we fought all day" (DeMallie 1984a, 274).

Gunfire actually erupted around 9 A.M., and the consensus is that the initial chaos lasted perhaps ten minutes and that sporadic gunfire followed. According to one soldier, Private Allen, fighting "lasted until about 4 or 5" in the afternoon, but Utley (1963) reported "everyone relaxed and set about the task of cleaning up the battlefield . . . close to noon." Historian Rex Alan Smith (1975, 196) added that a "sad caravan" of survivors headed for Pine Ridge around 3:30 in the afternoon with reporters filing their stories from Rushville, Nebraska, by 5 P.M. the same day.

The death of innocents at Wounded Knee has been especially troubling. Some accounts report soldiers wantonly killing noncombatants. Easier to substantiate were deaths that occurred when armed and unarmed women and children accompanied the men in taking flight. Many received deathblows from Hotchkiss shells that landed in the vicinity of Lakota who returned shots as they fled. Still others were felled by the chaotic crossfire.

The apocalyptic encounter included killing that took place some distance away from the conflict's well-known site. This led some to conclude that vengeful soldiers hunted down people who were far away from the action. However, Black Elk reported the lethal presence of combatant children at the event. Their role might not exonerate the army of all culpability, but it does reveal that everyone on the battlefield, regardless of age, was a potential threat. Black Elk recalled: "There were two little boys at one place. They had been killing soldiers all by themselves. We could see the soldiers they had killed. The boys were all alone there, and they were not hurt. They were brave boys" (DeMallie 1984a, 274).

The U.S. Army investigation includes testimony that soldiers sought to engage only warriors, but that (as also described by Black Elk) the battlefield included women, as well as children, returning deadly fire. Because of this, a court of inquiry exonerated the troops even though some of the participants in the engagement were recent recruits, whose behavior under fire garnered criticism from seasoned veterans. Isolated incidents prolonged the encounter and added to a death toll that should never have occurred.

Did the army's placement of artillery overlooking the camp mean that the U.S. soldiers had murderous intent before the confrontation even took place? Although Big Foot's people admitted to being treated well when surrendering, the Hotchkiss guns were an ominous presence that concerned them. They and critics of this arrangement did not know that army protocol required artillery to be ready for action when in the field. It was never simply placed under tarpaulins and left unattended. Battery personnel claimed that when finally discharged, the guns were aimed only at pockets of Lakota producing incoming fire.

Critics also later charged that the army attempted to cover up what could be considered a slaughter by emphasizing the valor of its soldiers. A matter of protest since its occurrence, the most Medals of Honor ever awarded for a single engagement in the history of the U.S. Army were handed out after Wounded Knee (three officers and fifteen enlisted men received the medal). However, a more mundane explanation of why medals were awarded mutes this critique.

The Medal of Honor was the only award that *could* have been conferred during this period of American history since a "certificate of merit" was the rarely given alternative. Consequently, men who received medals at Wounded Knee (less than 4 percent of the total) did not receive them for the reason (heroism) that soldiers would receive them in later periods. Rather, soldiers simply received a medal if cited by their commanding officer for any deed considered worthy of recognition.

Casualties also resulted from friendly fire, while other participants died at the hands of civilians who were present. A journalist, for example, acknowledged killing three Lakota. Still, what happened at Wounded Knee makes a persuasive case against Washington's over-reliance on military intervention to resolve conflict. Once committed to the field, the army might have done as well as could be expected. A vocal critic of the government and advocate for the Lakota he tried to shepherd, Father Jutz concluded in reference to the event, "I do not at all believe that any soldier killed or wounded a woman or child deliberately" (Kreis 2007, 152). As with military initiatives anywhere, though, actions came into play that bureaucratic directives could not foretell.

Big Foot's people were confronted with overwhelming odds, but this gave no assurance that the military's show-of-force strategy would be successful. Since many dancers thought the supernatural was on their side, no opponent was too intimidating to them. And yet, not everyone seemed to share this opinion. Helping one of the wounded, interpreter Wells recalled a person cursing the dead medicine man in gesture and in words. He translated what the person shouted in the direction of Yellow Bird, the slain medicine man: "I am sorry I cannot do more to you. If I could be taken to you, I would stab you! He is our murderer! Only for him inciting our other young men we would have been alive and happy!" (Smith 1975, 195). Along with other Lakota survivors, Big Foot's brother, Frog, corroborated the indictment shouted toward Yellow Bird.

Although Yellow Bird's contemporaries did not see him as a pacifying presence at the event, a reinterpretation of what happened at Wounded Knee a century later described his role differently (Ostler 2002, 342). It suggested that Yellow Bird was only trying to calm his people. This type of debate over what actually happened at Wounded Knee was nothing new. For years after his retirement, interpreter Wells avoided interviews about Wounded Knee. He found that writers sought sensationalism at the expense of what actually took place.

Wounded Knee Revisited

Since history is often told only from the viewpoint of those in power, what often is recorded is not the full story. A 1990 documentary, *Wiping the Tears of Seven Generations*, attempted to fill this void by presenting the viewpoint of Lakota descendants. These descendants were part of a memorial ride that traced Big Foot's journey to Wounded Knee a century earlier. However, in attempting to right the void, the film also offered perspectives that conflict with the experience of Black Elk and others.

The documentary cited Black Elk's memory, but added an account that is seriously at odds with the holy-man's philosophy and religious outlook. By doing so, it reinforced a misunderstanding of beliefs associated with ghost dancers like Black Elk and others. The video reported that just before the shooting began, a Catholic priest (unnamed, but who was Francis Craft) communally administered "last rites" to Big Foot's people. Since the priest did not ask for an interpreter, the documentary implied that he was trying to conceal what he was doing from those assembled. Suggesting collusion between this man and the army, the film further stated that when the priest finished his administration of the rite, an officer ordered the Seventh Cavalry, execution-style, to commence firing.

This depiction runs contrary to Father Craft's memory of the event. His involvement with Wounded Knee is well-known from depositions of Indians and non-Indians and from his diary (Foley 2009). Craft's vilification in the documentary is surprising since Black Elk recalled the priest's presence among his people as positive. He told Neihardt that Craft was a "very good man, and not like the other [white people]" (J. Neihardt 1961, 256).[1]

Craft was, moreover, fluent in Lakota and would not have needed an interpreter. According to his own, and other eyewitness testimony, Craft did not conduct any ritual prior to the eruption of gunfire. He was instead casually conversing with, and giving cigarettes to, some of the Indian men. Craft was at Wounded Knee because he had worked among the Hunkpapa, and both he and government officials thought his presence there might be helpful and pacifying.

Craft's portrayal in the documentary actually reflects a late twentieth-century rhetoric that was critical of Christian churches. This prejudice ironically targeted a man whose sympathy for Indians and ghost dancers was not shared by many. The priest visited dancers at a Rosebud camp and, unlike Father Jutz's appraisal, found their actions "to be all right, quite Catholic and even edifying."[2] Moreover, illustrating the priest's commitment to the Lakota, Craft, who was of Mohawk descent, asked to be buried with Big Foot's people if he did not survive wounds he sustained on the battlefield.

Although it offered a compelling account of this period in Lakota history, the documentary egregiously misrepresented Craft and did not adequately address the doctrine that dancers militantly professed. That is, biblical tradition was the source of core beliefs held by wisdom keepers of the ghost dance era. By not addressing this theology, the documentary implied that Black Elk's generation simply wanted a return of the old ways. While they did desire this return, it would occur by means of a theology that was itself changing with the times. Wounded Knee survivor Joseph Black Hair even said that Big Foot's people "nearly all belonged to some church" (McGregor 1940, 124). They thought of themselves as a kind of chosen people to whom the Son of God would soon come.

A century before the Big Foot memorial ride, Father Craft was already a target for the exact opposite reason than that cited in the video. He and the Jesuits bore the brunt of the era's infamous yellow journalism, or sensational stories unsupported by facts. Seen by some as too friendly with Indian causes, "Catholic priests" were said to be "worse enemies to the Government than old Sitting Bull was."[3]

The period, however, was rife with prejudice that was publicly aired. Interpreter Wells told of a Professor Bailey who visited Father Jutz at Holy Rosary Mission, and who was "hospitably entertained" by the Jesuits. Thereafter this same professor "assailed the Catholics . . . and accused them with responsibility for the war, and

falsely told how the priests received the confessions of the Indians
. . . and took payment in furs and bead work for forgiveness of their
sins" (Jensen 2005, 153). A newspaper editorial especially stands
out for its bigotry. Writing for the *Aberdeen Saturday Pioneer*, Lyman
Frank Baum (1856–1919) proposed "extirmination [sic] of the Indians" in order to protect settlers.[4] This seemingly genocidal sentiment, which was expressed by other journalists of the era (and no
doubt shared by a large portion of the public), besmirches an otherwise enchanting legacy bequeathed by the author of *The Wizard
of Oz*.

A century after Wounded Knee, the motion picture *Thunderheart* (1992) addressed important issues of late twentieth-century
reservation life. It did so by telling the story of a contemporary
Lakota who came to Pine Ridge where he found a polarized
community. He learned about his ancestor, Thunderheart, who
purportedly was a medicine man killed at Wounded Knee. Unfortunately, moviegoers were ill-served when the film associated
dancers solely with a nativistic doctrine.

Had *Thunderheart* better described the ghost dance period,
viewers would have learned that the early reservation's religious milieu was dynamic, not static, and evolving, not fossilized. The film's
concluding scene symbolized its theological shortcoming when it
showed Thunderheart's name etched on the stone memorial at the
famous gravesite. Just as the ghost dance was not portrayed accurately, so too is there no such name as "Thunderheart" on the actual monument.

Like *Thunderheart*, Howe's painting of the "massacre" and the
1990 documentary were *interpretations* of Wounded Knee. They
both sought to explain the pall that hung over destitute reservations.
Ultimately, what took place at Wounded Knee will remain a spring-
board for competing interpretations, and in the midst of these interpretations is Black Elk's elusive identity.

Competing Interpretations

Although *Black Elk Speaks* contains the holy-man's oft-quoted
memories associated with Wounded Knee, Neihardt's emotionally

evocative wording partly captured Black Elk's thought and partly did not. Black Elk did not think the ghost dance's apocalyptic promise was "beautiful" (DeMallie 1984a, 55). However, although the words were not Black Elk's, he did experience the horror Neihardt described:

> And so it was all over. I did not know then how much was ended. When I look back now from this high hill of my old age, I can still see the butchered women and children lying heaped and scattered all along the crooked gulch as plain as when I saw them with eyes still young. And I can see that something else died there in the bloody mud, and was buried in the blizzard. A people's dream died there. It was a beautiful dream. (J. Neihardt 1961, 276)

As popular as this passage became, it misled readers by implying the holy-man's late-life worldview was grounded upon the desolate killing field of 1890.

Black Elk's perspective was not a parochial one. He knew that comparable encounters were endured by people everywhere, and he was not consumed by the terrible memory of this event alone. The holy-man's vision was not frozen in the cold grave of Wounded Knee.

Black Elk was also aware of the conflicting accounts that Wounded Knee elicited. After all, given his version of what transpired, even his role that day is a mystery. It is not clear whether he was just a helpful bystander or mythic warrior.

Debate also exists over reference to the conflict as a "battle" or a "massacre." Ultimately, neither word adequately expresses the trauma this event visited on the people claiming relationship with those who died. Wounded Knee pitted opponents who had a history of conflict with one another against each other. Understood only in this way, its participants become faceless names or statistics in a history text. Their humanity, with all its pain and agony, hopes, dreams, fears and confusions, remains at an impersonal distance. But to the Lakota, the dead at Wounded Knee are relatives.

Over the years, analyses have assigned blame to one side or the other for what took place. Despite justifying its action, the army might never escape criticism for the death toll it inflicted. Similarly, Big Foot and his people could be faulted for blunders of thought and deed, but might also be honored for representing a Lakota effort, under oppressive conditions, to retain independence.

If Wounded Knee is seen as a conflict that victimized everyone, Black Elk's evaluation of the killing field can be better understood. His perspective transcended the debate since he came to understand the participants at Wounded Knee as players on a larger stage of human conflict that has existed in diverse places over time. His position was similar to what Arvol Looking Horse, keeper of the sacred pipe (the most sacred object within Lakota religion), stated in the 1990 documentary. He said that the memorial ride was not intended just to acknowledge Lakota anguish. It was also a Lakota plea for people everywhere to resist problem-solving through violence or the threat of it.

Black Elk's blessing would descend upon this broader vision that Looking Horse addressed. His evaluation was echoed by the Indian rock music band Redbone in its 1973 release ("Wounded Knee") that reached number one on the pop music chart in Europe. Black Elk might well have uttered the song's concluding line: "We were all wounded *by* Wounded Knee."

Like many who survived the experience, Black Elk did not remain locked within its memory. The holy-man eventually was able to find hope in a renewed religious commitment. He found resurrection from the ravine of Wounded Knee. In attempting to understand Black Elk's life more clearly, his descendants have sought to do the same.

CHAPTER 8

Conversion

In 1892, two years after Wounded Knee, when he was about twenty-six, Black Elk married Katie War Bonnet, and this union produced three boys. Never Showed Off was born in 1893, Good Voice Star in 1895, and Benjamin in 1899. *Black Elk Lives* (2000) noted this was a polygynous union that included a marriage to "Katie War Bonnet's sister." However, neither this marriage nor this woman's name appear in other Black Elk material. Still, *Black Elk Lives* named two children associated with this wife (Richard Black Elk Martinez, Jr., and Lillian Iron Bull).

As Black Elk's family expanded in the 1890s, memories remained within the Pine Ridge population of a wanikiye (savior) coming. Different forms of Christian practice made inroads into Lakota country and kept these memories alive. While the Native American Church (peyotism) drew some Lakota, Christian denominations began to claim a growing Native membership.

Because Catholic priests wore a black soutaine, or cassock, the Lakota called them black robes. Clothing worn by Episcopalians earned them the name white robes, while Presbyterians were called short coats. Others came to proselytize later on, but these three groups were the ones that initially came among the Lakota. They expanded the tribal repertoire of religious stories that fleshed out the theme of a savior returning. These hope-filled stories told of a creator who rescued other tribal peoples from a flood, feared enemies, and famine.

Black Elk's Medical Practice

Black Elk conducted his medicine practice as the reservation's religious landscape changed. He said that he committed this outreach "only to the weakest ones," and that a certain plant had been revealed to him for accomplishing the task (DeMallie 1984a, 236). Kills Enemy was with him one day in June of 1885 when birds revealed the location of this curative herb.

Since the plant was one Black Elk had never seen, its anonymity might have been the reason why he considered finding it a special revelation. It had two stems and flowers that were colored blue, red, white, and yellow. Although the description of it is not a perfect match, this was perhaps a variety of Columbine (*Aquilegia canadensis* or *Aquilegia brevistyla*).

Stanley Looking Horse—keeper of the sacred pipe in the twentieth century before his son, Arvol—told a similar story of a plant he mysteriously found that was necessary for curing a sick relative. In this case, however, he knew of the desired plant, and simply had been unable to locate it. He prayed for help and saw eagles flying in the distance. Driving in their direction, he got out of the car, and there found the herb he used to cure his family member.

In both examples, winged creatures were seen to be summoning the men to follow them. Black Elk and Looking Horse conferred supernatural significance on the beckoning birds, their appearance being an otherwise ordinary occurrence within the natural world. Acquiring knowledge in this fashion is what social scientists generically refer to as "divination," and forms of it are popular among numerous ancient and modern peoples.

Divination, or acquiring special knowledge by extraordinary means—in the case of Black Elk and Looking Horse, birds located the plants—has numerous secular and sacred forms. It entails a course of action that, to an outsider, appears random, as in flipping a coin. However, for holy-men like Black Elk and Looking

Horse, their experience was considered the answer to prayer and not a random act.

Augury through the assistance of birds is technically known as "ornithomancy." Using dreams or visions to prophetic ends—an especially important feature of the Lakota world—is known as oneiromancy. In addition to these forms of divination, which exist globally, Black Elk said there were other ways his people could discern future events.

The Lakota believed that one who was about to die could see future events. Black Elk also said that medicine men could tell what was to happen by deciphering petroglyphs in the Black Hills. Black Elk did not name the exact location of these inscriptions but they are believed to be in the Cave Hills. Another of these petroglyph sites was on the Rosebud River.

The First Cure

Black Elk performed his first cure when a man named Cuts To Pieces asked for his assistance. This doctoring occurred the same night that Black Elk discovered the special plant. He admitted to not really knowing how to conduct his ceremony, so his account of it shows how people of his generation learned their art. Like an intern, he drew upon what he witnessed other medicine men do.

In order to demonstrate that he was "really wanted" for this task, Black Elk asked that Cuts To Pieces bring him a pipe with an eagle feather on it (DeMallie 1984a, 236). Paying the practitioner with something of value when requesting a service was (and is) a time-honored custom. The family also presented him a horse, which he could accept four days after the cure was proven effective. After Black Elk ritually smoked the pipe with his parents and a visitor, he reflected on how, exactly, he would perform the ceremony (237).

The patient was a very sick four-year-old boy. Black Elk's medical equipment included a pipe, drum, eagle-bone whistle, wooden cup with water in it, and the herb. He was a novice who harbored self-doubt upon entering the family's tipi, and circling clockwise within it. Nonetheless, Black Elk proceeded and prayed while drumming. After singing, his doubt gave way to confidence, and when the little boy smiled at him, he knew he would be successful.

Black Elk performed the role of what ethnographic literature generically refers to as a "sucking doctor." Found in many cultures, this specialist administers treatment by appearing to suck an object from the patient's body. In doing this, the illness is removed.

Practitioners have reported that before the ceremony, they might cut their gums and hide a small feather on the wound to absorb the blood, thus making the feather unrecognizable. At the appropriate time in the ceremony, the specialist would appear to "suck out" a foreign substance—the bloody feather—from the patient and would spit it on the ground or into a fire for all to see. Those in attendance would witness that some foreign, or "evil," entity—the cause of the illness—had been removed (Santino 1982, 501).

Cultural outsiders might dismiss the practice as charade or intentional deception but might also learn about the therapeutic importance of a physician's bedside manner. Through the ceremony, those in need receive a dramatic assurance that the malady's cause has been addressed satisfactorily. The patient can be confident of relief, abetted through the administration of the healer's real, or placebo-like, curative tonic.

During his cure of the boy, Black Elk drank some water, puffed whiffs of smoke from the pipe, and felt the little blue man of his vision stir within his chest. Stamping four times in front of the boy, he then proceeded to suck "the north wind" through his patient's body. He had cut his gums and hidden a piece of cloth in his mouth, and then withdrew the bloody object to show he "had drawn something out of" the boy's body (DeMallie 1984a, 239).

Making a powder from his herb, he put the substance in hot water and from his mouth sprayed some of the liquid on the boy. He directed someone he described as a "pretty girl" to take it to the patient to drink. She assisted the child in rising and walking in the cardinal directions.

The boy eventually recovered and lived through young adulthood (but died before the age of thirty). After this first cure, Black Elk knew when his healing ceremony would be successful. His cup of water would reflect the patient's smiling face.

After this initial success, other Lakota medical practitioners who were known to invoke malevolent power acknowledged Black Elk's ability, recognized that he had strength, and steered clear of him. His career was, however, short-lived. A researcher found only one person who claimed to be a patient of Black Elk's (the man recalled being treated for a snakebite, a common enough ailment). People might have benefited from Black Elk's effort, but whatever he did as a healer was largely forgotten by the mid–twentieth century.

Later in life, Black Elk claimed that his medical practice had been successful. He told family members that he was adept in curing tuberculosis, and that the plant he used for its remedy could be found on a dark night. Black Elk would stand on a hill and scan the landscape looking for a plant that glowed (possibly the honey mushroom mycelium or fox fire, *Armillaria ostoyae* or *A. mellea*). The root structure of one of his most curative plants seemed to have arm and leg appendages—perhaps American Ginseng (*Panax quinquefolius*).

Beyond these anecdotal recollections, little else is known of Black Elk's medical practice. Although his ceremony reflected the conventional form employed by Lakota practitioners, his presence to others was therapeutic in other ways.

Heyoka

As a young man, Black Elk had been a *heyoka*, and aspects of this role seem to have stayed with him throughout life. Sometimes translated simply to mean "clown," the person who assumed the role of heyoka provided a complex mixture of religion and comedy. One did not just decide to become a heyoka, a position long before associated with being a successful warrior. Instead, dreaming of thunder or having a certain kind of vision required one to undertake the role.

The heyoka's most notable characteristic was to act contrary to what is expected, which is why the practice is sometimes referred to in ethnographic literature as the "contrary cult."[1] For example, one might complain of how cold it is on a hot summer day, and then dress in winter clothing, or greet someone by saying "good-bye," and vice versa. The heyoka is not unlike Iktomi, the Lakota trickster character of oral tradition. Like trickster characters found in oral literature worldwide, Iktomi performed creative deeds but also violated custom and often behaved in ways considered humorous or uncouth.

Tradition gives the heyoka a special place within Lakota culture. The initiate undergoes an elaborate induction ritual and has to observe many prohibitions. The role is a kind of supernaturally appointed position that one performs for the common good. The heyoka serves as a kind of Native therapist whose behavior provides a harmonizing element to the human condition, i.e., balances convention with its opposite.

Black Elk described to Neihardt the ceremony that initiated him into the role, which he continued to play, informally, throughout life. During the ceremony, he said that two men tied a slipknot around a dog's neck, pulled four times, and on the fourth jerk killed the animal. After the dog's hair was burned off and its body cleansed, the head, spine, and tail were removed.

A specialist sang for the occasion and then offered the head, spine, and tail to the four directions—first to the west, then north, east, and south—and then to the powers above and those below. After doing this, he approached a pot that had been placed in the middle of a circle and feigned three times throwing the head, spine, and tail into the boiling water. On the fourth approach, the parts were put into the water. The same procedure was followed with the dog's heart.

Onlookers did not have to pay strict attention to these proceedings. As the ritual unfolded, heyokas moved about the assembled group and entertained the people with creative jesting. Far from being a time of solemn, communal silence, the heyoka ceremony was an entrancing mixture of sacred and profane behaviors.

Inducted with Black Elk at this time was his friend, Kills Enemy. Both men had their heads shaved on the right side as an act of humility directed toward the west, from which came the power of the Thunder-beings. Black streaks of lightning were painted on top of a red color that covered their bodies. Holding a long, crooked bow with arrows, they sang a song in each of the directions. Poor, the man who was officiating, also sang, and the people danced.

Black Elk and Kills Enemy reached into the boiling pot as if fighting over the dog parts that it contained. Although onlookers thought that some wakan power prevented scalding, heyokas treated their arms with a protective salve. They harmlessly splashed water on the people until Black Elk charged the pot on horseback and skewered the head with an arrow. Kills Enemy used an arrow to get the heart. Other heyokas grabbed whatever meat they could grasp and divided it among the people, who considered it to be medicinal.

Black Elk's Blinding

Kills Enemy was also with Black Elk when the holy-man was partially blinded. This handicap came about in the decade after Wounded Knee when the holy-man was a heyoka. As with other aspects of Black Elk's life, what "really" occurred has been a matter of some dispute.

Kills Enemy's son thought that his father and Black Elk were upset when an owl kept them awake one night. The two men decided to shoot the owl but first had to make cartridges. Black Elk was standing close to a fire when making them. A spark ignited the powder and material flew into Black Elk's face, resulting in his blinding.

Black Elk's daughter, Lucy, told a different story. She said that her father and Kills Enemy were playing the role of heyokas, and Black Elk suggested they see how far a bullet would go down into the ground. When they smashed the loaded shell into the earth, it propelled debris upward into Black Elk's eye and his vision was never again the same.

Joseph Epes Brown offered still a different account. He said that Black Elk announced that he would make the earth rise up (having placed some gunpowder beneath the surface). When Black Elk used a cigarette to ignite the powder, the earth and powder flew into his face. However the event occurred, Black Elk was ever after visually impaired (a photograph exists that shows him wearing glasses).

On another occasion after they became heyokas, Kills Enemy and Black Elk approached a small puddle and acted as if it were a raging river. One jumped into the puddle and pretended to drown, so the other dove in to save him. Both men proceeded to splash around in the mud as if fighting a strong current. A typical heyoka stunt, their action provoked fits of laughter from onlookers.

Shooting a shell into the ground (or some other ploy), however, did not produce a similar response. It demonstrates that being an innovative heyoka was not without risk. Flaunting normative behavior was at the heart of the heyoka identity. One challenged people to look at reality in a different way. By doing so, the heyoka intended to open a portal to the Sacred.

As medicine man or as heyoka, Black Elk served the Lakota community while confronting challenges of his own. In the course of supporting a family, he was faced with the loss of his son Never Showed Off, who died in 1895. This was followed by the death of his wife in 1901. Left to care for two small children, a single father in his late thirties, Black Elk was burdened emotionally and physically. The holy-man also developed a chronic stomach disorder that required hospitalization.

Conversion

Beset with physical and emotional distress, Black Elk was spiritually restless in his role as a healer at the turn of the century. Respected elders came to his aid and provided counsel that offered the prospect of relief. Sam Kills Brave, especially, was instrumental in persuading Black Elk to reconsider what he was doing with his life.

Kills Brave was a principal leader of the reservation town of Manderson, South Dakota. He was a practicing Catholic, and the man who encouraged Black Elk to dispense with his yuwipi practice (the ceremony he performed in darkness, bound in a quilt, calling upon spirits). Kills Brave's advice was not taken lightly. It stayed with the medicine man as he answered a call one night in November of 1904 to doctor a young boy. In later years, Black Elk dramatically recounted what happened this night. Now regarded as his conversion experience, it is best understood as one incident in a process that had been ongoing for some time.

Family members found Black Elk's account both informative and amusing. For them, it was not a commentary on the confrontation of medicine men with missionary, but more the story of how their loved one became a catechist through the intervention of someone who became the family's respected friend—Father Joseph Lindebner (1845–1922). Black Elk's daughter, Lucy, provided the only account of her father's conversion experience, which occurred when he was in his late thirties:

> [He] walked over there carrying his medicine. . . . At that time, they walked those long trails if they didn't have a horse.
>
> When he got there, he found the sick boy lying in a tent. So right away, he prepared to doctor him. . . . My father was really singing away, beating his drum . . . when along came one of the black robes—Father Lindebner, Até Ptécela. . . .
>
> Father Lindebner had already baptized the boy and had come to give him the last rites. . . . He took whatever my father had prepared . . . and threw it all into the stove. . . . Then he took my father by the neck and said, "Satan, get out!". . . Até Ptécela then administered the boy Communion and the last rites. He also cleaned up the tent and prayed with the boy.
>
> . . . He came out and saw my father sitting there looking downhearted and lonely—as though he lost all his powers. Next thing Father Lindebner said was "Come on and get in the buggy with me." My father was willing to go along, so he got in and the two of them went back to Holy Rosary Mission.
>
> Até Ptécela told the Jesuit brothers to clean him up, give him some clothes—underwear, shirt, suit, tie, shoes— and a hat to wear. . . . They fed him and gave him a bed to sleep in. My father never talked about that incident, but he

felt it was Our Lord that appointed or selected him to do
the work of the black robes. He wasn't bitter at all.

He stayed at Holy Rosary [the Catholic mission] two
weeks preparing for baptism. . . . He gladly accepted the
faith on December 6, 1904. . . . After he became a convert
and started working for the missionaries, he put all his
medicine practice away. He never took it up again. (Steltenkamp 1993, 33)

Neihardt made no mention of this event, but did note that a
priest once intruded upon Black Elk's ceremony. He added that the
priest was later killed as the result of an accident. Implied is that
supernatural retribution brought about the priest's death. However,
this interpretation is probably not what Black Elk would have seriously asserted in 1931. The priest who died was not named in
Neihardt's notes, but Father Aloysius Bosch is the only possible
candidate. He was the only Pine Ridge priest who had an accident,
from which he never fully recovered. He died in 1903, five months
after being thrown from a horse in 1902.

Black Elk's daughter told the conversion story as if reporting
a humorous tale. She understood her father's encounter with Lindebner, whatever its particulars, as a special moment in her father's
life. It marked the beginning of a vocation he wholeheartedly embraced. By contrast, after learning of Lucy's account, Lakota author Ed McGaa creatively offered a new version and interpretation
of what took place.

For *Crazy Horse and Chief Red Cloud* (2005), McGaa offered
details about Bosch's death and involvement with Black Elk that
were nowhere else reported. Stating that Bosch *was* the intruding
priest (and not Lindebner), McGaa added that the priest was angry and that his horse was struck by lightning on a *cloudless* day. As
with Neihardt, he implied that Bosch's death resulted from his in-
terference with Black Elk's ceremony.

This embellished version also noted that "within a few years"
after this incident, "along came the overreacting Father Lindebner."
Then, Black Elk was "hauled into the Holy Rosary Mission to be
exorcised by one Father Zimmerman." McGaa reproachfully con-

Holy Rosary Mission, circa 1890. Courtesy of Marquette University Catholic Indian Mission Archives.

cluded that this is the flimsy basis for people saying "Black Elk was converted" (McGaa 2005, 81).

As for what actually took place within any of these vignettes, some things do not rely on speculation. When told the conversion story, other Lakota said that the portrayal of Lindebner conflicted with his reality. He was remembered as having a kind and gentle disposition, not that of a ruffian, and was a man with whom Black Elk fondly and fraternally associated.[2] His short stature even earned him the affectionate nickname of Até Ptécela, or "Short Father," which Black Elk's daughter used interchangeably with his more formal title. She recounted her father's *depiction* of Lindebner as an intrusive priest. This portrayal, and Black Elk's recasting of what actually took place, would have provoked laughter.

John Lone Goose was a young man and resident of Manderson at the time of Black Elk's conversion and associated with him until the holy-man's death. He understood that Black Elk's decision to become Catholic was aided by his conversations with Kills

Brave *and* the reputed interloper, Father Bosch! McGaa's association of Black Elk with an exorcism at the mission was not reported
by anyone who knew the holy-man because it simply did not take
place. In reality, the exorcist of McGaa's account, Father Zimmerman, was a friend of Black Elk's in later life. He was not involved in any manner with the baptism since he did not come to
Pine Ridge until 1930.

McGaa further claimed that medicine men like Black Elk
feigned conversion in order to avoid consignment to an asylum in
Canton, South Dakota. To avert this fate, they behaved *as if* they
were devout Christians. Mission records and clergy diaries are
silent on this matter, but McGaa further charged that priests acted
in concert with government agents to have uncooperative medicine
men sent to Canton for treatment.

McGaa's account is consistent with what Lakota elder Wallace
Black Elk (no relation to Nicholas) reported in his autobiography.
Consigned to a mental institution for a period of time, Wallace
wrote that a Jesuit priest, Father Bernard Fagan, abetted his per-
secutors. When told of Wallace's charge, Fagan good-naturedly
countered that nothing of the sort took place.

While McGaa spun a tale that contradicts what Black Elk's in-
timates knew about his life and thought, his account at least shows
how some people will vent their anger on the provocative topic of
religion and culture contact. Hoxie's *Encyclopedia of North American Indians* (1996) offered a point of view that was comparable to
McGaa's. In its entry for the holy-man, the encyclopedia reported
"the role of staunch Catholic was forced upon" Black Elk, and "he
played it well to appease his oppressors" (Hoxie 1996, 73).

Given the afflicted history of Indian peoples, this type of literature is not surprising. However, while there are many targets that
merit critical aim, the above evaluations are off the mark. A nephew
who received his instruction from the holy-man said that the encyclopedia's author "obviously didn't know Uncle Nick."[3]

Black Elk's conversion might not have occurred in the manner
he described to his daughter. His account simply might have been
his way of describing how "the Son of God had called him to lead
a new life" (Steltenkamp 1993, 36). He perhaps intended its dra-

matic content to illustrate the dramatic new direction he felt moved to pursue. Ultimately, the story's details are secondary to a spiritual formation that unfolded before and after the holy-man's baptism.

Black Elk's daughter said that her father understood his medical practice as being in the service of Wakan Tanka but that he also felt a call to do more. His understanding was that the Christian wanikye had "selected him" to pursue a different direction. After the Jesuits sent him to the hospital for treatment of ulcers, he returned a healthier man with an even clearer vision of what his life work would include.

After several months at the hospital, Black Elk came home and contracted a second marriage to the widowed Anna Brings White in 1905. Her maiden name was Between Lodge, and she had been married to a man whose last name was Waterman, from whom she had borne two daughters, Agatha and Mary.

CHAPTER 9

Catechist

When converging at the bedside of patients, clergy and Native healers learned one another's ways, and their dialogue often led to a rapport that blossomed into friendships. They were not always combative with one another during the contact period.

Both Catholic and Episcopalian missionaries sought medicine men to be converts during the early reservation period, and, as the Lakota religious universe expanded, many medicine men adopted some form of Christian practice. The term "conversion" is only more or less accurate for this adoption because their religious quest was ongoing. Black Elk's daughter offhandedly used the word "conversion" when referring to her father's experience, and it denoted Black Elk (and others) assuming an identifiable Christian practice. It was not a facile description of his (or their) entire abandonment of the Lakota religious universe.

From the missionary's point of view, enlisting medicine men as converts was a best-case scenario. These native practitioners were receptive to discussing matters of religion and, if receptive to baptism, could relate Christian teaching to a clientele that trusted them. In his notes, Jesuit Father Eugene Buechel (1875–1954) cited this as being the practice still in place in 1915.[1] However, by no means did the enlistment of medicine men as converts play out with every encounter. Sometimes there was friction in the exchange at a patient's bedside. Some medicine men would assume new roles and work for the church but then later return to their former practice. Not all experiences were the same, but some people, like Black Elk, became dedicated representatives of their respective denominations. People who knew them in the old order also trusted them in the new.[2]

Rather than describe Black Elk's role as a representative of the Jesuit mission, John Neihardt noted that the holy-man was "a kind of a preacher" (1961, vii) but said no more. His fleeting allusion appeared in his book's preface, was never explained, and was not questioned until decades later. Readers easily could dismiss the reference to "preacher" since Neihardt poetically portrayed Black Elk's life prior to Wounded Knee. The reference could have meant that Black Elk was a preacher of Lakota religion, a Christian evangelist, or someone given to being "preachy" when speaking with people. The impression Neihardt conveyed was that Black Elk was a "kind of a preacher" of pre-reservation ways. Only decades later would people learn the extent to which Black Elk was involved with the role of "catechist," which consisted of helping priests establish faith communities. Many laymen assumed the role, and it won Black Elk significant prominence within the reservation.

The Role of Catechists

Nicholas William Black Elk was baptized a Catholic in 1904 and immediately began working as a catechist. He instructed others as he had been instructed and assumed this role while supporting a young family. His responsibilities included the caretaking of the St. Agnes chapel in Manderson and serving as the priest's lay assistant when services were conducted.

When a priest was not present, Black Elk would lead scripture services, preach, instruct new converts, visit the sick, bury the dead, and baptize people who were close to death. As the first catechist at Manderson, Black Elk agitated for and oversaw the construction of a meeting hall. Since his residence was nearby, he maintained church property from his home base (when assigned outside their district, catechists were provided housing).

In detailing her father's activities, Black Elk's daughter recalled an era that people of a later secular period would find difficult to fathom. She described a different pace of life and different mind-set that characterized the reservation world of her catechist-father. "In the early life of the Sioux Catholics—they liked to hear about God and about Christianity," she said. "So they liked to have meetings" (Steltenkamp 1993, 90).

The period also was one in which missionaries discouraged interaction of their flock with people belonging to a denomination different from their own. This exclusivity disappeared with the ecumenism of later times, but it was not unlike social groups within the old Lakota order. Traditional culture saw one sodality require allegiance and foster competition with, or an identity distinct from, another. Catholics modeled two organizations on these traditional associations. They were known as the St. Mary's Society (for laywomen) and St. Joseph's Society (for laymen). Catechists were the lifeblood of these institutions.

The societies met each Sunday under the leadership of a president (who was called "grandfather" among the men's group and "grandmother" among the women's). Each meeting included praying, singing, instructing converts, planning church activities, and socializing. Black Elk's daughter stated that "members of the St. Mary's Society always [came] to him for advice and asked him what church work they should do in the future" (Steltenkamp 1993, 63). These groups also planned a yearly summer "congress" that drew together the Catholic population from all the Lakota reservations.

The Catholic Sioux Congress was held around the Fourth of July and drew as many as three thousand participants each summer. Missionaries designed this three-day event as an alternative to sun dance or Independence Day celebrations. It was an occasion for the Catholic population to celebrate its solidarity both spiritually and socially. Apart from planning this event, the societies and catechists also involved themselves with organizing holy day celebrations throughout the year.

Catechists spent much time traveling with priests, and close relationships often developed. Father Sialm was one such priest who reported in his diary a memory that Black Elk shared of Father Lindebner. It was a memory that made a lasting impression: "We were

Catholic Catechists – Congress 1911 – at Holy Rosary Mission

Catechists at the 1911 Catholic Sioux Indian Congress. Black Elk is sixth from left, wearing moccasins and his three-piece suit. Courtesy of Marquette University Catholic Indian Mission Archives.

three men at the little church at Potato Creek. Father Lindebner
cooked for us three with his little stove. He could cook for only one
man at a time. First he cooked and gave it to me. Then he cooked
for the second man. And lastly he cooked for himself" (Sialm
1923, 85). Sialm did not explain why Lindebner's simple courtesy
affected Black Elk as profoundly as it did. This type of considera-
tion for others won Black Elk's admiration for the priest he called
both "Short Father" and "Little Brother."

Fathers Henry Westropp and Eugene Buechel enjoyed a similar relationship with the holy-man. In the same vein, Black Elk's
wife, Anna, addressed Father Grotegeers (another Jesuit friend) as
"nephew." Since it was customary among the Lakota to use kin
terms when referring to someone, people like Black Elk did not find
it surprising to learn of Jesuit "fathers" and "brothers," and nuns
who were called "sisters."[3]

Ben Marrowbone was the widely respected nephew of an early
reservation leader named Calico, and a young man when Black Elk
was an active catechist. He was at one time a catechist himself.
Shortly before he died, he provided an account of what the role entailed: "We'd go to . . . every district . . . to every house in a district.
And . . . different people would want us to come in. . . . Father then
offered mass at that house and people nearby would come. They'd
explain their confession—their sins before God . . . so we tell
Almighty, and He forgives them. The people understood this and
they truly believed it" (Steltenkamp 1993, 54).

By the time researchers sought to learn more about Black
Elk's role within this period of Lakota religious history, the office
of catechist no longer existed. At the end of the twentieth century,
memories of Black Elk and the work of catechists were vivid only
among elders. In the absence of audio or video recordings, they
alone could convey a sense of the holy-man's style, and that of catechists generally.

At some point in his life, Black Elk learned to read passages
of scripture, prayers, and songs that were published in Lakota. The
"Jesuit Fathers of St. Francis Mission" published a Lakota prayer
and hymnbook in 1927 titled *Sursum Corda,* and Black Elk's copy
became well worn over time. It afforded him and others direct

A priest was told that the Lakota love ceremonies because they thought "the Creator always comes to ceremonies," according to the Creighton University online exhibit, "Fr. Eugene Buechel, S.J.—A Visual Biography." At this 1920 Catholic Sioux Indian Congress at Holy Rosary Mission, Bishop Lawler stands in the middle along with a man holding an openly displayed pipe (indicating the presence of this traditional prayer form within Christian gatherings). Black Elk is in the bottom row, third from left. Courtesy of Marquette University Catholic Indian Mission Archives.

Bottom, center Jesuit Fathers Buechel and *to Buechel's left* Lindebner. Courtesy of Marquette University Catholic Indian Mission Archives.

access to passages that they addressed in their preaching. A Manderson resident recalled:

> Even though they didn't have any formal education, those old converts were really trained to preach. . . . I read Scripture, but I can't remember the right words like they used to be able to do. . . . [T]hose old converts could really talk—especially about religion. . . . Nick was a catechist, and when he got up he really preached. People sat there and just listened to him. They could picture what he was talking about. . . . Nowadays we have education, but we're not that good. (Steltenkamp 1993, 121)

John Lone Goose spent many years associating with Black Elk and spoke with admiration for the man who was his religious mentor:

> . . . I remember every detail of what he did because I was with him—not every day—but every time the Father would come over, or when he would teach somebody who wanted to be a Catholic. I was there to help him.

The priests gave him instructions in the faith and Nick said he wanted to teach God's word to the people. . . . [H]e learned what the Bible meant, and that it was good. He said: "I want to be a catechist the rest of my life. I want it that way from here on!" So he went around . . . all those districts. . . . Lots of people turned to the Catholic Church through Nick's work.

He never talked about the old ways. All he talked about was the Bible and Christ. I was with him most of the time and I remember what he taught. He taught the name of Christ to Indians who didn't know it. The old people, the young people, the mixed blood, even the white man—everybody that comes to him, he teaches. . . .

He was a pretty good speaker, and I think Our Lord gave him wisdom when he became a Christian. For even though he was kind of blind, his mind was not blind. And when he retired and was sick, he still taught God's word to the people. He turned Christian and took up catechist work. And he was still on it until he died. (Steltenkamp 1993, 54)

Kills Enemy (Black Elk's lifelong friend) and many others joined him in this type of work. William Cedar Face, Louis Mousseaux, Silas Fills The Pipe, Frank Gallego, Joseph Horn Cloud, James Grass, John Fool Head, Willie Red Hair, Ivan Star Comes Out, and Daniel Broken Leg are just some of the men who served as catechists at Pine Ridge. Black Elk's experience was not unique but was representative of men such as these who embraced roles within the different denominations.

Letters from Black Elk appeared in a missionary publication named *Sinasapa Wocekiye Taeyanpaha* (*The Catholic Herald*). This newspaper began in 1892 on the Devil's Lake Reservation, and was published in Lakota. In his letters, Black Elk described various aspects of his work:

Remember that I am just a common man like you. But I was installed as a catechist and I have received instructions. . . . I am a Catechist and that job is to pray with

people—teaching them how to pray—and this is what I am
doing. So if I should come to your house, don't be afraid
of me—because I am one of you. . . . [W]e should tell the
younger generation about the St. Joseph and St. Mary Society, we have learned that this is the organization of the
Holy Family. In the Bible, Jesus told us that "You should
love your neighbor . . . ." So remember if you get in trouble with your neighbor, remember that God has said, "Love
your neighbor." So whatever you have said, or if you did
some bad thing to them, go over there and please tell them
that you are sorry. (Steltenkamp 1987, 258)

In addition to their involvement with formal gatherings, catechists also conducted an "after hours" ministry. They might be
called in the middle of the night to visit and pray with a sick person.
At other times, the catechists might conduct a prayer service on their
own or lead the community in songs that were written in Lakota.

Father Westropp's description of Black Elk matched what late
twentieth-century Lakota elders recalled of the holy-man of their
youth. In a publication that detailed Jesuit activities at Pine Ridge,
the priest referred to him as a "fervent apostle" and "second St.
Paul" (Steltenkamp 1993, 65) who was responsible for many converts. Singling out Black Elk long before books made him famous,
Westropp wrote:

. . . Gladly abandoning wife and family for weeks at a time
to help the missionary in his work . . . is a . . . [former]
ghost dancer and chief of the medicine men. His name is
Black Elk. . . . Though half blind he has by some hook or
crook learned how to read and he knows his religion thor-
oughly. . . . On a moment's notice he can pour forth a flood
of oratory holding his hearers spellbound. There are few
that can resist him and none of whom he is afraid. (Steltenkamp 1993, 65)

Black Elk's labors were not limited to his people alone. The
holy-man spent time at other reservations in South Dakota and, in

Black Elk preaching at Joe No Water's home in 1928. Courtesy of Marquette University Catholic Indian Mission Archives.

1908, he reported success with the Winnebago of Nebraska and Arapaho of Wyoming. Describing his work among the latter, he said, "With all our might we taught them about church work and now about half of the people believe" (DeMallie 1984a, 18). His experience made him reflect aloud that those who argued the most became the easiest to convert. His skill was impressive enough for the missionaries to select him and three others to travel east on a fund-raising tour.

On the tour, Black Elk visited New York, Boston, Washington, Chicago, Lincoln, and Omaha. The overwhelming response he recalled was one of warm welcome and applause. Even the incarcerated at Sing Sing prison appreciated what the holy-man preached to them around the year 1913:

> You came to this country which was ours in the first place. We were the only inhabitants. After we listened to you, we got settled down. But you're not doing what you're supposed to do—what our religion and our Bible tells us. I know this. Christ himself preached that we love our neighbors as ourself. Do unto others as you would have others do unto you. (Steltenkamp 1993, 67–68)

Red Feather, Crazy Horse's brother-in-law, spoke as candidly as Black Elk about his Christian faith when interviewed by Crazy Horse researcher Eleanor Hinman in 1930. She asked him to recount his memories of the Lakota leader, and he responded as if to imply that people ordinarily lie when interviewed about such things. He reminded Hinman of the ground rule he would observe: "I will tell you the true facts about Crazy Horse because I am a Catholic now and it is part of my religion to tell the truth" (Paul 1998, 196). Black Elk at Sing Sing prison and Red Feather with Hinman both professed values (e.g., the golden rule and honesty) that their audiences probably did not expect to hear.[4]

Missionary journeys often enough included difficult travel. Accompanying Father Westropp to the Cheyenne River agency, Black Elk and the priest came to a fast flowing and deep river. Black Elk told Westropp that crossing it would not be possible, but the priest assured him that "God is going to help us. He'll take care of us" (Steltenkamp 1993, 60). It was not long before the men were swept down the river along with their horses, buggy, and provisions. Fortunately, Black Elk and the priest were rescued by friendly people who provided them with dry clothing, something to eat, and a place to stay.

Westropp recounted another experience with Black Elk that reveals the type of lighthearted banter that could characterize their interaction while going about religious work. The priest wrote:

> Once after having returned from what he called a scalping-tour . . . we had baptized a couple . . . we were drawing close to the house of Silas Fills-the-Pipe, another catechist. "Little Owl" (my Indian name) he said, "Let us sing the war song, the song of victory," and so we ended it with a few whoops that brought Silas to the door of his cabin. "I thought the way you sang that you had killed some white people," he said. "Yes," replied Black Elk, "we have taken the scalps of a few devils." (Westropp n.d.(a), 8)

Good-natured jesting clearly had its place within work that often enough included grueling trips and grim encounters with the many faces of poverty.

Although he experienced success as a missionary-catechist, Black Elk also suffered personal loss. In 1910, his step-daughters died of tuberculosis while a son, Henry, died in infancy the same year. The death of his mother in 1915, a woman who had been a pillar in his life for half a century, was especially felt. The birth of a daughter, Lucy, in 1907 was a consolation, as was the birth of Nicholas Jr. in 1914. His eyesight problematic, Black Elk named his daughter after Saint Lucy. Within popular Catholic piety, she was the patron saint for afflictions of the eye, and traditional Lakota would have regarded such a saint as a "spirit helper." To Black Elk, Saint Lucy's help could be particularly useful since he was partially blind.

Black Elk was also a victim of the tuberculosis epidemic that took a high toll in the early twentieth century. Stricken with the

In this 1911 photograph of catechist Black Elk and his family, his wife wears a woman's hairpipe breastplate, which daughter Lucy models in miniature form. Courtesy of Marquette University Catholic Indian Mission Archives.

disease, his mobility was limited, and by 1916 his journeys to other reservations were no longer a regular part of his routine. For many years, he was the catechist at Oglala, a reservation community, where his grandson, George Looks Twice, continued the family tradition into the twenty-first century by overseeing the church property there.

Black Elk's work at Oglala included visiting the sick, spiritual counseling, helping priests with the administration of sacraments, and caring for the church's upkeep. The spirit of his presence there was partly communicated in Father Buechel's diary entry for December 23, 1928. He wrote: "Mass, sermon & 12 Holy Communions at Oglala. Drove home. On the way, Black Elk & I prayed for Mrs. Charles Eagle Louse who is sick" (Steltenkamp 1993, 58).

Not all activity was as serious as the above. Father Henry Grotegeers once gave a ride to Black Elk on his motorcycle. As they neared Oglala, the priest was unable to stop, so he rode it to the racetrack and went round and round until deciding to return to Holy Rosary Mission. Black Elk held on tightly until Grotegeers ran it off the road and came to a crashing halt. Both were thrown off the bike (but unharmed) and had an experience they later could laugh about in the telling.

Since a catechist's salary was not great—over the years it ranged from $10 to $25 per month—the job's rewards were to be found in the ministry itself. But Joseph Epes Brown thought otherwise when evaluating the role in 1948:

> The Catholic Church among the Indians in the early days gained many followers, by making catechists of the old men, tempting them with money, good clothes, and a house, and the opportunity to travel. These old men—Black Elk among them—made hundreds of converts, but now that they have gone, participation in the Church has fallen off, and a vacuum has been left. Let us hope it shall be filled by the renewal of their own Way. (2007, 116)

While Brown's posthumously published letters do not report a similar charge against other church groups, the same conceivably could have been said of them all. However, it is difficult to regard any of the different missionaries as purveyors of temptation. They were unable to provide themselves or their converts with much of *anything* material.

Brown's evaluation was not shared by anyone who knew Black Elk, but there was precedent for it elsewhere. The term "rice Christian" was associated with people in Asia who affiliated with a Christian denomination in exchange for material gain. Brown apparently thought that something similar might be at play among the Lakota. However, because their religious order had representatives throughout the world, Pine Ridge Jesuits were knowledgeable of missionary experiences abroad. They were not blind to the phenomenon of "rice Christianity," and their diaries attest to this. Enticing people to join their church via rice or some other form of material well-being was not a conversion strategy employed by Pine Ridge Jesuits.[5]

Adopting the catechist lifestyle brought Black Elk an evident satisfaction. His zeal was expressed in letters that appeared in missionary publications, and he regularly proposed new trips to different reservations and return visits to others. Black Elk's daughter, Lucy, summed up what everyone acquainted with him knew: referring to his work as a catechist, she simply said, "He sure was interested in that kind of life" (Steltenkamp 1993, 630).

Hearth

The domestic scene during Black Elk's first years as a catechist was much like later ones. A snapshot of daily life for his family at Manderson included living in a three-room log house with one room reserved for the holy-man's mother. Black Elk's pay for being a catechist was not much, but correspondence between the priests indicated that he did well. No one went hungry because the family garden yielded potatoes, corn, and beans. Other vegetables were planted and filled the cellar each year. Black Elk also owned livestock that included horses, pigs, chickens, a milk cow, and, at one point, fifty head of cattle.

On any given day, friends or relatives, many of whom came of age in the pre-reservation era, would visit and be served coffee or wild peppermint tea. One family friend and visitor went by the name of Coffee. He was from the Rosebud Reservation and was Crazy Horse's nephew. Lakota hospitality was extended to him as it was to others, and in exchange Coffee would chop wood. A moderate cigarette smoker, Black Elk also might smoke a pipe with visitors. Elderly guests would use Lakota words that the young people, themselves bilingual, did not always understand (Black Elk only knew "a little" English). A twentieth-century Lakota vocabulary did not contain all the words that were used at an earlier time.

People seeking counsel were also regular visitors at the homestead. Others would receive advice even if they did not request it. One such case involved a relative who was remembered as being prone to complain about others. Always quick to find fault with whatever certain people did, she seemed eager to hear and spread the most recent rumor. Black Elk gently suggested that her habits of speech were producing results that she did not intend. He told her a parable drawn from everyday life: "A dog is really happy when it finds a bone. The dog picks it clean and then puts it where he can find the bone later on. He does this with each one he finds until he has collected a whole pile of them. He thinks he has a mountain of treats, but the fact is he only has a pile of dried, rotting bones"(Steltenkamp 1993, 90–92).

This indirect form of communication was normative within Lakota tradition. Instead of directly confronting and chastising the woman, Black Elk told a story from which she might draw her own conclusions. A member of the dog nation proudly collecting meatless bones was a powerful image. It might have reminded her of the well-known story of the Lakota's sacred pipe coming to the people (wherein the antagonist misbehaved and turned into a boney skeleton). Both stories equated bones with ignorance and wrongful or unproductive behavior. Moreover, Black Elk's point was a forceful one since family members recalled that the woman's tendency to gossip and complain was curbed after speaking with the holy-man. Her habit curtailed, she eventually became a welcome visitor at the Black Elk home. Others, too, benefited from the holy-man's counsel.

Recipients of *The Catholic Herald* regularly would see his name appended to some article, and in one issue he submitted a lesson based upon the Titanic sinking. Black Elk said that wealthy people thought they could become even more wealthy (and always be secure) by building a ship that would not sink. However, he wrote that "the boat they made sank from blindness"—i.e., it hit an iceberg that the captain did not see (Westropp n.d.(a)).

For Black Elk, the Titanic and its owners served as a metaphor that reflected his spirituality. That is, placing confidence solely in material well-being amounted to placing confidence in a ship that would sink. Black Elk then said that unless believers "stay in our ship" and "be close to our Savior," they will be unable to stand up "when . . . struck by something large," i.e., an iceberg-like problem in life (Westropp n.d.(a)).

Instruction by way of story was also apparent in the account of what Black Elk said was a "well known" incident among members of his generation. He told of a man who was "not a good warrior" and who was a "smarty" (the word given by his translator). After the man had teased his brother-in-law beyond propriety, the

brother-in-law reacted to the insult by heedlessly going after
Shoshone opponents. They, in turn, slaughtered the thirty Lakota
who accompanied him. Black Elk said that this battle saw "the
greatest number of Sioux [ever] killed" (DeMallie 1984a, 351).

The story was no doubt "well known" because of the lesson it
demonstrated. Boasting, foolhardy taunts, and the inability to ignore a slight were behaviors that brought disastrous results. The
tale's point was self-evident, and Black Elk was a skilled storyteller
who drew upon a vast library of oral literature. With experience in
Europe, urban areas in the East, and life in the pre-reservation era,
Black Elk had firsthand knowledge of other cultural traditions. His
social universe was broader than most people's, and it was this
broader experience that both Indians and non-Indians tapped in
speaking with him. It made him a valuable resource.

Unlike his father, Black Elk held no ill will toward the settlers
who seemed to inundate the plains. He compared their arrival to
a flood over the land that forced both Indians and animals to seek
islands of safety. He saw their great numbers and insisted that his
children be able to speak English and learn how to get along with
the newcomers. Thinking that education could accomplish this, he
respected the aging warrior-leader Red Cloud for asking Jesuit
priests to establish a school on the reservation.

Some commentators have suggested that Red Cloud only
requested Jesuit presence as a kind of passive resistance to the government. President Grant's "Peace Policy" earlier had assigned different Christian denominations to work on different reservations,
and Episcopalians were given Pine Ridge. In light of this, perhaps
Red Cloud's petition for a Jesuit, not Episcopalian, mission on the
reservation was really just an attempt to impede the federal government's initiatives among his people.

According to this thesis, if the government wanted one thing,
Red Cloud would request something else. The case could be made
that he never really wanted black robes to work among his people
but was instead jockeying for position on some other issue. Contrary to this type of speculation, Lucy said that her father held Red
Cloud in high regard because both men knew that a black robe
school included religious instruction.

This position was echoed in a remark made by Catholic bishop Martin Marty in an obscure, German-language mission publication (*Die katholischen Missionen*). The comment shows that Black Elk and Red Cloud were not alone in their thinking positively of what the black robes could offer. When recounting his interaction with Sitting Bull, Marty reported that the holy-man spoke of a positive encounter with DeSmet years earlier. The summer before his death in 1890, Sitting Bull requested of Marty the presence of a black robe church and school among his people (Kreis 2007, 149).[6]

Lakota leaders might not have been able to define what doctrinal differences separated the Christian groups, but some knew that black robes brought with them an educational system that included religious instruction. Father DeSmet had been a welcome Jesuit visitor at many Lakota camps when Red Cloud was young, and he left a positive impression on the senior generation. Recalling the man's presence, Red Cloud thought his people would be well served if priests like DeSmet came among them and established their schools.

Since Red Cloud's relationship with the Jesuits continued long after his request for their presence on the reservation, Lucy's account appears to have the ring of truth. A Jesuit diary written at the time of Red Cloud's death noted that he remained "a good Catholic" until the end (Perrig, n.d.). Given the period and the source, this observation would have been based on religious behavior that the priest thought was important enough to note. The diary thus provides a glimpse into the private life of a Lakota leader that is fairly absent in history books and biographies of the man.

When Red Cloud took the name "Peter" at his baptism, it was probably symbolic. The Jesuits understood him to be "first" among his people just as they understood Peter to be "first" in rank among the apostles of Jesus. When Red Cloud died in 1909, there was some pressure to bury him at Fort Robinson, Nebraska. However, Black Elk's close associate, Father Lindebner, conducted a service at Pine Ridge that was well attended, and a blizzard decided against the Fort Robinson option. Police accompanied the cortege to the

Holy Rosary Mission where Red Cloud was interred after another service in the church there. Ever since that time, the old warrior's grave has been on a hill overlooking the mission grounds where many of his descendants, and Black Elk's, have attended Red Cloud Indian School.

CHAPTER 10

The Two Roads Map

As Black Elk undertook his work as a catechist, the black robes presented him with something besides the educational opportunities he and Red Cloud had endorsed. They introduced him to a new type of winter count—one that, rather than marking significant events in Lakota history, seemed to shed light on the visions he had received throughout life.

A catechetical tool used by Jesuit priests, this winter count of sorts was known as the "Two Roads Map." It illustrated such biblical stories as Adam and Eve, Noah's ark, and the Tower of Babel, while also noting the seven deadly sins and the seven sacraments. The Two Roads Map fell within a genre of teaching devices, often patently sectarian, used by different Christian groups. Studies refer to these instructional aids as "ladders of salvation" (Pipes 1936 and Prucha 1988). Although the name of the teaching tool was a household phrase for Lakota converts during the first sixty years of the reservation, it was largely unknown by the end of the twentieth century.

While the Two Roads Map used by priests at Pine Ridge was both colorful and comprehensive in detail, extant examples of "ladders" used elsewhere often are crudely drawn and juvenile in comparison. The different denominations used these "picture catechisms" to communicate their theology. In Black Elk's case, priests taught catechists who, in turn, used this instructional aid to

Catechist Black Elk teaching the Two Roads Map to Broken Nose children, circa 1928. Courtesy of Marquette University Catholic Indian Mission Archives.

teach others. The map's arresting depiction of human, animal, and otherworldly creatures condensed Catholic teaching into pictures that a good teacher could amplify in words. By the time Neihardt interviewed the holy-man, this new, Christian winter count had become interwoven within Black Elk's understanding of the Sacred. Strangely enough, by discussing the holy-man's childhood vision in *Black Elk Speaks*, Neihardt introduced readers to the ideas in the Two Roads Map without realizing it.

The Two Roads Map and the Boyhood Vision

In *Black Elk Speaks*, Neihardt depicted Black Elk's childhood vision as exercising profound influence on the holy-man throughout his life. Although Brown, by contrast, spent no time addressing the experience, Neihardt strove to show Black Elk's felt sense of supernatural assistance that the vision promised. That is, after contracting a fever and lingering at death's doorstep for twelve days, young Black Elk, instead of dying, came to consciousness with a vivid memory of what he had seen. Whatever the source of Black Elk's experience, be it the supernatural or his illness, Neihardt believed the vision warranted new attention.

By recounting Black Elk's vision, which Brown did not even discuss, *Black Elk Speaks* introduced readers to a world of images and symbols that formed the landscape of the holy-man's private experience. Neither Neihardt nor his readers knew that the vision included elements depicted on the catechetical aid that had been used by the holy-man for three decades before he met the poet. This aid, the Two Roads Map, played a significant role at the time of Black Elk's baptism and afterward.

Interpreting the Vision

The Two Roads Map featured ideas and images that both subtly and overtly paralleled those in Black Elk's vision. A partial listing of them includes Thunder-beings, flying men, a daybreak star, a rainbow, tree imagery, circled villages, a black road, a red road, friendly wings, a blue man in flames, people mourning, a history of the people, and a young man appearing to be ill. While similarities within the map and vision might amount to what psychologist Carl Jung referred to as "archetypes" (i.e., images and symbols common to all people and residing deep within the human psyche), Lucy said that her father learned the vision's term "black road" when he became a catechist and learned about the map.

Because of this correspondence between the Two Roads Map and the vision, questions have been raised about the accuracy in the naming of what Neihardt referred to as "The Great Vision." What the poet thought he recorded and what Black Elk intended to communicate might have been two different productions. Instead of solely recounting an unaltered vision from a boyhood experience, the holy-man might have provided the poet with a synthesis of religious images that engaged him from boyhood through adulthood—that is, vision images fused with images from the Two Roads Map.

The idea of Black Elk fashioned by Neihardt was of a holy-man extolling cultural practices of old and locked within the memory of the pre-reservation era. However, Black Elk seems to have had in mind a larger audience for his life story than his people alone. Neihardt, as writer, drew upon Black Elk's early life for material to present his reading audience. Black Elk, as catechist, enlisted Neihardt to instruct readers he would otherwise never have the opportunity to meet.

For Black Elk, this enterprise was a new type of missionary journey. His religious thought would be transported to new audiences by way of a book. This larger audience that Black Elk foresaw was implied by what appears to be a merging of the map and vision in his account and in what he directly stated to Neihardt. Outside the finished text, but noted by Enid, was Black Elk's comment that he "wanted the world to know about it" (i.e., his life story), not just his people. This desire merged the universal, evangelistic nature of the map with the private, vocational nature of his vision.

Neihardt's emphasis was that Black Elk's vision, about to vanish with the holy-man's impending death, could be an inspiration for his people. Black Elk went a step further and was catechizing "the world." Still a catechist instructing, he wanted others to benefit from his life's vision.

Two Visions

Black Elk corroborated a broader understanding of the vision when he told Neihardt "I hope that we can make the tree bloom for your children and for mine" (DeMallie 1984a, 44). DeMallie said their partnership was sealed when the holy-man bestowed on Neihardt the name "Flaming Rainbow" (37) during a naming ceremony. The poet would "serve as his spokesman through his writing" (37), his words taking the vision outward just as flames along a rainbow would blaze forth.

DeMallie, however, also noted that Neihardt "could not fully comprehend the meaning of the vision" (DeMallie 1984a, 37) when this naming ceremony occurred. After the ceremony, the poet still seemed to conceive of Black Elk's vision account in narrower, more ethnocentric terms. He wrote his publisher that his work would be "the first absolutely Indian book thus far written" (De-

Mallie 1984a, 49) and planned its title to be "The Tree that Never Bloomed" (a metaphorical reference to the economic and social blight affecting the Lakota).

The book's title was ultimately changed, but Neihardt's emphasis remained nativistic. The work's oft-quoted concluding lines were not Black Elk's words, but the poet's opinion of what the holy-man "would have said if he had been able" (McCluskey 1972, 23):

> With tears running, O Great Spirit, Great Spirit, my Grandfather—with running tears I must say now that the tree has never bloomed. A pitiful old man, you see me here, and I have fallen away and have done nothing . . . here, old, I stand, and the tree is withered, Grandfather, my Grandfather. Again, and maybe the last time on this earth, I recall the great vision you sent me. It may be that some little root of the sacred tree still lives. Nourish it, then, that it may leaf and bloom and fill with singing birds. Hear me, not for myself, but for my people; I am old. Hear me that they may once more go back into the sacred hoop and find the good red road, the shielding tree!

Neihardt's interpretation of Black Elk's thought ultimately limited the holy-man's vision, even in what were purported to be Black Elk's words. In reality, Black Elk's vision remained a global one—with the holy-man thinking that what he expressed could be a portent of hope for both his people and all others.

The Red and Black Roads and the Flowering Stick

Important images in Black Elk's vision are the red and black roads and a flowering stick. Understanding these images generically—as Neihardt intended them to be understood—yields a far different vision than if they are taken within the context of Black Elk's life.

In terms of the roads, the red road generically is one of peaceful virtue and the black generically of difficulty. By contrast, the two roads illustrated on the sides of the map are designated as a "way of good" and a "way of evil," and are not colored red or black. However, there are red and black sections on the map that stand out more prominently than the portion designated as the two "ways." People are shown walking in the center of the map on a vertical black-and-red path. Some viewers might have thought the prominent red-and-black portion was the two roads (or additional ones) since humanity is depicted walking its length.

This vertical path on the map, however, depicts significant Judeo-Christian moments throughout history. The black section refers to the centuries before, and the red section the centuries after, the Christ's coming. Because of these associations, Black Elk's words take on more meaning than the generic interpretation originally offered in Neihardt's interpretation. Black Elk said, "I'd bring my people out of the black road into the red road" (on the map, the black section leads into the red). That is, he would be a leader of his people into the Christian era, not in the sense of an evangelical preacher, but by being a Lakota elder who fused the best of old and new understandings of the Sacred (DeMallie 1984a, 293).

This interpretation is implicit within Neihardt's field notes but is not so apparent in *Black Elk Speaks*. These stenographic notes include the holy-man's metaphorical reference to a "stick," which is, ultimately, Black Elk's reference to the Christian cross. Within the notes, a passage reads: "'Behold it, from there we shall multiply; for it is the greatest of the greatest sticks.' This stick will take care of the people. . . . We live under it like chickens under the wing. We live under the flowering stick like under the wing of a hen" (DeMallie 1984a, 129). Within *Black Elk Speaks*, this passage reads: "Here we shall raise our children and be as little chickens under the mother *sheo*'s wing" ("*sheo*" footnoted as meaning "prairie hen"). This misleading translation fell far short of what Black Elk meant (J. Neihardt 1961, 34).

What seems the quaint example of a country metaphor within the holy-man's vision was instead his citing of Matthew 23:37 and Luke 13:34. The stenographic notes contained Black Elk's direct quotation of this passage, but *Black Elk Speaks* did not. It is this scriptural reference that Black Elk used to explain the meaning of his vision. The holy-man said that his people would live under "the stick"—"like chickens under the wing . . . like under the wing of a hen." The scripture passage refers to Jesus telling people that he wanted to care for them as a hen would her chicks.

For one to miss Black Elk's biblical allusion has the further consequence of one missing the holy-man's interpretation of "the stick" and its role in the future of his people. A rich symbol, it conceivably could refer to an ordinary cherry branch stick used in religious ceremonies, trees or growing things, a cane to lean on, Wakan Tanka, shelter, the Lakota nation proudly flourishing, or it could be a metaphor for the Christian cross. In light of Black Elk's quoting scripture in association with "the stick," it is likely the latter. His reference to and paraphrase of Christian teaching is straightforward.

The holy-man said that his people will depend on the sacred stick (the cross or Christ presence) and that it "will be with us always" (Black Elk's quote of Matthew 28:20, which reports Jesus saying, "Behold, I am with you always"). He concluded his narration to Neihardt as if preaching as a catechist: "From this we will raise our children and under the flowering stick we will communicate with our relatives—beast and bird—as one people. This is the center of the life of the nation" (DeMallie 1984a, 130). Black Elk further reinforced imagery of the cross and brought the motifs of his vision and the map together when he said that the black road intersected the red road. That is, death (black) and life (red) merged within the cross's meaning.

After this part of the vision, the stenographic notes offer a degree of clarification that is not helpful. The holy-man purportedly said that the tree (or stick) was the nation, and that it never bloomed because white people came on the scene. However, if he earlier stated that the people would live *under* the stick, the account is all the more confusing. How could the people live under the nation? The tree could, as stated, be a symbol having more than one meaning (as both cross and as a people flourishing), but Black Elk concluded this section saying that if the tree had bloomed, he or his descendants would have been great chiefs!

These concluding remarks straddle the line of being either jocular or the unclear abbreviation of an extended discussion. They read as if Enid took notes quickly as Neihardt, Black Elk, Ben, and others exchanged comments. Stark references to becoming a chief and the toll taken by the presence of "white people" need qualification that is never provided.

Given the interview setting, perhaps the commentary was interrupted. Perhaps those people present were editorializing on what Black Elk said, or maybe the opportune moment simply did not present itself for follow-up questions. Fortunately, the broader context of Black Elk's life helps clarify what he was trying to communicate.

The Broader Context

Neihardt already knew this broader context. He thus excluded from his book what seemed a hostile attitude toward white people (since the poet knew of Black Elk's transparent goodwill toward all). The vision showed how the sacred powers intended to help the holy-man serve others, so Neihardt rightly deleted this garbled portion of the transcript that conflicted with that vision and reality of the holy-man's life.

Neihardt appears to have been unaware, however, of the map's existence or the role it played in Black Elk's thought. That is, the holy-man brought his life's cumulative visions to the conversion experience, and they were given new substance upon his learning of the Two Roads Map. However, even if Neihardt knew of the map, telling of the holy-man's life as a catechist would have conflicted with the nativistic image that he was crafting.

This discussion further indicates why the stenographic notes cannot always be taken at their face value. What Black Elk said to his son, what Ben told Neihardt, and what the poet eventually directed Enid to write was part of a process that left gaps. By contrast, Black Elk's daughter was direct in speaking about her father's vision and took exception to people misinterpreting it:

> The past couple of years I've been shocked to hear people say that my father never actually believed in the Catholic religion. I know they're really making a mistake. . . . He had

that vision and learned it was to be the Christian life of all people. At the time before he died, he . . . said he didn't do his part in accomplishing this and that the tree was dying. People were not walking the right path. But he still hoped the tree would be able to give forth its branches before it was entirely dead. I know this is what he meant. (Steltenkamp 1993, 141)

Lucy owned a clear sense of her father's teaching, but even her words require comment. Her catechist-father's early enthusiasm for all people following the wanikiye (savior) was reconfigured over time. Initially, the "Christian life of all people" entailed his commitment to building membership in the St. Mary and St. Joseph societies. As years passed, he remained a devout catechist but appreciated that other sincere and virtuous people might never formally associate themselves with his form of religious practice. While not indifferent to their choices, he still could bestow his blessing on those who sincerely embraced other religious forms. Besides symbolizing the cross, the image of a flowering tree also served as a visionary metaphor showing that "the Christian life" can have many branches that bear fruit, regardless of what name they bear.

Lucy said that her father's vision for the Lakota was depicted on a beaded, circular medallion that she asked her daughter to craft. On the medallion, a cross—what the vision cites as a "blooming tree" or "sprouting stick"—was at the center of seven tipis (which, camped in a circle, represented the Lakota nation's "hoop"). Forty years earlier, Black Elk's ghost dance vision seemed to forecast this understanding: "I saw the tree in full bloom. Against the tree I saw a man standing with outstretched arms. . . . [T]welve men said 'Behold him!'" (DeMallie 1984a, 263). Black Elk's latter phrase is an "Ecce homo!" allusion to John 19:5. That is, "Behold the man" is another example of Black Elk's familiarity with scripture: it was Pilate's reference to the scourged Jesus.

Taken together, Black Elk's visions were, ultimately, neither parochially Lakota nor insularly Catholic. Rather, they entailed a cross-fertilization of Christian and Lakota traditions that was enriching to both—a position shared by Black Elk's nephew, Frank

Black Elk's daughter, Lucy Looks Twice, said this medallion represented her father's vision, with the cross within the nation's circle and at the center of the Lakota's seven divisions. Photo by author.

Black Elk's friend, John Lone Goose, at a Rushville, Nebraska, nursing home in 1974. Photo by author.

Fools Crow, a late twentieth-century Lakota holy-man. Black Elk envisioned a spiritual "tree" whose shade could in some way be a refuge for both his and Neihardt's children and all people. The map offered a way for Black Elk and all people to understand their place in that refuge and offered a guide for remaining under it through life.

John Lone Goose, a long and close friend of the holy-man, reverently recalled Black Elk's use of the Two Roads Map (Steltenkamp 1993, 101): "He'd teach them that Map many times. He carried one. So every time we go teach, he'd go down the Two Roads. He taught them how to go to heaven and how to be a Christian man. Father gave him a Two Roads Map, and he taught from it the rest of his life."

Ironically, it was in *Black Elk Speaks*, and not the stenographic notes, that the holy-man seemed to explain, by discussing his vision, the impact of the Two Roads Map on his thinking: "It was the pictures I remembered and the words that went with them. . . . It was as I grew older that the meanings came clearer and clearer out of the pictures and the words; and even now I know that more was shown to me than I can tell" (J. Neihardt 1961, 41). DeMallie reported that this quote and other Neihardt material is nowhere to be located (presumably the poet, if not putting words in Black Elk's mouth, acquired or remembered commentary that took place outside the interview setting). While he was apparently referring to the vision, Black Elk could just as well have been describing his experience of the map with its "pictures" and "words" and the instruction he received.

Neihardt enlisted Stephen Standing Bear to sketch images of Black Elk's vision, and these were inserted within the text of *Black Elk Speaks*. Although they did not illuminate Black Elk's experience or thought, they did reinforce the book's nativistic cast. By contrast, inclusion of the Two Roads Map would have communicated a truer sense of the holy-man's religious worldview.

Black Elk's Path

The Two Roads Map showed how Wakan Tanka gave the two-legged beings a sacred path to walk. It identified this path as the path of Jesus (the "good red road"). It was Black Elk's path, and one that he knew was not chosen by everyone. Still, he led by example and even good-naturedly admitted that his vocation to make the tree bloom "was next to impossible, but there was nothing like trying" (DeMallie 1984a, 293).

The "red road" phrase became one of the holy-man's most enduring legacies. However, shorn of its association with the Two Roads Map, the "red road" was depicted in *Black Elk Speaks* as simply the road of virtue on which Black Elk tried to lead his people by way of restoring traditional Lakota lifeways. This red road would lead to a better life now, and to the life that awaited them in eternity. It could simply mean this, of course, but according to his daughter and others, Black Elk intended it to mean much more (Steltenkamp 1993).

"Red road" references multiplied after Neihardt first brought the phrase to light, and the term is often said to be a widely used image within "Indian religion" (all Native traditions often are lumped into this one nonspecific designation). A popular "twelve step" drug rehabilitation program even adopted the name. It was not, however, a pan-Indian term from antiquity. Rather, the origin of the "red road" phrase was within the missionary labors and language of Black Elk, the catechist.

Black Elk's red road was a Catholic one, but his ultimate concern was not entirely parochial. He bestowed his blessing on many travelers whose varied visions of the Sacred moved them forward. What was important to him was that they made the effort. This was the concern that remained with him until the end.

CHAPTER 11

Holy Humor

Stereotypes of religious figures often depict them as being serious and humorless. Zen teachers are thought of as solemn purveyors of one-line meditations. Popes issue stern rebukes, ayatollahs are angry, and the militant adherent to Islam is as ingrained an image as the Christian preacher associated only with hellfire and brimstone. Following suit, films and books have long typecast American Indians as stoic and somber individuals.

Black Elk's portrayal occupied a premier niche within each of these sober depictions. As both a religious figure and American Indian, he came across as fairly void of light-heartedness. However, just as the other stereotypes need qualification, so does Black Elk's. While Neihardt and Brown rightly showed that he was a very devout man, there was more to his personality than they revealed. Their reference to Black Elk by his last name alone relegated him to the nineteenth century even though for almost fifty years everyone called him "Nick."

More surprising than Black Elk's use of a first name is the sense of humor for which he was also known. Lucy did not recall her father being a detached and unsmiling mystic, but, rather, a "dad" who was more down to earth. Others spoke of him being "a really good fellow" whose wit was as memorable as his wisdom. People remembered the mystical sage for his comic behavior.

When Lucy spoke of her father's life, she instinctively thought of humorous incidents associated with him. Listeners could laugh heartily at what she narrated, years after the incidents occurred. No one ever directly linked Black Elk's comic persona to his early-in-life heyoka participation, but an association between his sense of humor and conventional heyoka practice seems apparent in the stories that follow (e.g., both employed humor that went contrary to what was expected). It is not surprising that the holy-man used techniques from an earlier period since they worked equally well in the later one.

Although absent in *The Sacred Pipe*, the holy-man's humor is detectable in *Black Elk Speaks* and Neihardt's notes. However, if Neihardt even recognized this quality within his subject, he chose to de-emphasize it and render a more contemplative Black Elk. Because the holy-man's sense of humor was often understated, readers are on their own to detect when it comes into play—both in Neihardt's field notes and in *Black Elk Speaks*.

For example, one instance occurs in the holy-man's memory of his sojourn in Europe. Recalling the gravity of his illness when staying with his host family, Black Elk reported that they purchased a "very expensive" funeral casket. He then casually remarked that he wished he had died in Europe because he would have been laid out in a "good coffin" (DeMallie 1984a, 253). With humorous understatement, he mused that since he was now back home at Pine Ridge, he was resigned to settling for a casket of much poorer quality.

Black Elk's subtly jocular tone is again evident in his account to Neihardt of his ghost dance vision. Recounting the solemn context, Black Elk told of being swept into a futuristic Lakota camp that was well-supplied with game (in stark contrast to the famine his people were then experiencing). Instead of maintaining the tragic tone of his account, the holy-man mused, "I was very happy to see that, and I'm hungry for some of that meat right now" (DeMallie 1984a, 261). Neihardt left no record of his reaction to this understated observation, but Black Elk probably intended to elicit at least a smile from his visitor.

In describing his ghost dance vision, Black Elk again reported being in a village where he saw "plenty of meat there—buffalo all over." Rather than sustain the sober tone of his narrative, he re-marked, "I was hungry and they should have fed me then," as if he could have gained real nourishment from an envisioned feast (De-Mallie 1984a, 264). In these ways, Black Elk wryly wove together the mythic with the mundane, or comedy with tragedy. This was the art of a heyoka.

Another portion of Neihardt's book also offers glimpses into Black Elk's personality. After the gripping account of Wounded Knee, *Black Elk Speaks* takes readers into the conflict's bleak af-termath. The serious tone of Black Elk's account made it easy for readers to overlook the ludicrous elements it contained, and that appear to have been missed even by Neihardt. These humorous el-ements appear unexpectedly, examples of what comedians consider to be an essential skill of their craft: timing.

The holy-man stated that during the battle, he and a friend, Red Crow, paused to eat (an unlikely behavior in the midst of skir-mishing). Bullets whizzed around the tipi, and one nearly struck Black Elk. The holy-man casually mentioned that had a bullet then killed him, he probably would have died with beef jerky in his mouth. His absurd reflection matched the absurdity of what was taking place around him.

In telling this anecdote, Black Elk revealed a trait that made him an accomplished storyteller. Heyoka-like, he could always temper his tale of tears with a touch of levity. However, when Nei-hardt reported the holy-man's comments in *Black Elk Speaks*, he left readers not attuned to this aspect of his subject's style to regard the passage as some kind of solemn pronouncement about dying while dining or about having an ever-present appetite. This un-derstanding was not at all what the holy-man intended to com-municate.

Even when interviewed by Neihardt again in 1944 during World War II, in which many Lakota served, Black Elk could sat-irize a difficult subject. He did this when reporting that Plains Indian sign language designated his people as "cut throats" (a fin-ger motion across the throat indicated that they severed the heads of enemies). He said the Lakota believed that by decapitating an enemy they would frighten their opponents into disengaging from war. Concluding this reflection, he commented, "[I]t seems the heads grew back on, for we are still having war" (DeMallie 1984a, 313).

Black Elk's sense of humor not only came to the fore in ordinary conversation, but it also was evident in stunts he performed. When he preached, he was gifted in knowing how to get the assembly's attention. On one occasion, he stood before the congregation while wearing his wife's coat. People in attendance maintained a respectful silence and watched their spiritual leader reverently return to his seat. Upon apparently detecting the apparel mix-up, he looked startled and surprised. As if realizing he had worn this clothing by mistake, he feigned a reprimand of his wife. Churchgoers watched Black Elk tell Anna to please hang her wardrobe in a place separate from his and therefore spare him embarrassment of this sort in the future. Black Elk thus creatively employed the heyoka style of breaking from expected behavior in the novel setting of a Catholic church.

Similar examples of the holy-man's humorous antics were also elicited in less formal contexts. When called to accompany a priest on a pastoral call, Black Elk rushed to dress. Hurriedly opening his suitcase to find "clean clothing," he put on his underwear and then presented himself to the priest and his family garbed in his wife's bra! Chastising Anna for not separating their apparel was again part of a performance that this time had everyone laughing (Steltenkamp 1993, 59). Apart from wearing his wife's clothing, Black Elk pulled other stunts such as putting his left shoe on his right foot and right shoe on his left.

In another instance, returning home late one night, Black Elk found that his wife had turned out all the lights and it was extremely dark. Awakened by her father shouting "hey" outside, Lucy roused her mother. Upon opening the door and turning on a light, Anna saw Black Elk about ten feet from the house facing the opposite direction. This was his good-natured way of showing her the need to leave on a light. These kinds of physical joking could occur in the midst of formality or during the course of some everyday event. People remembered these occasions, and their memory of what Black Elk said at the time was aided by his humorous antics.

While Neihardt chose to portray a more serious and stoic holy-man, he did report in his book that Black Elk spoke of "truth" coming into the world with two faces (J. Neihardt 1961, 193). One of the faces wept and the other one laughed, but both were ultimately the same face. The holy-man said that when people are too discouraged, the laughing face is what they need to see. Similarly, the weeping face could serve as a caution to those who feel overly secure and content. Despite Black Elk's evaluation, Neihardt and Brown bequeathed a portrayal of him that pretty much reflected the non-laughing face.

Horses

While much of Black Elk's personality was displayed before a human audience, his sense of humor was not reserved for his dealings with other two-leggeds alone. Enjoying a special role within the family—and receiving the brunt of some of Black Elk's playfulness—over the years were Baloney, Brownie, and Button, his horses.[1] The popular assumption that Black Elk's mysticism detached him from more superficial pursuits is particularly countered by the holy-man owning Button, who was a racehorse! Button, however, served double duty as a workhorse.

One day at the general store, when the holy-man was using his horses for their more practical purpose, he remained so long inside that his team and buggy walked home without him. (Black Elk often got absorbed in conversation with people and paid no attention to time.) Not to be outdone by his team, he went to the store on another occasion, then returned home and left his horse tied at the rail! People thought these incidents reflected a personal relationship that Black Elk maintained with his horses, and they with him. The tit-for-tat behavior of the two-legged holy-man and four-legged horses was seen as a conscious interplay between the two parties.

Another time, arriving home late one night, Black Elk let go of the rope to his light-colored horse, Baloney. After all, he knew that Baloney never moved unless told to do so. Getting the gate open, Black Elk turned around to go back for Baloney but was confronted by a big white face and dark eyes—what he thought was a ghost.

Black Elk riding his horse named "Baloney." Courtesy of Marquette University Catholic Indian Mission Archives.

Terrified, he instinctively punched the face that stared at him nose-to-nose. Off went Baloney, not a ghost, and he did not return until the next day.

To Black Elk's Lakota peers, that he would have such a seemingly special relationship with these four-legged creatures was not surprising, and was in some measure attributable to his boyhood vision (Thunder-beings had a special relationship with horses, too). This vision had revealed to him an herb that gave him the power to heal sick or injured horses, and assured him that his horses would have good wind and not wear out. People who bet against Button in races were not aware of the assistance his owner was able to provide.

Iktomi

With no written language, oral narrative—or storytelling—was important within traditional Lakota life. Black Elk's daughter said that for the senior generation, listening to stories was "like reading a book." This oral literature composed a cultural repertoire that extended into Lakota prehistory.

That long-ago era came to life for young Black Elk when his mother told the tale that follows. It is a story that he, in turn, told to young members of his family in the twentieth century. Stories such as this one influenced the thought and behavior of Black Elk and his age-mates, but television, radio, movies, and popular music would influence Lakota youth in succeeding generations. Oral traditions were displaced by other media that relegated the former to being a thing of the past, and of interest only to anti-quarians.

The following narrative reports an adventure of Iktomi, the Lakota version of a trickster character, a literary figure found in cultures worldwide. A trickster's deeds often contain humorous elements, and trigger much laughter among audience members (a humor that is often lost on modern listeners). These actions also often account for why different aspects of creation or culture came into being. Heyoka behavior, for example, was associated with Iktomi's, so it is not surprising that Black Elk's repertoire of oral narratives included this one.[2]

> One day, Iktomi was walking along (he's always walking along and wanting to be where the people are camping). Anyway, he was walking along the creek when all of a sud-

den he came upon a big giant, a great big giant. He called him "Iya" because he'd eat anything—even people [*i'yaka* means "glutton"].

The giant was sleeping, and every time he'd breathe out, his breath would knock over Iktomi (who was very small by comparison). The giant awoke and Iktomi asked him: "Brother, what are you doing here?" The giant responded: "Oh, I'm tired, and thought I'd lay down here and rest. Who are you?"

"I am Iktomi, the one responsible for putting created things in their place. When I put this world together, I even made real big things like you." The giant said that he thought Iktomi looked familiar, but wanted proof of his identity. Whereupon, Iktomi breathed upon the giant, and the wind of his breath knocked the giant over. When the giant sat up, Iktomi drew his fist back, and punched him in the nose—knocking him over again.

"Okay, okay, stop," said the giant, "I remember now. You're who you say you are." Iktomi then said: "Look what else I can do." He got into the creek, and ran above the water just like that spider you sometimes see on a pond who runs above the water. After Iktomi did this, the giant was afraid of him.

Iktomi then said to the giant: "Brother, when you get up from a nap, I know you're hungry, and I know just what you'd want to eat. There's a bunch of people camped not far away from here. We can go there, and you could start eating people from one end of the camp, and I could start on the other. How does that sound to you?" The giant smiled, and thought this was a pretty good idea.

As they set out, Iktomi turned to the giant: "I want to ask you something. What frightens you?" The giant thought for a moment, and said that he was always frightened by the sound of loud drumming. People who hollered and screamed also sent shivers down his back. "Oh," replied Iktomi, "you're really my brother. Those are the very things that scare me."

Now in the afternoon, people in a camp usually are resting, or taking a nap. So just to be sure that their coming would be a surprise, Iktomi volunteered to go ahead and see that the people would be caught with their guard down. He said to the giant: "You wait for me here and I'll come and get you." So the giant waited as Iktomi set off for the camp.

Upon his arrival, Iktomi looked around, found some men who were awake, and said: "There's a big giant, and he's going to attack you. However, he's terrified of drums and hollering. When I come back with him, I'll give the signal for all of you to holler out, beat on all the drums you can find, and make as much of a commotion as you can. If you do as I say, the giant will drop dead of fright, and you will all be spared."

He went back to the giant and said: "Everything is ready. They're all quiet and resting in their tipis. Let's go." When the giant started toward the camp, his weight made the ground shake. Strangely enough, he made the kind of noise which he said frightened him. All of a sudden, the ground stopped shaking, trees stopped popping, and branches stopped cracking as the giant arrived at the camp. However, he never got a chance to do anything. He never even got one bite of human flesh.

When the giant came to the camp, Iktomi signaled everybody to begin hollering. Even the children screamed and wailed. Drums were pounded and people shouted out, or made whatever horrible sound they could think of. The giant went into a frenzy, and dropped dead. Iktomi said: "Cut open his stomach. I think he's got a bunch of people in there." They slit open his stomach, and sure enough, a lot of people came out.

That's a story which tells of how Iktomi saved the people. It's an example of him doing good. At other times, he tricks them, and does the wrong thing. That's why they call him Iktomi—a tricky clown, a clown who does things the opposite of what he's supposed to do. Sometimes his adventures are all right, and don't cause any trouble. At other times, he really messes things up.

Drawing upon the trickster tradition, Black Elk employed his heyoka identity in order to incarnate the "good" that Iktomi was capable of performing. Garbed in a woman's coat within the solemn confines of a country church, casually recalling that he might have died with a mouthful of dried meat, or musing that he would have had a better coffin if he had died in Europe, Black Elk brought smiles, heyoka-like, to many anguished faces that looked to him for hope or encouragement.

An Insightful Catechist

While Black Elk injected humor into his calling, deftly weaving the comic into everyday life and experience, he remained in tune to the seriousness of his work. Like others, he was a gifted and insightful catechist–holy-man. Many in his audience took to heart the counsel he provided, but others did not. He found it curious, however, that people who argued with him the most about some religious matter were, in the long run, the easiest to convert!

An aged cousin of the holy-man (who was a young girl at the time of Wounded Knee) respectfully described him and his work twenty-five years after his death. She said: "He was a really good fellow. He'd preach about the Gospel. He'd say to 'bring up children according to God's laws. Only Almighty God can change the way things are.'" Outspoken in her criticism of a religious laxity at the time that disheartened her, she said, "People heard him but did not listen" (Steltenkamp 1993, 155).

This woman, who in the 1970s was a matriarch of the St. Agnes church and nearly one hundred years old, spoke on behalf of those who knew Black Elk on personal terms. He was a man for whom humor and sober concern about matters of faith intertwined—despite the one-sided image of him readers would embrace for years after he was made famous by Neihardt and Brown.

CHAPTER 12

Neihardt's Visit

In the 1960s and 1970s, when *Black Elk Speaks* became "the bible of the hippies" (Steltenkamp 2003, 153), people were eager to learn more about the holy-man and John Neihardt's relationship with him. The poet's account of his 1931 visit had previously seemed straightforward. However, questions arose over time that stirred wonderment about Neihardt's portrayal.

In his preface to the "life story" he wrote, Neihardt said that he had sought a member of the Lakota's senior generation who could tell him about the ghost dance religion. The "Field Agent-in-Charge at Pine Ridge Agency" directed Neihardt to Black Elk.[1] His recommendation that the poet speak to the holy-man was not surprising—others would have made the same suggestion. Nick Black Elk was a much-respected elder, whose involvement with religion was known to Indians and non-Indians alike. Not only this, Black Elk was the patriarch of an extended family that the agent knew would be an amicable and trustworthy host, providing genuine hospitality to the inquiring guest.

Accompanied by his son, Sigurd, and a longtime friend of the holy-man, Emil Afraid of Hawk (whom Neihardt referred to as "Flying Hawk"), Neihardt met Black Elk in August of 1930, when the holy-man was about sixty-five. When they met, Neihardt was not aware of the extent to which the holy-man was involved with church work. He did not know that the man he would interview was a world traveler and articulate catechist familiar with the old and new ways of Lakota life. Being on unfamiliar ground among a people not his own, Neihardt no doubt felt trepidation appearing out of nowhere and seeking information. But his social discomfort was dispelled by a man long accustomed to making strangers feel at ease. The poet described his first encounter with Black Elk, who could relate easily to outsiders, as a matching of kindred spirits. Black Elk may well have imparted to him a sense of ease. In a passage suggesting the holy-man was clairvoyant, the poet even reported that Black Elk somehow knew he would visit.

For Black Elk to have told Neihardt he anticipated his arrival seems to have been a social convention that denoted hospitality. Joseph A. Zimmerman (1885–1954), a Jesuit priest and friend of Black Elk's, recounted a similar but less dramatic encounter several years later. After being away for three years, the Jesuit returned in 1937. He later wrote that the "veteran catechist" greeted him upon his return, saying, "Every day I saw you in my prayers. I knew you would come back. When I looked and saw you, I could not believe my eyes and tears rolled down" (Steltenkamp 1993, 88). While this vignette profiles the experience of a priest with whom the holy-man fraternally interacted, it is comparable to Black Elk's greeting of Neihardt, a stranger, and later Brown.

Buoyed by their first meeting, Neihardt was eager to arrange another visit. Given an advance by his publisher, the poet wrote Black Elk in November, outlined what his project would include, and said he would pay him "well for all the time that [he] would give [him]" (DeMallie 1984a, 29). While Neihardt offered payment, Black Elk told the poet that, regrettably, he was often paid for his medical services with gifts of horses instead of cash. Whether he was serious, joking, or indirectly suggesting that Neihardt provide monetary support, his comment would have been easy to overlook were it not for his conversion story reporting that for lack of owning a horse he had to walk a long distance to where his patient lay ill. The stenographic notes imply that his success as a healer should have provided him with a herd from which to choose a ride and therefore made walking unnecessary.

Regardless of all this, Neihardt proposed that he visit again in April the next year, but *Black Elk Speaks* reported that the holy-man requested a second visit when they first met. The congenial first visit was no doubt a mixture of Neihardt wanting another one and Black Elk's family graciously extending a welcome. The holy-man's relationship with the poet was built upon a combination of Neihardt's solicitation, Black Elk's willingness to communicate, finance, and friendliness.

Neihardt arrived at the Black Elk homestead for the second visit on May 9, 1931, and the family remained true to its reputation. New accommodations had been specially prepared for the poet; his stenographer-daughter, Enid; and his fifteen-year-old daughter Hilda. Although Emil Afraid of Hawk had served as interpreter during their first meeting, Black Elk's son, Ben, assumed the role for this occasion.

Fluent in Lakota and English, Ben translated the words of his father, and Neihardt phrased them in a readable fashion that Enid then committed to paper. This process resulted in a depiction of the holy-man that eventually won many admirers. However, when the life story was later read to holy-man Frank Fools Crow, enough nuance existed within Neihardt's portrait that Fools Crow simply observed, "That is not my uncle" (Mails and Chief Eagle 1979).

Long after *Black Elk Speaks* had become a classic, people began to ask why the "life story" treated only one-third of Black Elk's life. Neihardt stoked concern over this partial telling when he replaced the words "as told to" (the author) in his subtitle with "as told through" in the 1961 edition. Readers could only wonder what was being left unreported, what possibly was misrepresented, and why Neihardt even made the qualification he did.

Revisiting Neihardt's Work: A New Source

Not until publication of *The Sixth Grandfather* (DeMallie 1984a) were Neihardt's notes accessible. The best index to what Black Elk said during the men's interview, these notes were in need of much explanatory material that their editor (anthropologist Raymond J. DeMallie) ably provided. If Fools Crow found Neihardt's book lacking, he might have detected his uncle in the interview transcripts. However, even they are not without problems.

The stenographic notes are not an exact transcript of questions and answers that were part of a back-and-forth interview. Instead, commentaries sometimes appear to be paraphrases of longer narratives. This might have resulted from the interview forum requiring Neihardt to summarize accounts in order to acquire a story line.

The brevity of Neihardt's visit no doubt required gathering information at inconvenient times. Factors come into play when visiting someone's home (especially in a different culture), and it is not easy to fix a deadline while simultaneously enjoying relaxed and uninterrupted conversation or reflection (Brown recounted this very problem in a letter written during his visit seventeen years later). Nonetheless, the task was completed, and a snapshot of Black Elk's early life was preserved for posterity.

Revisiting the Visit

The poet's meeting with Black Elk read as an uncomplicated encounter of mystical magnitude between two men from different cultural backgrounds. This was a more appealing scenario than the fuller context of the situation, which might have distracted readers. Underlying the interview was a familial dispute that lay outside the scope of Neihardt's vision for the project. Perhaps he was not aware of the conflict. Given where he wanted to take the text, explaining Black Elk's earlier life, there is a clear reason why he would not have committed it to paper if he knew of it.

While DeMallie speculated that other catechists "were opposed to—or jealous of—the book" (DeMallie 1984a, 62) that was being planned, Lucy understood the matter differently. She thought that her father's friend and fellow catechist, Emil Afraid of Hawk, would be the interpreter, and she did not think that her brother, Ben, should serve in the role. She and Emil shared concerns: Would the poet treat only Black Elk's early life experience? Would he include Black Elk's adult years as a catechist? Would Ben's ideas be interlaced with her father's? (Emil later achieved modest fame as translator for *The Singing Sioux Cowboy*, a popular Lakota language text.)

Ben, however, apparently had concerns of his own. DeMallie quoted a letter from Ben in which he wrote to Neihardt that Emil was "loading the old man [i.e., Black Elk] about lots of things. The old man felt uneasy for awhile. But he is perfectly satisfied, very glad to hear you are coming again" (DeMallie 1984a, 62). Familial nerves apparently were frayed, temporarily, when Emil and Lucy dissociated themselves from the project and Ben assumed the role of translator.

Black Elk's daughter recounted this altercation for *Holy Man of the Oglala* (1993), but Hilda Neihardt offered another perspective on it. As a fifteen-year-old, she was probably too young at the time of the visit to appreciate what transpired among the adults, but she later said that the holy-man wanted Ben to serve as interpreter because the arrangement would be optimal for the flow of communication. The oral tradition related to Ben serving as the interpreter that Hilda inherited did not include Lucy's commentary. Ultimately, both women stated what they knew of a transaction that was decided by the holy-man, Neihardt, and Ben.

Lucy's dispute with Ben is actually suggested within *Black Elk Speaks* when the holy-man reports his experience at Wounded Knee. Black Elk mused, "At this time I had no children and maybe if I had been killed then I would have been better off" (DeMallie 1984a, 275). The reflection seems enough out of context to suggest its origin was the family's real-life quarrel.

When the book's publication (1932) justified Lucy and Emil's concerns about the completeness of Black Elk's portrait, disappointment was expressed in a declaration attributed to Black Elk and dated January 26, 1934, titled "Black Elk Speaks Again—A Final Speech." This document told of the holy-man's conversion, his work as a catechist, and his fidelity to the Catholic faith that he had taught for thirty years. Black Elk signed the document, which included the witnessing signatures of Lucy and Father Zimmerman (DeMallie 1984a, 59).

A more harshly worded criticism of Neihardt's work was made in a letter addressed to "Dear Friends" and dated Sep-

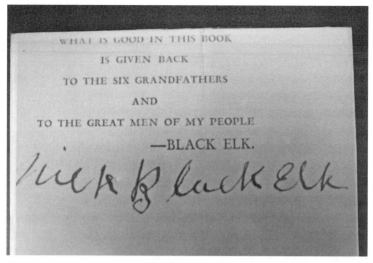

WHAT IS GOOD IN THIS BOOK

IS GIVEN BACK

TO THE SIX GRANDFATHERS

AND

TO THE GREAT MEN OF MY PEOPLE

—BLACK ELK.

Black Elk's signature on the dedication page of *Black Elk Speaks* in a copy of the book within the Jesuit library at Holy Rosary Mission on the Pine Ridge Reservation. Photo by author.

tember 20, 1934 (Steltenkamp 1993, 85). Black Elk claimed that Neihardt had promised to pay him half the book's profit, but that he had received nothing. He further charged that the book perpetrated an injustice against him for not mentioning his many years of labor as a catechist. DeMallie speculated that this second statement perhaps was written by Lucy, with encouragement from the priests (1984a, 62n).

While Lucy and the priests' close involvement in the situation is a possibility, this scenario is just as likely not what took place. The German-born Jesuit Placidus Sialm was especially critical of *Black Elk Speaks* for not treating the holy-man's entire life, but he and the other priests were not privy to all the letter's details. In other words, they were not present when Neihardt visited, so they could not have had firsthand information about what arrangements had been made. The Jesuit library at Holy Rosary Mission also contained a copy of the book with Black Elk's signature, which would seem an unlikely addition to the library's collection if the priests considered the work such a disservice. Lucy herself never claimed a role in composing the letter. In the end, neither of the documents received attention until first brought to light in *The Sixth Grandfather.*

The concerns raised in these statements, however, bear on a re-mark Enid jotted down when her father conducted the interview. In the note, which was overlooked when *Black Elk Speaks* was writ-ten and not mentioned when it was published, she wrote, "When we're through with the story, Black Elk wants to put in just a few words" (DeMallie 1984a, 43). Since "the story" already purport-edly represented many "words" drawn from the holy-man, Black Elk's desire to add "just a few words" is telling. Given the content of the interviews, he must have known that the book would not treat his entire life. According to Lucy, this was the concern he eventually wanted to address in the declaration and letter.

Black Elk's daughter did not see Enid's notes but echoed the same concern when she said: "My father related to John Neihardt an addition to his book, but they never put it out. Afterwards, he realized this and wanted the last part of his life also told—his life as a Christian man praying" (Steltenkamp 1993, 20). Enid's brief note therefore gives substance to the idea that the book's limited scope was a matter that the holy-man himself wanted to clarify. The post-publication statements were then not a question of priests ag-itating for a retraction or of Black Elk being pressured to reform his way of thinking by them and his daughter. His interrogator was acquiring much information about his early life and thought, but Black Elk himself wanted to be sure that his entire tale was told.

A "vaguely unpleasant subject"

More than sixty years after the poet's three-week visit, his daughter Hilda addressed it in *Black Elk and Flaming Rainbow* (1995). Since *Black Elk Speaks* came to be understood as more than the simple telling of a life story, *Flaming Rainbow* sought to an-swer questions that had arisen over the years. It was a recitation of memories Hilda had carried since accompanying her father to the Black Elks' home as a fifteen-year-old. A second book, *Black Elk Lives* (2000), was a follow-up to this reminiscence, and it was supplemented by information provided by Ben Black Elk's children and grandchildren.

Perhaps unintentionally, Hilda revealed in *Flaming Rainbow* that Neihardt influenced what Black Elk and others chose to share during the three-week visit. Her father wanted the story of a medicine man whose narrative was unambiguous. The holy-man and his son understood what their guest wanted and complied with the request. Hence, Neihardt poetically sketched a portrait of Black Elk's early life without reference to anything that took place after Wounded Knee.

According to Hilda, however, Black Elk did tell her father that he joined a "white church" (H. Neihardt 1995, 119). ("White church" was Hilda's term, not Black Elk's.) Since she and her father regarded the holy-man's catechetical work as "that sensitive, vaguely unpleasant subject" (1995), this might partly explain why Neihardt was silent about the rest of Black Elk's life. For Black Elk, however, his life as a catechist was not at all a "sensitive, vaguely unpleasant subject." DeMallie concluded that Neihardt found Black Elk's vision so intriguing because he found Christian practices so "stultifying" (DeMallie 1984a, 47). This was not Black Elk's position, but years later, institutional affiliation would also be found more sterile than stimulating by persons who presided over the emergence of New Age religion (which helped popularize *Black Elk Speaks*).

While the New Age movement was to unfold decades after Neihardt's visit, there existed a readership in the 1930s that was drawn to the idea of old-time Indians collectively regarded nostalgically as "the vanishing American." For these readers, an account of Black Elk's catechist life paled in comparison to a work that focused on "the Wild West." This was the ready-made audience for which Neihardt wrote, an audience for whom the holy-man's church work could not compete with reminiscences of Little Bighorn, Buffalo Bill, and Crazy Horse.

Decades later, however, the writer's daughter expressed the matter differently. Hilda said that when her father inquired about Black Elk's life as a catechist, the holy-man remained silent. Hilda may have been too young at the time to appreciate the social dynamics at play, but in later years she drew this conclusion: "What he did not find it necessary to say left us with a strong sense of where his true beliefs remained" (H. Neihardt 1995). She said that her father understood Black Elk's silence "all too well" and that her father "said no more."

Lakota social interaction, however, often includes silence, which does not always translate into the Western aphorism that it means consent. The poet had represented himself as seeking a Native elder whose recollections were solely from of old, so Black Elk, his friends, and son accommodated him as gracious hosts. The holy-man's silence was most likely his show of respect for visitors who he knew were not interested in reporting his life as a catechist. He courteously agreed to provide the biographical information they sought, and he requested, to no avail, that an addendum be included.

What Black Elk Sometimes Said and What He Meant

John Neihardt spoke of *Black Elk Speaks* as "a work of art with two collaborators" (Holloway 2003, 20). As a result, the holy-man of the book and the real-life holy-man are not the same. The poet chose themes he wanted his "life story" to include, and Black Elk provided information that covered a range of topics that the writer recast.

In fact, if isolated from the rest of his life, some of Black Elk's statements in the transcripts of the interviews could be understood as candid, broad-stroke indictments of everything associated with non-Indians. These utterances were by no means defining moments, but they lend some credence to Neihardt's portrayal of Black Elk as a dejected elder. Still, they are best understood within the broader context of the holy-man's life.

One such moment of candor occurred toward the end of the 1931 visit. Ben might have made additions to what his father said or Neihardt might have augmented the translation, but some of Black Elk's comments reveal a man whose familiarity with mainstream religious and secular teachings enabled him to indict the "wasicu" (i.e., "whites") for not observing these same doctrines.

The wasicu only brought misery to his people—a people who *could* observe the teachings.

> The first thing an Indian learns is to love each other [John 13:34]. . . . The next thing is telling the truth [Ninth Commandment]. Whatever they say, they stand by it. We should treat our fellowmen all alike. The Great Spirit made men all alike [Declaration of Independence]. Therefore we made a mistake when we tried to get along with the whites. We tried to love them as we did ourselves [Gospel of John]. On account of this we are now in misery. They were men like us in all but color and therefore we wanted to like them and get along with them . . . the white race has done great wrong to the Indians. (DeMallie 1984a, 289)

Black Elk's account here is comparable to what he preached at Sing Sing Prison and in eastern cities, and to what he addressed with Neihardt, Brown, priests, and Lakota elders when speaking about matters related to the Sacred.

Black Elk's final 1931 experiences with the poet reveal his dissatisfactions of another kind. The day before parting, Neihardt's entourage took Ben and his father to the Black Hills where photos could be taken of the holy-man praying on Harney Peak. Stopping at a carnival, they treated Black Elk to a ride on the Ferris wheel which, as luck would have it, came to a halt when the holy-man was high in the air. Although he shouted for the ride to end, Black Elk was not persuasive, and so was forced to endure the full circuit (DeMallie 1984a, 47).

That night, the group attended a movie that featured a scantily clad heroine. Her portrayal prompted a solemn-faced Black Elk to grip the arms of his theater seat and utter "bad, bad" (DeMallie 1984a, 47). In the morning, the group climbed Harney Peak, conducted the photo shoot, and put together a transcript of Black Elk praying. After this, *Black Elk Speaks* awaited to be written.

CHAPTER 13

Sanctity

John Neihardt visited Black Elk in 1930 and 1931 and concluded that the senior generation of Lakota was preoccupied with waiting for "yesterday," the pre-reservation era of its youth. His melancholic observation could have described many Pine Ridge residents at the time since socioeconomic conditions were not good. Widespread unemployment and alcoholism, much poverty, and few opportunities for social interaction characterized life for a large segment of the population.[1] It was easy for people to imagine better times existing elsewhere or in an earlier age. Elders, as more aged members of the community, were especially affected by conditions beyond their control. Their mobility often limited, they had few leisure opportunities away from the homestead.

In recalling the period when Neihardt visited, Fools Crow labeled the 1930s as "the worst ten years" he could remember (Mails and Chief Eagle 1979, 148). The times were oppressive enough that the holy-men from different religious backgrounds (Catholic, Episcopal, yuwipi, etc.) gathered to address their people's plight. Black Elk was about seventy years of age when he attended this meeting, and all agreed that "shameful behavior was everywhere" (Mails and Chief Eagle 1979, 149).

The leaders' gathering as a group was an exercise in religious tolerance that was normative for the Lakota. The group's consensus-based "solution" also reflected Black Elk's influence:

Fools Crow said that the holy-men affirmed one another's effort to walk a sacred path and acknowledged that if a solution were to be found, it was "not in [their] hands" (Mails and Chief Eagle 1979, 149). The best they could do "was to fall back on [their] prayers" (again, in Lakota, one's "way of prayer" referred both to the praying one did and the religious tradition one practiced). The ecumenical group made a decision that was neither sectarian nor nativistic. The participants simply admitted that the people needed more than ever a corporate commitment on the part of holy-men to continue their religious exercises unselfishly on behalf of the people. Their effort in this fashion was consistent with the idea of bringing to bloom the flowering tree of Black Elk's vision.

As the reservation community struggled with weakened socioeconomic conditions, Black Elk underwent his own setback. In 1933, two years after Neihardt's stay, Ben Black Elk wrote to the poet that his father was not the "man he used to be" (DeMallie 1984a, 59). This remark was occasioned by a wagon accident that sent Black Elk to the hospital with two fractured ribs. There he received what was then commonly referred to as "last rites," the Catholic sacrament for the seriously ill.

Black Elk's weakened physical condition prevented him from performing the outreach that typified his earlier years. Some days he felt better than on other days. Like anyone who has undergone hardship, he could candidly point to disappointments of a religious or social nature. However, discouragement did not define Black Elk's personality or his evaluation of what he did as a catechist, contrary to what some writings on him suggest.

Although church membership had increased and care of the faith community was now overseen by a younger generation of clergy and lay assistants, the holy-man still would be asked to address meetings of the societies or to assist with the celebration of holidays and feast days each year. As an active catechist, Black Elk was responsible for visiting the sick and comforting the bereaved at funerals. In retirement, he informally continued this practice until his death. Throughout these activities, Nick Black Elk remained a welcome guest at homes and a hopeful presence within the community.

At St. Elizabeth's church in Oglala, South Dakota (1936). Black Elk is second from right, wearing glasses and holding his prayer book. Courtesy of Marquette University Catholic Indian Mission Archives.

In the 1930s Black Elk likewise continued an interest in the community of the larger world around him. During this period, he befriended Gutzon Borglum (1867–1941), the chief sculptor of Mount Rushmore.[2] Along with family members, friends, and reporters, Black Elk ascended the faces in a gondola two days before the monument's dedication in August of 1936. *The Sixth Grandfather* reported that this experience stirred fear within the holy-man. However, like portrayals of Black Elk's personality and life in literature earlier, even the account of this occasion is open to reinterpretation.

A family member reported that Black Elk planned to sing as the group ascended. However, as the cable car went higher, Black Elk remained quiet and Ben's sister-in-law asked him why he was not singing. According to *The Sixth Grandfather*, Black Elk replied to her, "Tell them I'm too scared" (DeMallie 1984a, 65). Perhaps this is exactly what occurred and nothing more came into play. On the other hand, the incident makes one wonder why he would say this only to the young woman within such a confined space and not also tell the others.

Perhaps his reply was instead a grandfather's way of offering consolation to his granddaughter, letting her know that she was not alone in feeling the way she did without singling her out. Perhaps he said this to break what might have been real tension felt by the group as a whole. Or, since Black Elk was skilled at choreographing performances, he might have realized that singing on the ride up would not fit the occasion or would be an unnecessary distraction. He perhaps decided that singing was better suited for the ceremony at the top. It would be surprising for Black Elk to have been too paralyzed with fear to sing at this time when performing the "death song" was so ingrained a cultural tradition at moments of greater duress than this one.

The holy-man's literary representation has stirred debate, and this simple incident is an example of why his identity is difficult to apprehend. His fear apparently abated when the car stopped. Wearing a buffalo headdress, he then sang and prayed with a pipe for the assembled. No fear was cited during the descent.

The Summer Showman

From 1935 until infirmity took its toll on Black Elk a decade later, the holy-man spent his summer months at Alex Duhamel's "Sioux Indian Pageant" (one of many business ventures that had been operated by the entrepreneurial Duhamel family since the beginning of the twentieth century). This pageant took place nine miles south of Rapid City, South Dakota, at what became known as Sitting Bull Crystal Caverns. A major tourist attraction by the late twentieth century, the caverns owe their name to Black Elk.

The Duhamel family history tells of Alex visiting "Nick's place" (i.e., Black Elk's home at Manderson, South Dakota) in the 1920s and informing the holy-man that his family was going to open the caverns for tourists (D. Lewis 1993, 119). Alex told Black Elk, "People are very interested in learning about the old Indian ways and perhaps we could develop some kind of a play to tell their story" (118). According to Alex, Black Elk then suggested that the site be named after Sitting Bull. Ever since this visit, the caverns have been known by that name.

At the Sitting Bull Crystal Caverns, where the holy-man had camped in the company of relatives and others, Black Elk again became an admired showman. The pageant, which began in

1927, included a variety of people reenacting different Lakota customs, and Black Elk's daughter, Lucy, remembered her father as having "the main part" as a medicine man. Each show began with Alex's son Pete saying a prayer in Lakota. Alex's son Bud assumed the role when his father and brother (Pete) died in 1941.

The Indian pageant consisted of twelve "acts," which respectfully showcased traditional Lakota religion. Bud Duhamel acknowledged that in "the 30s and 40s, most of the old Indians had become Christians—but they could still remember how it was in their old religion" (D. Lewis 1993, 126). In depicting that "old" tradition and lifestyle, the show included portrayals of a camp on the move, a sun dance, a medicine man's healing ceremony, mourning and interment rituals, rabbit and buffalo dances, the pipe ritual, and an Omaha war dance, along with vocal performances. Black Elk was perfectly suited for the role of performer since he had been a kind of lifelong performing artist as a showman with Buffalo Bill, a medicine man, a heyoka, and a catechist. His involvement also provided income and an enjoyable break between what were always long and hard South Dakota winters.

For his performance, Black Elk used his well-honed skill to instruct audiences on matters of the spirit, although he served neither as an evangelist for Lakota religion nor for his Catholic practice. On one occasion, audiences laughed with Black Elk when his grandson, George Looks Twice, climbed onto the burial scaffold and fell asleep. Prior to this occurrence, George had played a sick child who his grandfather healed.

The pageant prompted positive interaction between visitors and Lakota culture, as well as between Black Elk and Alex. During the pageant, visitors mingled with Black Elk and other Lakota families, who were camped at what was called the "Sioux Village." Friendly conversation and hospitality characterized their interaction—generating within tourists an appreciation for Indian culture, and within performers nostalgic memories of their youth.

Many pageant viewers went away with an enduring memory of a spectacle that delivered what it promised. Advertised in an idiom that later generations would consider inappropriate, the pageant nonetheless impressed visitors who watched the proceedings with

Black Elk, dressed for the Duhamel pageant, in 1937. Photo by Walter "Ben" Hunt. Courtesy of Marquette University Catholic Indian Mission Archives.

Black Elk with his grandson, George Looks Twice, at the
Duhamel pageant's "Indian Village" circa 1940. Courtesy of Vern Ziebart.

"silent respect" (D. Lewis 1993, 120). Promotional material read:
"Interesting, historical, educational, glamorous, colorful, excitement, no fairy tales or mythical acts." Potential audience members
were advised to come "see the mighty Sioux on the trail with their
travois and ponies as you would have seen them sixty years ago. Set
in the center of the Sioux nation the war cry of the last savage min-
gling with the soft beat of the tom-tom will make your blood tin-
gle" (D. Lewis 1993, 128). Taken on the road to neighboring

states, the show featured Black Elk as an important part of the entourage. However, when the pageant began drawing small audiences during World War II, it was discontinued.

Over the years of their interaction, Black Elk and the Duhamels
formed a close relationship. Bud Duhamel considered it a great
honor when Black Elk said that he would privately induct him into
the tribe by slashing Bud's wrist and his own.[3] Bud recalled Black
Elk saying that as their wrists bled and the blood joined together,
they became "blood brothers." Black Elk presented Duhamel an
eagle feather and bestowed on him the name "High Hawk." The
Duhamel family history does not say whether Duhamel's strong
Catholic practice helped forge this bond between the men
(Duhamel was a fourth-degree "Grand Knight" in a Catholic
men's fraternity known as the Knights of Columbus). Duhamel attributed to Black Elk the following counsel that accompanied the
giving of the feather:

> The Indian Nations developed specific religious cere-
> monies not only to the spirit of the living, but also for sup-
> port on the pathway to eternal life. The most significant
> was the reward of the Eagle Feather which symbolizes the
> patterns of humility and obedience to the Creators to aid
> their fellow man in faithfully carrying them out.
>
> The Eagle Feather given to you this day protects you
> in your present spiritual life and beyond. It is to go with
> you on your journey into the hereafter as proof of your
> worthiness. (D. Lewis 1993, 124)

In terms of Bud's new name, "High Hawk," before and after Black
Elk's time, it was not uncommon for Lakota elders to bestow a
name on non-Lakota whose friendship they valued. This courtesy
is not the same as the "making of relatives" ceremony but was a gesture of amity extended to appreciative recipients (e.g., all the early
Jesuits had Lakota names).

Black Elk left a lasting impression on the Duhamels for other
reasons, too. Bud Duhamel recalled that one of the performers,
Henry Horse, became seriously ill. When the Sioux Sanatorium, a
medical facility, offered no hope for Henry's recovery, Black Elk

collected herbs and roots and made "a stew" of them. He and Bud administered the mixture to the patient, who, in three days, was restored to health and was again dancing in the pageant.

Bud also claimed that when, on one occasion, a fire burned out of control in the Black Hills, Black Elk quickly organized a number of Lakota to perform a "sun dance" to avert the threat. Within a day and a half, rain came and extinguished the fire. Memories of this nature moved the Duhamels to value Black Elk's friendship with them as much as he valued theirs (D. Lewis 1993, 124).

The Death of Anna Brings White

In 1941, when he was about seventy-five years old, Black Elk suffered the painful loss of his wife, Anna. What little is known of her was reported in a missionary publication, *Indian Sentinel,* after her death on February 19 that year. Her obituary revealed how priests and lay people alike saw the Black Elk household as a kind of "mission center." According to the account, Brings White, a beloved matriarch, created a "welcome home for the missionary" where she addressed the priests in kinship terms. She made her house a gathering site at which people prayed and sang hymns. Her loss was "a great sorrow" for the holy-man, according to the obituary.

Three months after Anna's death, Black Elk willingly agreed to address a Memorial Day assembly. It was a twentieth-century Lakota custom for an older church member to speak at the cemetery on the holiday. On this occasion, Catholics would celebrate a mass, and people would tidy the grounds and pray for the dead. Under a hot sun, Black Elk performed the task but later collapsed at home. He recovered, but the experience reminded everyone that he still felt the loss of his wife. He moved from Oglala to Manderson where he stayed intermittently with Ben, Lucy, or Nick Jr. until his death nine years later.

Manderson Memories

Now relocated near the church he helped found (St. Agnes), Black Elk was committed to the role of loving grandfather and re-

Front, center, Black Elk and his wife, Anna; Lucy (her hands on a boy's shoulders); and other parishioners after a "home mass" near Oglala in 1937, four years before Anna's death. Courtesy of Marquette University Catholic Indian Mission Archives.

tired catechist. Each Sunday at Manderson, weather permitting, he walked about two miles to church. Cane in hand, he would join John Lone Goose at the general store. As the men walked together, they prayed aloud the rosary. At St. Agnes, Black Elk needed a younger person's assistance when kneeling and rising since he insisted on receiving Communion on his knees at the rail. He periodically would address the congregation and sometimes chastise them for not being as responsible as they should be in caring for the church.

At home, Black Elk would pray on everyone's behalf before eating. His daughter, Lucy, recited a prayer that he reportedly uttered on Thanksgiving. She might have heard it enough times that it stayed in memory. It flowed from her as if she were reading a text (Steltenkamp 1993, 118–19):

> I am talking to you, Grandfather Great Spirit, on this day.
> Pitifully, I sit here.
> I am speaking for my relatives, my children,
> my grandchildren, and all my relatives—wherever they
>   might be.
> Hear me, Grandfather, Great Spirit.
>
> With your help, our needs are taken care of.
> You have helped us in the time of want during the past.
> And on this day we wish to thank you.
> Hear me, O Great Spirit.
> This day is a day of thanksgiving.
> The nations of living things the world
> over—and we the two-leggeds, along with the
> children and the smaller ones with them—come
> to you today to express thanks.
>
> In the future, make us see again a red day of good.
> In the past, you have preserved us from evil
> on this red road. Keep us on this road, and do not let us see
>   anything wrong.

I, my children, and my grandchildren shall
walk—led like children by your hand.
You have helped us in all things.
And Grandfather, Great Spirit, through your power
alone we have survived.

Grandfather, Great Spirit, you have come and
put us down—gathered together on mother earth.
And while we continue in this world you provide
food for all living creatures.
So we give you thanks on this day.
Grandfather, take pity on me.

One day, we shall go and arrive at the end of the road.
In that future, we shall be without any sin at all.
And so it will be in the same manner for my
grandchildren and relatives who will follow as well.
We give you thanks, Grandfather Great Spirit.
I am sending this prayer to you.

Identified with praying on special and ordinary occasions,
Black Elk also was associated with being a devoted grandfather. The
holy-man's grandchildren recalled a man who would one day be a
well-known religious figure, but who to them was their dear
babysitter. Brown described well the beloved elder whose presence
brought joy to youngsters: "He loves children, & when they are
about they are all over him—he is kindly, gentle, with a most mar-
velous sense of humor" (Brown 1947a).

When not reading his prayer book, which was written in
Lakota, he would have a rosary in one hand and cane in the other
as the children played, rode their tricycles, or rode a horse he
walked for them. Come bedtime, it was customary for him to sing
them to sleep with a song from the Latin mass. He also sang a
church hymn in Lakota. Decades later, this song was still used at
services attended by the then-elderly children born to members of
his generation. Its English translation is:

O God most good
Who wants to make himself known,
All rejoice rightly,
He asks of you your hearts.
You Lakota are a nation,
Quickly may they come together;
Jesus would have it so,
Because he has called you all. (Steltenkamp 1993, 56)

Throughout his life, the holy-man learned many prayer-songs, and his last years saw him draw upon one of them in trying to avert a storm that threatened. He was not skeptical when told that Jesus could quell storms. After all, the heyoka claimed similar power.

Taking his pipe to a hill and facing the west, he sang: "I said I am a Thunder Being nation. You will live. I said I am a Thunder Being nation. You will live" (Steltenkamp 1993, 117). His daughter said it seemed that clouds rushed off in other directions when Black Elk sang this way.

On another occasion, when a storm frightened his grandchildren, Black Elk stood outside, singing: "They will dance. Those make me live. They are coming" (DeMallie 1984a, 218). The clouds moved away after he addressed them in this fashion. The children were calmed, and witnesses smiled and shook their heads in wondrous disbelief. Singing songs from the Latin mass or from a vision demonstrated an eclectic religious repertoire that even his granddaughter tapped. Relatives believed that on one occasion she followed his example when a storm approached, and sang one of his songs. According to family witnesses, the thunder and wind immediately subsided (Steltenkamp 1993, 117).

CHAPTER 14

Sacred Pipes

In the fall of 1947, Joseph Epes Brown went in search of Black Elk and found the holy-man staying with "extended family" members who were digging potatoes somewhere in Nebraska (Brown 1989, xii). Brown carried some misgiving since Neihardt had said that Black Elk would not speak with him. Entering the holy-man's tent, he presented Black Elk with an Assiniboine ceremonial pipe.

Comparable to what Neihardt and Zimmerman reported earlier, Brown said that "the old Sage" asked why he had been so long in coming. Given the similarity of the meeting accounts, the holy-man's customary, disarming hospitality appears to have followed a formula. He was able to convey an immediate sense of welcome by communicating in some way to visitors that he was expecting them.[1]

Brown intermittently stayed with Black Elk that winter in Manderson, and was a guest of Ben's family. Putting together a book from his interviews, he hoped his work would help revitalize traditional Lakota religious practice and was pleased that his presence had an effect on Ben. Brown wrote that his efforts had "done Ben much good" and that Ben "bit by bit" came "to realize the truths that underlie his own rites" (Brown 2007, 115). As he finished writing *The Sacred Pipe* (1953), Brown was optimistic that his work would help "many" Lakota "awaken" to "the glory of their heritage" (Brown 2007, 115).

Brown's letters (2007), published sixty years after his work with the holy-man, reveal his interests at the time of his visit.[2] The letters also provide a sense of the social scene that was not described in *The Sacred Pipe*. In them, Brown reflected on what prevented the religious revitalization he sought from "going ahead" at the time. He sensed an "inertia" that was "very great among the majority of the people." Brown hoped he might help dispel this social malaise by starting a fraternity of religious specialists that would be known as the "Order of the Pipe."

As Brown interviewed Black Elk, Ben again served as his father's interpreter, and their collaboration produced *The Sacred Pipe*. It eventually became a canonical text for people interested in American Indian religion. Most of the rites discussed in the book already had received attention in anthropological literature, but Brown's description of them struck a resonant chord with readers. He devoted a chapter to each sacred ceremony that the holy-man described. The book owes much of its strength to Black Elk's interpretation of the rites, but this also has been its challenge. Namely, the book is a highly detailed work containing long prayers and descriptions of rubrics that might be cumbersome for casual readers. On the other hand, this comprehensive treatment, its footnotes and commentary, might be valued by researchers. Years after *The Sacred Pipe*'s publication, Brown regretted not presenting the material differently. Regardless, the book has been a rich source of reflection for a wide array of readers.

The rites Brown detailed in *The Sacred Pipe* were a fixture of the nineteenth-century Lakota religious world but were not the totality of Lakota ceremony. Brown only focused on the "sacred pipe" and seven important rituals within which it was employed. Other researchers had reported much of this information, but Brown popularized it by relating it through the warm and wise words of an aged holy-man. By doing so, he personalized Indian ceremonialism that previous literature pigeonholed as unremarkable tribal practice.

Brown did not address to what extent Black Elk's interpretation of the rites was actually his Christian reinterpretation of them. Like Neihardt, he made no reference to the holy-man's Christian practice. By the time Brown visited Black Elk in 1947, many Lakota had integrated the old and new to such an extent that "sharp differences between traditional religion and Christianity began to blur" (DeMallie 1984a, 92).

Brown's main contribution is probably his introducing readers to the pipe itself. It was an instrument of private prayer and public ritual that experienced renewed usage in the late twentieth century. *The Sacred Pipe* contributed to this resurgence since it became, according to comparative religion scholar Ake Hultkrantz, "the most widely read work on Plains Indian religion" (Capps 1976, 91). People had been long familiar with the term "peace pipe," but Black Elk imparted to audiences new appreciation for a sacred instrument, with a deep history, and its ritual use.

Sacred Pipes

Throughout Indian America, variously designed pipes have been used for religious functions or for leisurely smoking. Different peoples maintained one emphasis or the other. Pipe antiquity is evident in the numerous bowls that have been excavated from many sites across the continent.

While other Indian nations own a comparable heritage about how their pipes came to them, Black Elk popularized the Lakota pipe tradition. It was his account that stirred many people's interest in Native practice. As a result, the Lakota's story of their pipe's arrival has become a valuable addition to the world's collection of sacred literature. Black Elk recounted for both Neihardt and Brown the well-known story of how his people received the sacred pipe.

To Brown, he said that early one morning, two Lakota men went hunting, and as they stood "on a hill looking for game, they saw in the distance something coming towards them in a very strange and wonderful manner":

> [T]hey saw that it was a very beautiful woman . . . bearing a bundle. . . . Now this woman was so good to look at that one of the Lakota had bad intentions and told his friend of his desire, but this good man said that he must

not have such thoughts, for surely this is a *wakan* woman. The mysterious person was now very close to the men, and then putting down her bundle, she asked the one with bad intentions to come over to her. As the young man approached the mysterious woman, they were both covered by a great cloud, and soon when it lifted the sacred woman was standing there, and at her feet was the man with the bad thoughts who was now nothing but bones, and terrible snakes were eating him.

The woman told the good man that she would come to his village and tell them "something of great importance." True to her word, she brought to his people the gift of the pipe. It would assure the people that Wakan Tanka would hear their prayers. She also said that in the course of time other rites would be revealed. When the woman departed, she was transformed into a buffalo calf—eventually disappearing over a nearby hill. This is why the pipe is sometimes called the "Sacred Calf Pipe." (Brown 1953, 3–4)

Details vary little within the plot from one telling of this story to the next. Black Elk, for example, informed Neihardt that worms crawled from the skeletal remains while Brown's account has snakes take the place of worms.

Some Lakota believe that the story of the pipe's coming took place as told. Others say it was not an actual historical event but should be understood as the inspired vision (dream) of a holy-man. Understood literally or symbolically, recognition of the pipe's sacred importance was a major moment in Lakota history. Just as the sacred writ of world religions has inspired followers to draw guidance from it, so did the oral tradition that told of the sacred maiden's gift. Transcending self-interest, choosing to do good over evil, recognizing the Sacred beneath surface appearances, and giving one's life in service of the community are some of the themes that Black Elk learned from this oral tradition as a youth.

While the pipe ordinarily served a role in communal ceremonies and private prayer, it also appeared at other times that non-

Lakota initially might find surprising. An example of this kind of usage occurred during a tense moment when an army column confronted Crazy Horse. The Oglala leader approached the officer in command and said: "Let's dismount and have a smoke. Even a man about to die takes time to smoke" (Clark 1976, 63).

Offering of the Pipe

When it came time for Lakota to smoke a pipe, they undertook an offering ritual Black Elk described to Brown that had been revealed by the mysterious maiden, who was named "White Buffalo Cow Woman." Ever since her coming, this ritual has been observed with minor variation when one prays privately with a pipe or when it is used in ceremonial contexts. Because they are descendants of the sacred woman's gift, all pipes are believed to carry the original's power. In rituals, the stem first is pointed toward the four cardinal directions (beginning with the west, then the north, then the east, and finally the south), toward the sky, and then toward the earth. Lastly, it is smoked.

This pattern (west, north, east, south, sky, earth) is a predictable, ritual, and narrative structure in the Black Elk literature. However, a variant pattern also exists. The pipe sometimes is offered to the heavens first, then the cardinal directions, and then the earth. Other nations follow this pattern, but some peoples, such as the Anishnabé, begin in the east instead of the west and proceed clockwise (or, according to Black Elk, "sun wise"). Pawnee ritual orientation has the nuance of featuring a northeast, southeast, southwest, and northwest directionality.

The pipe user places a pinch of tobacco in the bowl and prays with each gesture if the bowl has not been filled prior to the offering. The Algonquian word *kinnikinnik,* meaning "what is mixed," became an early pan-Indian reference for what is smoked, but Lakota also used the word *chanshasha.* This mixture was a blend of tobacco with red alder, red osier, or dogwood.

Pipe stems have varied in size but those in ceremonial use are between one and two feet long. According to Black Elk, the stem represents all things that grow from the earth, and it might have

decorative incising such as a turtle or buffalo form. Adornments
such as feathers or animal parts might be attached to the stem, and
their meaning is associated with the owner's experience of the Sacred. Black Elk said that twelve eagle feathers were attached to the
original, first sacred pipe, and that they were meant to remind the
person who was praying that their thoughts should always be lofty
ones, rising as high as the eagle. This original pipe was kept and remains on the Cheyenne River Reservation, so it is possible that
Black Elk was only told what it looked like and never saw it in person. His nephew and much-respected holy-man, Frank Fools
Crow, did not see the original pipe until he was in his eighties
(Mails and Chief Eagle 1979, 203). One observer associated the
pipe with twelve golden eagle feathers while another in 1941 reported seeing six that were stained red.

Pipe Bowls

Just as there is an account explaining the pipe's coming to the
Lakota, a sacred story also reported what material was to be used
for making the bowls. Different versions exist, and Black Elk did
not provide one. A well-known story reported that long ago all the
Indian nations were warring with each other, and Wakan Tanka took
pity on them. Called to gather at what was a sacred stone area, the
nations were told about the ground on which they stood. It held a
crimson-colored stone that reminded the people of blood. From it,
they were to fashion their bowls. Whenever the sacred stone was to
be used for the smoking ritual, people were supposed to lay down
their arms and not permit hostility to occur. Ever since receiving
this gift, Indian nations have observed this mandate. An account of
a Lakota incident illustrates the letter of this law, if not its spirit:

Digging at a quarry in Wisconsin one day, a Lakota man no-
ticed an Anishnabé man doing the same and approached his traditional enemy. After a greeting, the two men smoked and then
parted company. After separately digging for stone, they rode off
the sacred area and then fought until one man was victorious and
in the possession of a scalp (West 1934)!

Only a few quarries for the reddish-colored rock, known as pipestone, exist, so the stone is rare. The premier cache is in southwestern Minnesota, at a site artist George Catlin (1796–1872) visited in 1836. He fielded complaints from Mandan, Ponca, and Sauk Indians that the Dakotas were prohibiting access to the site. A Mandan leader even asked that Catlin get the president to intervene so that his people could once again visit the pipestone area.[3] The Yankton ceded the parcel to the government for a monetary settlement in 1928, and it was placed in the care of the National Park Service. It became Pipestone National Monument in 1937. Native artisans continued to craft the stone with reverence, but some Indians have charged that its commercial exploitation should not be permitted.

While some bowls are yellowish or black in color, most are made of this stone. Sometimes the figure of an animal is carved on the bowl, while others are smooth and plain. Catlin's name eventually came to identify the reddish stone so that it is commonly referred to as both pipestone and "catlinite." Black Elk reported that the original pipe bowl has a buffalo calf carved on it that represents all four-leggeds.

Praying with the Pipe

Prayers in *The Sacred Pipe* are the holy-man's illustration of what people could say when enacting the ritual. A prayer's content was not fixed, and, as with specialists in any religious tradition, some Lakota practitioners were more adept than others in spontaneously composing them. One prayed within the constraints of a ritual's accepted structure, but different circumstances required creativity. Imaginative or inspirational phrasing was as much valued among the Lakota as peoples elsewhere.

Within the rites Black Elk described to Brown, the pipe was not the focus of attention, and it should not be understood as something the people worshipped. Instead, rituals included singing, gestures, praying, and commentary that occupied the attention of those gathered. While use of the pipe began ceremonies and punctuated the flow of what transpired, another feature of Lakota ceremonialism was incensing, colloquially known as "smudging." During this ritual, a practitioner wafted wisps of smoke emanating from burning twists of sweetgrass or cedar over the group gathered. This purified the assembly, the sacred area, and the pipe itself (Mooney learned in 1891 that the use of cedar chased away evil powers while sage drew in good ones). The rubrics of smudging would rivet everyone's attention during a ceremony, and the practitioner's gestures, like the use of the pipe, reminded people that something very sacred was taking place.

Although different individuals invest the pipe with their own meanings and rote prayers are not the custom, some understandings of the pipe are commonly shared. When offering the pipe, for example, one invokes the supernatural powers that reside above, below, and in the cardinal directions. Tobacco grains accompany these offerings, and these grains represent all created things and all the intentions of the assembled. The pipe ritual thus includes all space, all creation, and all the personal concerns brought by participants. Rising smoke represents the ascent of all this to Wakan Tanka.

Humility and dependence upon the creator define a reverence that was profoundly evident in Black Elk's account to Brown of the pipe's significance. His reflections became an important source of inspiration for a late–twentieth-century pan-Indian movement. Since his contribution, new meanings have been added to the pipe ritual that was already dense with associations.

The Pipe and Weather

The pipe also has a sacred relationship to storms. Among the Lakota, a particularly potent manifestation of the Sacred is the Thunderbird of the west (Wakinyan Tanka), who protected the pipe. Since the Thunderbird's glance was lightning, it was like the pipe itself in connecting heaven and earth.

Lakota oral tradition reports that the Thunderbird will strike lightning upon anyone who does not respect the pipe. Some adherents say that the pipe is "alive" and must be shown strict reverence or else it might punish one who does not observe decorum. However, this type of threat of retribution does not appear to be part of Black Elk's theology. He made no reference to stories that circulate regarding the pipe's avenging power. One of these stories told of people stealing the original pipe from its keeper. They were later found dead. Lightning dealt their demise and the pipe mysteriously returned home.

Brown heard of comparable incidents. One account dealt with two men who created drawings of the original pipe and made money by showing them to tourists in Rapid City. On the men's trip home, lightning killed them and their drawings were destroyed. On another occasion, the Pine Ridge Indian agent reportedly had two policemen confiscate the pipe, which he contemplated giving to a museum. Leaving the pipe in his office, he could not sleep all night because of the sound of a buffalo calf bellowing in his office. In the morning, he had the policemen return the pipe. Lightning killed one of the officers later that year, and one died of some disease (presumably because of his complicity in taking the pipe). Five decades after Brown wrote of these incidents in letters home, his editors checked their veracity with pipe-keeper Arvol Looking Horse (born long after the incidents purportedly took place). The editors stated that Arvol "confirmed them" (Brown 2007).

Although Black Elk did not reference stories of the pipe wreaking vengeance, he did tell less dramatic stories about the pipe that were typical of those that others told. He remembered when storms arose and pummeled everything but the sacred space that was the site of a ritual in progress. Later in life, he prayed with the pipe for rain if it was desired or to avert a storm that threatened.[4] In such instances, like Native peoples elsewhere, Black Elk regarded the presence of an eagle soaring overhead as a good omen. It signaled that the enterprise would be successful. The eagle's association with Wakinyan Tanka (the great thunderbird of the West who protects the pipe) made its appearance a sign of the Thunderbird's heavenly, protective presence.

Ritual Colors

Although Lakota religious specialists had long associated colors with the four directions, it was Black Elk material that brought new attention to this ceremonial feature. He associated black with the west, white with the north, red with the east, and yellow with the south. With Black Elk–related books commanding such respect in the twentieth century, these associations assumed authoritative status. They came to be considered by many readers the only "sacred" colors that "Indians" associated with the directions, with each color tied to the direction to which Black Elk consigned it (even though he substituted blue for black on occasion).

This kind of material in the Black Elk literature cast universal appeal as people sometimes said that these four colors represented the "four races" of humanity. This association suggested to some that from earliest times Native America understood humanity to consist of four color groupings, and categorized it accordingly. One often hears that the ritual use of these four colors is a Native acknowledgement that there is a unity in humankind's diversity.

The meaning of the four colors expanded, and it was not uncommon to hear within Indian circles that if these four colors were mixed, the result would produce a shade of skin that was identifiably "Indian" (a tannish or dark tone can result depending upon the amount of each color in the mix). A widespread Indian folktale has a comparable motif. It told of the creator "baking" the different peoples of the world into existence. In the oven too long, some were burned black. In the oven for too short a time, some were white or yellowish. Baked just perfectly were Indian peoples, a reddish shade. Black Elk material brought the ceremonial use of color to the consciousness of many readers who found the topic fertile. However, subsequent studies tempered the intriguing conclusions that this topic tended to spawn.

Other Indian religious specialists, for instance, revealed that they varied their association of colors with the directions. Black, white, red, and yellow were in broad use among the Lakota and other nations, but green, blue, or brown were sometimes substituted for one of them. These three colors were often used in place of black, which is, technically, not a color. Linguists also found that many languages only contained a few color words.[5] Studies further showed that if a language had one color word, it would be "black." If a language had two color words, they would be black and white;

if three, black, white, and red; if four, black, white, red, and yellow. Linguists reported that this color hierarchy of black, white, red, and yellow prevailed in languages worldwide. The words for these colors were followed by green, blue, brown, purple, pink, orange, and gray, in that order. Black Elk and others essentially used color words that were within a language that did not have a large color lexicon.

The Lakota Pipe's Antiquity

Some say that the Lakota pipe revelation occurred in the long-ago and misty past, but Black Elk estimated the pipe's arrival among the Lakota to have occurred "about eight hundred years ago" (DeMallie 1984a, 284n). Winter counts place its coming at 1540. Archaeological excavations have dated the use of Minnesota pipestone to as early as 900 A.D. while a Nebraska site has been dated to the thirteenth century.

Black Elk learned the history of the sacred rites from Elk Head, the original pipe's keeper in the 1920s. When Black Elk's daughter, Lucy, met Elk Head, she feared being in his presence. Her father dispelled her fear when he casually told her to say "hello" and shake the man's hand. At the beginning of the twenty-first century, the pipe's nineteenth caretaker was Arvol Looking Horse.

For many years, the original pipe has been kept at Green Grass, South Dakota, on the Cheyenne River Reservation. Some Indians have sought for its formal placement within a shrine that would be uniquely Indian in design. Others have resisted this effort and prefer that inquisitive visitors be prevented from gaining access to the gift brought by the sacred maiden long ago. Debating how best to care for the pipe is nothing new. In a letter to Father Gall, Brown said that Black Elk and "some other old men" planned to "take" the pipe and "give it to a qualified person to keep." Black Elk reportedly said that such a person "should be one who is always praying" (Brown 1947c).

CHAPTER 15

Sacred Rites

The Sacred Pipe played an important role in acquainting non-Indians with American Indian religious traditions. As Brown hoped, it also inspired Native people to enliven those traditions anew. Given the book's influence within this revitalization movement two decades later, it is surprising that Black Elk's initial reflection in the work did not elicit curiosity.

In the foreword of *The Sacred Pipe*, he stated: "We have been told . . . that God sent to men his son, who would restore order and peace upon the earth; and we have been told that Jesus the Christ was crucified, but that he shall come again at the Last Judgment. . . . *This I understand and know that it is true*" (Brown 1953, xix; italics added).

Nothing more was said about this testimony since Brown followed Neihardt's lead and was silent about Black Elk's Christian practice. Brown understood Black Elk to be "one of the last of the *wischaka* [*sic*] *wakan*" (i.e., holy-men), and that this particular holy-man "was envious to re-establish an order of the Pipe." Since Brown thought this was "of the greatest importance" (Brown 1947b), he proceeded in the following chapters to spell out a wealth of detail related solely to the traditional Lakota religious universe.

In his correspondence with Father Gall, Brown explained that "these people & most of the Indians here are Catholic—out of a certain sort, i.e., they recognize the truth wherever they find it & so know that their ancient way was also the true one" (Brown 1947b). Brown reported that he and Black Elk could not "talk" to one another because of the language barrier, but he did not think direct communication was necessary. Ben was his able interpreter and Brown considered himself to be "of one mind" with Black Elk (Brown 1947c). By the time Brown met Black Elk, the holy-man had spent more than forty years as a catechist and had internalized a spirituality that reflected both his Lakota and Christian upbringing. Brown sought to record what he thought to be Black Elk's pristine recollection of seven traditional rites—to which he devoted a chapter each.

The Keeping of the Soul

"The keeping of the soul" rite is part of Lakota mourning customs. Brown's coverage, however, did not address all these customs. By contrast, Neihardt recorded Black Elk's frank recollection of ritual weeping: "I cried all day there. It was hard work crying all day, but this was the custom. This is the way I had to cry: 'Hownh, hownh—My cousin, he thought lots of me and I thought lots of him.' I did not feel like crying, but I had to do it all day" (DeMallie 1984a, 207). Other patent expressions of loss included cutting a finger off, usually at the last joint; slicing pieces of flesh off the arm; and cutting hair. *The Sacred Pipe* focused on what might be considered the essentials of Lakota grieving ceremonialism.

Black Elk addressed burial and mourning when Neihardt interviewed him in 1944, but he did not provide the poet with the full description or meaning of the soul-keeping ritual that Brown later reported. Neihardt, like the Duhamel pageant, only offered a cursory account. The holy-man told him nothing about how the soul was kept, but only reported that the deceased was placed on a scaffold—which accounted for disposal of the body alone—and that relatives would then mourn their loss for four days. Black Elk did, however, mention that if the living sincerely made the effort, they could change their bad habits during this period of mourning and become better people (DeMallie 1984a, 381–82).

Black Elk said that his people originally kept "only the souls of a few" great leaders, but "later we kept the souls of almost all good people" (Brown 1953, 11). Lakota belief held that a soul would wander the earth (which is what normally would occur with the soul of a bad person) if the rite were not performed on its behalf. In 1890, the government prohibited this ritual of mourning.

Black Elk told Brown that the maiden who brought the pipe also instructed the people how to conduct this rite. It involved clipping a lock of hair from the deceased and incensing it with smoke from sweetgrass.[1] Prayers were made to the powers above, below, and in the four directions. The hair was wrapped in buckskin (a sacred bundle) and placed in a *wanagi tipi* (spirit house). The lock of hair in buckskin represented the soul that was being kept.

Keeping of the soul (and other rites) included several taboos. The word "taboo," which comes from a Polynesian lexicon, is used by anthropologists when referring to diverse prohibitions found within a culture. Violation of a taboo is thought to bring serious consequences and to incur some kind of spiritual (or social) debit.

Black Elk said that the one who kept the soul must be a virtuous holy-man. A taboo that the soul-keeper had to observe was that he should not touch a knife for any reason during this mourning period. The keeper also should not fight or be in contact with blood. Instead, he should pray constantly, be a role model for others, and always carry the sacred bundle in the crook of his left arm, closest to his heart.

People believed that the habits they established during this mourning period could remain with them, contingent upon one's sincerity and resolve. As a result, family members of the deceased must perform praiseworthy deeds, entertain noble thoughts, and speak in a sacred manner. By comporting themselves this way, they help their loved one make the transition from this world to the next. By maintaining a sacred lifestyle, the family also contributes to the well-being of the larger community. Black Elk reminded people in mourning to remember: "Your hands are *wakan*; treat them as such! And your eyes are *wakan*; when you see your relatives and all things, see them in a sacred manner! Your mouth is *wakan*, and every word you say should reflect this holy state in which you are now living." The holy-man's counsel clearly reflected his vision of the sanctity to which he thought all people were called.

As part of the soul-keeping ritual, a woman also cares for the sacred bundle. On good days, the bundle is placed on a tripod outside the tipi with its legs facing north, east, and west. The opening to the south is the direction in which departed souls return to Wakan Tanka (represented by the point where the tripod legs meet). A thong hangs toward the ground from the apex, and this symbolizes the journey taken by the soul from the earth to Wakan Tanka. People come to pray in the presence of the bundle and bring it gifts. These will later be given to the needy. Since Black Elk's time, this distribution (colloquially referred to as a "giveaway") has been extended to anyone who had a special relationship to the departed.

The Releasing of the Soul

Holy-men determine the day on which a soul is released, and they make the pipe offering to commence this rite. Crying as she gets the sacred bundle, the keeper's wife brings it to her husband, who addresses the soul and reminds it of the love and good care it has received. The pipe offering again occurs, along with many prayers, and the keeper cries. The community follows his lead with keening. People also might cut short their hair or lacerate themselves.

At the end of the ceremony, the celebrant aims the bundle toward the sky and asks the soul to help the nation. As the bundle emerges out of the tipi, the soul is released, and the bundle is no longer sacred. The soul then travels the "spirit path" (the Milky Way) until meeting an old woman at the place where it divides.

In earlier times, all Lakota wore a blue spot on their forehead so that this woman would know them. To the right, she would send those who had lived well. To the left, she would send those who must wander until sufficiently purified. Only then could they go to the "land of many lodges." References used in the late twentieth century to this place were "Spirit Land," "spirit world," "Deer Land," and "Deer-killing Land" (Stolzman 1986, 197), but not "happy hunting ground."

With a loved one no longer in their midst, Lakota people in mourning compose an emotionally afflicted community. However, instead of feeling helpless, adrift, and emotionally disoriented, they observe rites that call them into action. Those left behind can extend one last act of caring or respect toward the departed. Not only will their loved one benefit from this corporate observance, but those left behind, too, can become better people as a result.

Inipi: The Rite of Purification

The rite of purification is a sauna-like, sacred experience that takes place in what is commonly referred to as a "sweat lodge" (J. Neihardt 1961, 166). Besides the classic form practiced by the Lakota, three other types of induced "sweating" were undertaken by Native peoples. One included placing a blanket on heated stones. A person would then lie on the blanket. Another was a "dry sweat" that involved using heated stones without sprinkling water on them. While open-fire sweating also took place, the Lakota form was the most popular. For it, people gathered in an igloo-shaped structure made of willow. Within this chamber, people would purify themselves so that they might know "true life" and come closer to Wakan Tanka, "who is all purity" (Brown 1953, 32).

Different terms for the ceremony (stone bath, sweat booth, sweat bath, vapor bath) appear in literature that preceded and followed the holy-man's description of it. Popularity of *The Sacred Pipe* among both Indians and non-Indians eventually made the ritual commonplace within urban and reservation settings. It became a practice undertaken by young and old, and men and women alike, when just years earlier it had been a custom preserved by relatively few.

In the late twentieth century, this purification rite became a pan-Indian ceremonial expression of ethnic solidarity. Practitioners also began to serve as religious advisers to interested non-Indians and popularized the ceremony among them (making the rite an Indian contribution to the non-Indian world of religious questing). Meanwhile, some practitioners objected to non-Indians adopting the ritual and claimed proprietary rights to the use of any Native religious form.

Black Elk assigned religious meaning to every artifact and action of each ritual. Given his detailed account, Brown surprisingly omitted a description of the lodge's covering (even in the sketch that accompanied the account). Buffalo hides initially served this role, but blankets, comforters, and other materials have replaced them in use. The entire universe came to be represented within the sweat lodge. The natural elements, four-leggeds, two-leggeds, and supernatural powers were all participants in this prayerful ceremony. Its rules required strict compliance or else the rite's efficacy would be compromised. However, Black Elk's interpretation of the rite is not the only one.

Anthropologist and Jesuit Father Raymond A. Bucko analyzed a vast literature related to the ceremony, and placed Black Elk's account within a broad, historical context. Comparing the tradition with its late twentieth-century practice, he showed that changing circumstances required practitioners to adapt. Black Elk spent a lifetime doing this within many spheres of activity and was not alone in the effort.

World religions often have codified, or printed, texts that specialists consult and follow, but Lakota religion did not have these written sources. It relied upon oral tradition and experience. Retaining continuity with a rite's essentials, specialists also adjusted to changing times. The challenge was to balance tradition with a sense of the sacred that the tradition was intended to impart. As with any religion, if tradition itself became an uncompromising deity, the wakan would be lost.

Was buffalo the only meat that could be used in a ceremony? Could beef replace it? Could chokecherry juice be replaced by something else? Muslims perform ablutions with water, but sand came to be employed when circumstance dictated its use. Some Christians drink grape juice instead of wine, as was used at Passover, for their Communion services.

When John Neihardt visited in 1944, Black Elk stared tradition in the face and humorously favored necessity. He was about to tell the story of a Lakota mythological figure but recalled that it was his people's custom to tell that kind of story only on winter nights. He said that if nighttime stories are told during the day, "you will get long hair on your bottom" (DeMallie 1984a, 395). After careful reflection, Black Elk decided to tell the story anyway. Able to discern essentials from nonessentials, he decided in good conscience that expedience permitted telling the tale.

Black Elk's decision was like that of an Anishnabé holy-man who likewise justified reporting a similar story. He said that the taboo applied only if one told it in the Indian language. He would tell the tale in English, so it could be told on a summer day. Both holy-men were skilled in discerning the spirit of the sacred from the law of tradition that might, at times, stifle it.

Black Elk's account of using the sweat lodge stressed positive themes that were high-minded (e.g., the lodge's darkness represented ignorance, and participants sought to purify themselves of it so that they might emerge into the light). However, the historic record reveals the rite also was employed for less noble purposes. It also formerly involved conjuring illness to come upon someone, addressing unrequited love, and compelling marriage upon the unwilling.

Black Elk provided an uplifting account that was rich with symbolism. Participants were shown at the center of an interplay between light and darkness, hot and cold, laughter and tears, and purity and impurity. Going into the lodge, people entered a kind of womb from which they exited reborn and renewed to begin life afresh.

Since Black Elk's time, practitioners have tended to invoke the ceremony's benign expressions detailed by Brown. It was a prayerful ceremony undertaken by people in need, for helping someone who was ill or for simply acquiring a sense of general well-being. Black Elk said that people often performed the sweating ceremony on a daily basis and that its restoration would be a good thing. Given the resurgent interest in the sweat lodge rite, his counsel was heard.

Hanblecheyapi: Crying for a Vision

Throughout Native America and described at length by Black Elk is what much other literature refers to as the "vision quest." The

Lakota knew about this rite before the coming of the pipe, and both men and women "lamented." Success depended upon the character of the person, so not everyone received a great vision. Black Elk was insistent that performing the rite would not just magically transform a person whose life was floundering in some fashion. It was important that the lamenter find a wise elder who could help guide and interpret his or her questing experience.

The holy-man likened the vision quest to a "retreat" conducted by priests for laypeople. On a retreat, the same kinds of prayer, fasting, and spiritual direction took place. In 1906, Father Buechel wrote in his diary: "Nick Black Elk had come to collect money at an issue in Rosebud. As it came off later, he made three days retreat. I gave [it] to him. He asked 'How is it about eating during the retreat? The Indians do not eat during their recesses'" (Steltenkamp 1993, 64). Black Elk appreciated that both traditions included an isolation and discipline that helped one experience union with Wakan Tanka and all creation.

Black Elk said that people lamented when preparing for war, asking Wakan Tanka to find a cure for a relative, or giving thanks for some favor received. Other reasons for lamentation that were not mentioned by him included naming a child, acquiring a protective design, being successful in the hunt, entering a secret society, mourning appropriately, or seeking help to exact revenge. Apart from these pragmatic interests, the holy-man thought that the rite's foremost role was to help one seek the strength to perform good deeds.

The ritual included a person going to a protruding rock, mountain, or hill away from the camp (Black Elk said that women quested closer to the village than did men). The individual remained within a small area, its length and width large enough to accommodate a person resting. This space had a pole in the center and poles in each direction.

There in solitude, clothed only with a breechcloth and with hair hanging loose on the shoulders, one sought a vision. Abstaining from food and water could induce hallucinations, but acquiring a "vision" generally entailed having a dream. The seeker intentionally looked pitiable so that the Sacred-beings would be more inclined to give assistance and establish a relationship (Plenty Coups, an Apsáalooke, reported cutting off a fingertip in supplication while on his quest).

Everything that occurs during this period of seclusion can help the lamenter. If, for example, a storm's Thunder-beings instill fear, this can reveal the paralyzing power of Wakan Tanka. It is a lesson in humility, since by comparison the lamenter is made to feel very weak.

Brown learned that something very practical could be acquired when questing. He was present when Black Elk's friend, Little Warrior, came off the hill. Appearing "more dead than alive" due to the cold weather, Little Warrior said that the experience provided him a cure for tuberculosis (Brown 2007, 121).

Black Elk said that when the lamenter walks away from the pole in each direction, the movement represents how people walk away from Wakan Tanka throughout life. At these times, one thinks he or she is alone and independent. The person must learn to return to the source of all life, Wakan Tanka, which the central pole represents.

No prayers appear in Black Elk's description of the ceremony, but he insisted that one should take time in making them. During this period, which generally lasted two days, the lamenter must be especially attentive to all creatures that draw near because they might bring a message. No creature, be it an ant or a mouse, is too lowly to be the bearer of some lesson the lamenter needs to learn. Still, the lamenter might not acquire a great vision, even after many attempts.

Crazy Horse's custom was to lament several times a year. Through these quests, he acquired what Black Elk called "power and holiness" (Brown 1953, 45). These occasions brought Crazy Horse inspiration from a badger and a rock, and his name was derived from the vision of a prancing horse. It was also from vision experiences that he learned to take gopher mound dust and put it on his horse and on his scalp. Less tangible mediators for him were "the day" and a "shadow." One of these prayer experiences revealed an amulet that protected Crazy Horse. He would sling a piece of buckskin around his neck and on it was a small white stone that hung under his left arm. Many thought that this stone helped make Crazy Horse bulletproof, his death by a bayonet giving credence to this belief.

Red Feather told Father Buechel that he quested at least five times in his youth forty years earlier. Saying that he "did not 'see' or 'dream' strange things," Red Feather reported that on one quest he heard the grunting of buffalo when buffalo were nowhere around. Despite having no vision, he told the priest that his prayers "were heard." After all, he had lived a long life and still owned "many horses and cattle" (Buechel n.d.).

Black Elk repeatedly encouraged perseverance in questing. His most defining observation about the rite (and about one's religious practice as a whole) was stated twice in this account. He said that a person should realize "*Wakan Tanka* is always anxious to aid those who seek him with a pure heart" (Brown 1953, 66).

Wiwanyag Wachipi: The Sun Dance

The longest chapter in *The Sacred Pipe* is devoted to Black Elk's description of his people's longest ritual, the sun dance. Practiced by twenty to thirty Indian nations, the ceremony has Siberian parallels. Before the modern period, its enactment at Pine Ridge in 1881 saw nine men undergo the piercing that it included.

The Lakota sun dance was outlawed in the 1880s, but this prohibition was not enforced until 1904. The dance was reinstated in the late 1920s and then formally by the Indian Reorganization Act of 1934. The late twentieth century witnessed its revival, and Black Elk material gave significant impetus to this development.[2]

Revealed in a vision to a man named Spread many years before Black Elk was born, the sun dance would help the Lakota since they had become lax in their religious practice. It was a "new way of prayer" (Brown 1953, 68). A "new way of prayer" is, literally, how Black Elk's generation also referred to the different denominations they joined. Having a way of "prayer" was understood as something one should have (it would be beneficial for the individual and everyone else).

As with the other rites, Black Elk assigned meaning to all elements within the sun dance. The drum, for example, was important because its roundness represented the universe, and its sound was both its beating heart and the voice of Wakan Tanka. As with so much of what Black Elk said, the interpretations he offered were not necessarily standardized. The content of a holy-man's reflection did not have to echo another's. Their thought drew upon a lifetime of religious experience in two traditions.

Black Elk also said that one should reverence the cottonwood tree. It was used for the sun dance because it always looked up to the heavens (and so provided a good example for people to imitate). Like the pipe, it focused on the powers above. Similarly, the tree's voice prays when wind rushes through its branches and reminds the people that they should also pray. It gave shelter to bird nations just as the specially chosen cottonwood sheltered the Lakota who placed it in the center of this sacred ceremony.[3]

Seeing the tree as a person praying was a perspective that Black Elk bequeathed to his daughter. Reflecting on her youth, she recalled going into the family garden to "shake hands" with the corn stalks. In doing so, she would say "good morning" to what she called "these creatures" and "pray" with them (Steltenkamp 1993, 75). Lucy's memory revealed that the cottonwood was just one of many inhabitants residing within the Black Elk family's religious landscape.

Held in late June or early July, the sun dance consisted of two periods with each lasting four days. The first period was for preparation and the second for the dance itself. Participants would be people who, in time of need, vowed to undergo the rite.

Black Elk described the sun dance of his childhood, but over time different practitioners modified it. One's vision could supersede tradition. This permitted latitude in how one danced, what one sang, what gestures one employed, or what designs one painted on one's body.

While the dance included body piercing, comparable (or more severe) forms of mutilation are common to other religious traditions.[4] Leashed to a central pole by cords attached to their pectoral region, dancers moved to break free of the connection. They also might make flesh offerings cut from their arms or drag buffalo skulls attached to their back. If release did not come in the course of dancing, friends or relatives could cut or pull off the attachments, and it was not unusual for participants to faint when undergoing the rite.

Brown sought to report the sun dance's "pure" form, and did not note Black Elk's interpretation of the rite. Lucy said her father thought Christianity fleshed out traditions that the Lakota practiced, and that he understood the sun dance to be a Lakota imitation of the sufferings Jesus endured (e.g., a crown of sage dancers wore was the rite's parallel to the crown of thorns Christ wore). Black Elk also associated the sun dance with the Christian notion of a self-sacrifice that relieved the suffering of others.

The holy-man was not alone in making this association. Red Feather described these same ceremonies to Father Buechel, and he shared Black Elk's opinion that "many of the old Indian rites are similar to those of the Catholic Church" (Buechel n.d.). When addressing groups on the East Coast, Father Craft (the priest at Wounded Knee) would say that Lakota traditions paralleled the sacraments (e.g., the rite of "making relatives" was similar to baptism, the sun dance to Communion, keeping the soul to anointing the sick, sweat lodge participation to penance, etc.).

At the 1881 ceremony, one of only nine dancers was able to pull free of the piercing; the others required help. Publicly restored in 1928 as part of a tribal fair without piercing, the sun dance became a popular social event at Pine Ridge for many years. By century's end, many sun dances with piercing were being conducted on the Pine Ridge Reservation and throughout the plains. The dance had become more popularly practiced than ever before and returned to being solely a religious exercise.

Hunkapi: The Making of Relatives

Father Buechel wrote in 1915 that the only person remembered as performing the *hunkapi*, or making of relatives ceremony, was a man named Brown Wolf. The priest noted in his diary that Brown Wolf was "a Catholic" who had died years earlier (Buechel n.d.). Black Elk material helped the ceremony's reemergence such that some form of the ceremony again became commonplace.

The holy-man stated that hunkapi created a threefold peace. The first was what a person experienced in realizing oneness with Wakan Tanka. The second was a peace that existed between two people, and a third is what existed between two nations. The third cannot take place without the first two, and by striving for this peace, one has "done the will of the Great Spirit." This goal was at the heart of a senior Black Elk's worldview: "The first peace, which is the most important, is that which comes within the souls of men when they realize their relationship, their oneness, with the universe and all its powers, and when they realize that at the center of the universe dwells Wakan Tanka, and that this center is really everywhere, it is within each of us" (Brown 1953, 115).

Black Elk's account might be his reinterpretation of what earlier existed. The rite originally might not have been as universal in its orientation as he described it to be (since the Lakota customarily fought people whose language they did not understand). However, adapting tradition to new understandings was his prerogative. Not noted by Black Elk, but reported by Buechel, was that a red stripe was painted on the forehead and cheek of the person who was made a relative and that several stripes were worn as a badge of honor.

Relatedness is also at the heart of an utterance that is not in the Black Elk literature. Heard most often within the darkened confines of a sweat house, the phrase "*mitak oyasin*" (all my relatives) became widely used after Black Elk's time. Within the sweat house, social distinctions evaporated and gave way to a communal sense of dependence on the Creator. Union with others might not be the felt experience of participants outside the ceremony, but the sweat house elicited this sentiment as they bonded to one another inside it.

Sometimes meaning "this is for all my people," sometimes "for all you people," and sometimes with the more inclusive accent of "all *are* my relatives," the saying can be an affirmation of family or community, an assurance to participants that they are not alone, or the assertion that everyone is related (H. Neihardt and Utecht 2000, 158).[5] A visionary insight, "all are my relatives" enjoins participants to transcend self-interest and behave toward others in the respectful manner that a familial relationship requires. Thus, when

praying *"mitak oyasin,"* one reminds listeners to actualize its promise in the deeds they perform. One symbolically and reverentially
is invoking the *hunkapi* ceremony.

Ishna Ta Awi Cha Lowan: Preparing a Girl for Womanhood

Cultures everywhere have so-called rites of passage. These ceremonies mark a person's transition from one social identity to another. Preparing a girl for womanhood is the description of a Lakota
rite of passage that has parallels in cultures elsewhere. It takes place
just after a young girl has experienced her first menstruation.

The Lakota ceremony affects a broad range of behaviors and includes what social scientists refer to as the "menstrual taboo." This
prohibition, which is not a phrase used by Indian people, is most evident when women are absent from ceremonial participation. Some
people who look at the taboo from outside the tradition that observes
it might evaluate the taboo as a form of patriarchal oppression. Those
within the tradition regard the taboo as a defining mark of gender
that must be reverenced in an appropriate, sacred way.

Among these people, a woman's monthly flow of blood required a segregation that, seen in a positive light, recognized the
special birthing power of women. A menstruating woman must not
be present at certain rituals or may not touch certain objects. It is
thought that her special power at this time might disrupt other powers and bring affliction of some sort. The mysterious quality is emphasized and the taboo's restrictive nature is not considered.

Arguments that dismiss a taboo's observance as passé might
themselves be dismissed with no justification other than a man or
woman saying "something will go wrong if we don't do this," "we have
always done it this way," or "it is our tradition." Others might offer
an explanation they say is a traditional one or that is based on their
personal reflection (e.g., the sacred mixes with the mundane when
some say that good spirits avoid unpleasant odors that might exist
with dried blood). Ultimately, modern practitioners are confronted
with the option of interpreting the menstrual taboo in some new way,
ignoring it, or retaining the time-honored tradition (Stolzman 1986).

Ordinarily, an older woman would instruct a young girl in matters related to her new status. This woman would tell the girl that the people depended upon her for survival just as all people were dependent upon the earth's fertility for survival. Like the earth, this young girl had a sacred power to bring new life for the people, so she must reverence her new, generative ability entrusted to her from the Creator.

The man leading the ceremony makes a bundle out of sweetgrass, cherry tree bark, and the hair of a live buffalo. Holding it over the head of the young girl, he informs her that she is a tree of life standing between heaven and earth. As a woman with power from above, she must live in a sacred way. He would then rub the bundle on all sides of the girl so that the powers of the direction were part of her.

Red Feather told Father Buechel that the master of ceremonies prayed over girls so that they would have a long life. An old man performed this ritual, and Red Feather said that the old man would "receive a horse and other things for his service" (Buechel n.d.). As with other occasions, a banquet would conclude this rite.

Tapa Wanka Yap: The Throwing of the Ball

Black Elk also described to Brown a sacred game that had not been played for many years. He said that because the buffalo people did not have hands to catch a ball, they gave this game to two-leggeds in a vision to Moves Walking. Its enactment culminated in the throwing of a ball in the cardinal directions and straight up into the air. When the game ended, a feast was held and the poor received presents.

Black Elk interpreted the ball as being both the world and Wakan Tanka (who is everywhere, thus in all the directions). The ball's descent from the four directions represented the power of Wakan Tanka descending upon the people. Buechel said that in a time of sickness or trouble, one would vow to stage the ceremony on behalf of the poor—but only if the sickness or trouble was overcome.

In concluding his reflections, Black Elk acknowledged a hierarchy in creation (Brown 1953, 138): "of all the created things or beings of the universe, it is the two-legged men alone who, if they purify and humiliate themselves, may become one with—or may know—*Wakan Tanka*." He then sadly reflected on his people's waning spiritual fervor. He believed that religious commitment produced virtuous living, and he associated virtuous living with the sacred ball. However, to his great disappointment, he said it appeared that some of his people were "not even trying to catch it" (Brown 1953, 138).

A New Audience for Black Elk

The Sacred Pipe did not receive much attention when first published in 1953. When reprinted in 1971, it drew readers who Brown described as engaged in "a serious reevaluation of the premises and orientations" of American culture. He said that for many people, modern America had begun "to represent diminishing attractions" (Brown 1971, xv–xvi).

Black Elk's foreword for the first edition of *The Sacred Pipe* especially spoke to people seeking the sacred in everyday life and in an endangered natural world. The holy-man pleaded for his audience to appreciate Wakan Tanka, whom he described as "within all things; the trees, the grasses, the rivers, the mountains, and all the four-legged animals, and the winged peoples; and even more important we should understand that He is also above all these things and peoples" (Brown 1971, xx). This perspective also provided the environmental movement with a spiritual grounding that many found inspirational.

Brown cast Black Elk's spirituality within the framework of seven Lakota rites. Authors previously had reported Lakota ceremonialism, but *The Sacred Pipe* brought it to life. Brown revealed a holy-man who saw the sacred in everything and who urged others to do likewise. His narrative to Brown in the last years of his life was one more effort to help people live in a wakan manner.

CHAPTER 16

The Land of Many Lodges

A fter Brown's departure in the spring of 1948, Black Elk slipped and broke his hip. When not bedridden, he used a wheelchair. During this period when he was in his eighties, the holy-man was not absorbed so much with thoughts of how people sought the Sacred but that they even tried to search for it. Despite Black Elk having this concern about others' spirituality, what Brown described as Black Elk's "kindliness" was not affected. Others, too, remembered a holy-man whose disposition remained positive through days that only became more difficult.

Black Elk's physical deterioration continued after his fall when he suffered a stroke that left him partially paralyzed. He had trouble feeding himself and, although resistant to the decision, was hospitalized in Rapid City where his grandson, Benjamin Junior, was being treated for meningitis. However, the holy-man was one night mystically present at home when his son-in-law, Leo Looks Twice, returned to the family cabin. There Leo heard but did not see the holy-man singing a death song. Leo said aloud, "I hear your voice, but I hope nothing bad happens in our family" (Steltenkamp 1993, 127). He retired for the night and concluded that his father-in-law was preparing them for someone's death. Shortly thereafter, Benjamin Junior died.

Since Western medicine was unable to save Ben's son and had not improved his father's condition, Ben suggested that Johnson

Little Warrior, a healer, be contacted. This was a natural sugges-tion—working with Brown had helped Ben become active in what Brown described as "encouraging" people "to take up again the old ways." Perhaps this man could heal Ben's father by means of a traditional Lakota healing art for which he was known (Brown 2007).[1]

Little Warrior impressed Brown as being "as holy as Black Elk," while Ben also held him in high regard (Brown 2007). Lucy asked her father if he had confidence in his old friend (who also had been a performer in the Duhamel pageant, and belonged, Lucy said, to another Christian church). Although he respected Little Warrior, whom he called "cousin," Black Elk was not interested in having his friend doctor him. Nevertheless, Lucy said that Ben was curi-ous about traditional Lakota practices and so encouraged his father to be treated by Little Warrior. Black Elk consented, and Ben con-tacted the healer. The session, which took place at Lucy's home, be-gan with cleansing and praying in a sweat lodge.

These activities had remained a part of Black Elk's life as a cat-echist. Lucy recalled an earlier sweat lodge experience with her father that she did not wish to repeat but found humorous in ret-rospect. She said that her father shouted from within the lodge ask-ing her to open the flap. Unwilling to be involved with the "males-only" ritual that was taking place, she did not do as he requested until hearing him yell, "Hurry up or we'll all burn up in here" (Steltenkamp 1993).

Another sweat lodge occasion took place when Black Elk ac-companied Brown to Denver. The holy-man felt unclean in their rundown hotel, so thought it wise that they purify themselves there in the room. Extending blankets over chairs in front of the fireplace, he constructed a hot chamber wherein they observed the purification ceremony.

Although he had taken part in these experiences in the recent past, Black Elk did not want to participate in the lodge when Lit-tle Warrior came to doctor him. Instead, three older men underwent the ceremony and prayed on his behalf. Little Warrior then pro-ceeded to treat his aged friend within the completely darkened con-fines of the cabin.

Black Elk's friend and healer, Little Warrior, circa 1948.
Courtesy of Marquette University Catholic Indian Mission Archives.

As with comparable yuwipi ceremonies, this one included little
glimmers, or flashes, of light that appeared during the ritual. They
were understood to be Little Warrior's "spirit-helpers" lending assistance. Brown observed Little Warrior's ceremony a year earlier,
and on that occasion it included shaking rattles and drumming. He
further stated that an owl was Little Warrior's spirit helper.

Hanging within Lucy's house was a picture of what Catholics
refer to as the sacred heart of Jesus. Intended to represent the love
of Jesus for all people, the picture has long been a staple of popular Christian art. Hanging next to the picture was a rosary. Before

the ceremony began, Little Warrior said that some practitioners tell their sponsors to take "holy pictures" off the wall during these ceremonies but that he believed in doing the exact opposite. Little Warrior told Lucy that the sacred picture and rosary would help heal his patient. He asked everyone to pray to the sacred heart and to pray the rosary throughout his ceremony. Lucy reported that his spirit helpers did arrive and that they made these objects appear to glow. She understood the glimmering lights to be "worshiping" the picture and rosary (Steltenkamp 1993, 124).

Administered by the spirit helpers, Little Warrior's therapy apparently involved a form of physical manipulation. Afterward, Black Elk was tired but good-naturedly said that he had been "roughed up" during the ceremony (Steltenkamp 1993, 125). He told his doctor-friend that if there was to be a "next time," Little Warrior's spirits should not treat him so harshly.

Little Warrior (who died in 1953) and Black Elk interacted with the Sacred in similar ways. Little Warrior spoke to Lucy about praying, and she said his counsel was comparable to her father's: "When you pray, the good spirit is always going to help you. In the morning, when you get up, stand in the doorway and pray that the day is a nice quiet day. Give thanks for the day—for coming through the night" (Steltenkamp 1993, 125). He offered the caution that one should not go out at night unless necessary because that is when "bad spirits" prowl.

A custom Lucy learned from her father that Little Warrior also observed was to place a morsel of bread, fruit, or meat outside the house. In doing so, one would offer it to the good spirits and make a request of some kind in exchange for the gift. In the morning, it also was customary to take a drink of water, thank "God" for it, and pour some of the water outside for the good spirits in gratitude for a new day. When bedding down at night, one also was to thank the "Great Spirit" for the day just ended.

Priests and Medicine Men

Medicine men apparently could be as off-putting and sectarian as their clergy counterparts. However, they could also be like

Little Warrior and Black Elk and at ease in the company of priests
like Buechel. These three could pray with the rosary or pipe or participate in different rituals while some of their confreres would not.
Brown reported Black Elk saying that if priests were angry at the
pipe practice, it was "proof of their ignorance" (Brown 2007, 105).
Fathers Gall and Buechel probably shared this sentiment. Unlike
Father Sialm (who was known to argue with Black Elk), these men
appear to have focused on similarities of religious thought instead
of their differing expressions. (A testimony to their friendship,
though, Black Elk and Sialm remained amicable with one another
despite their disagreements.)[3]

Religious debate does not seem to be fertile ground for nurtur-
ing a relationship, and the holy-men were not immune to disputes
over their differing practices. Father Zimmerman, for example,
stands out in this regard. Black Elk tearfully welcomed this admired
friend upon his return in 1937, but a decade later, Brown's experience of this same priest was not as positive. Zimmerman visited
Black Elk during Brown's visit and argued with Ben and his father
about a pipe ceremony that they had staged. The priest was opposed
to their investing time with the old tradition at the expense (he
thought) of their Catholic practice. Still, illustrating the complexity
of all the holy-men's relationships, Black Elk and Zimmerman
respected one another despite their differences.[4] Pete Catches also
held the memory of Zimmerman in high regard, even after he was
no longer affiliated with the church. The son of a catechist, and once
a catechist himself, Catches later became a medicine man of some
renown, and his son followed his example. Pete practiced a yuwipi-
like ritual known as the "eagle ceremony." Even then he admitted
"praying to" Zimmerman because he thought the Jesuit holy-man
was in heaven, and could render assistance from that sacred place
(Steltenkamp 1993, 84).

Like their Native counterparts, non-Indian holy-men were
not carbon copies of one another. Fathers Sialm and Zimmerman
related to Black Elk differently than did Fathers Lindebner and
Buechel. Still, Lucy said that her father "got along" with all the
priests (Steltenkamp 1993, 79). He especially seems to have valued
his relationship with Father Gall. The only record of Gall is within

One-time catechist turned medicine man Pete Catches, Sr., prepares to pray with the pipe in beginning the Catholic Sioux Indian Congress at Manderson, South Dakota, in 1973. Photo by author.

Brown's letters published after his death. In them, Brown refers to the priest as Black Elk's adoptive son. Edited references to the man are ambiguous and vague enough to make readers wonder if Gall was perhaps the product of Black Elk's relationship with the woman he romanced while in Europe.[5]

Outside these letters, and absent from other publications related to Black Elk, Gall was Erich Schuon, brother of the philosopher-artist Frithjof Schuon. Born January 26, 1906, in Basel, Switzerland, to Paul Louis Schuon and Marguerite Marie Benoit, he became a Trappist monk at the Abbey of Scourmont in France (where he took the name of Father Gall, and where he died in 1991). In 1947, Brown told Black Elk of Gall's interest in Indian culture and religion, and that the priest wanted an Indian name. A surprising coincidence linking the men is that an uncle of Black Elk's named Swan had proposed to Gall's grandmother when she was visiting Washington in 1868.

Brown's primary relationship was with Father Gall's brother (who informed Brown of the priest's "very real interest in the Dakota"). Learning that Gall wanted to acquire an Indian name, Brown wrote the priest saying not only that this would "be possible" (Brown 1947a), but that he could also "become a member of the Sioux nation" (Brown 1947b). The priest was grateful for Brown's kindness, but Brown expressed gratitude for Gall's "influence" that became "most beneficial to *our* mission." He told Gall that the Jesuits had "been fighting Black Elk for many years" because "they fear the fact that he still follows his 'heathen' practices, & firmly upholds the validity of his own ancient tradition." Brown told Gall that "it means much" to Black Elk "to be encouraged in his old ways by a Christian Father" (Brown 1947c).

Black Elk proceeded to name Gall "Lone Sioux" but later thought that he should have named him "Two Men" since, he said, "in appearance" Gall was "a white man, but in reality" he was "an Indian" (Brown 2007). According to Brown, the holy-man also said that when the priest died, his body would remain with the white people, but his "soul shall return to" America. Black Elk thought that the priest "shall always really be a Lakota" (Brown 2007, 113).

Both Indian and non-Indian practitioners could be rigid and doctrinaire about their religion, with little tolerance for ecumenism. Others were like Black Elk, Buechel, Little Warrior, and Gall. They fell within a category of holy-men whose understanding of the Sacred made them build upon the good they perceived in one another's traditions. This was a position that gained ascendance in the late twentieth century, the Black Elk literature contributing to its spread.

Preparing for Death

Black Elk's family members were impressed with what Little Warrior accomplished through his healing ritual. Black Elk's mouth was not as crooked as it had been before the ceremony, and he seemed to be able to feed himself more easily. However, not long after this healing took place, a broken hip, age, and tuberculosis combined to bring about the holy-man's final days.

In his last months, Black Elk, who was about eighty-five years old, practiced a devotion that had been part of Jesuit tradition since 1675. It was a piety that included reception of Communion on the first Friday of nine consecutive months. This was done because the visions of a French nun, Margaret Mary Alacoque, promised that one would not die in disgrace or without a last anointing if one received Communion on nine first Fridays. Devotees thought that the practice assured one of finding refuge in the "sacred heart of Jesus" when they died.

Jesuit Father Peter Price was the priest assigned to Manderson when Black Elk requested, and received, the sacrament of the sick (for the fourth time). In those final months, he asked Price to say mass on each first Friday of the month at Ben's home. Lucy recalled that during this period, her father always held a rosary and prayed with it. Ben's daughter, Olivia, also remembered Black Elk having a pipe, which she said came into Lucy's possession when the holy-man died. Relatives asked if they could do anything for him, but his response was simply that they say their prayers and faithfully receive the sacraments. He assured them that he was ready to pass on and that they should not be overcome by grief at his passing.

As his condition deteriorated, Black Elk told Lucy that he was consoled by a "holy-man" who visited him "from overseas" every day at three o'clock (Steltenkamp 1993, 129). He said that the two of them would pray together. Family members did not know who this person was, but Frithjof Schuon (Father Gall's brother, the well-known philosopher-artist) thought Black Elk might have been referring to him. Schuon thought so because he and his wife daily prayed the rosary for Black Elk at their home in Europe about that time of day (Black Elk, however, made no mention of a woman also being present).

Brown understood that Black Elk's report frightened family members, but Lucy's recollection was different. She said the envisioned visitor could have been a Jesuit since her father referred to him as a "*wicasa wakan*" (holy-man). This was the Lakota reference for priest, and many of the early Jesuits with whom Black Elk had worked were from Germany. Perhaps his visitor was Father Gall.

Only Black Elk detected the presence of this visitor, who family members, whatever their reaction, did not dismiss as hallucination. Black Elk simply perceived reality in a manner different from others. His experience of visions (as a child or adult) is perhaps best understood through an incident that occurred in 1947, three years before he died. Brown wrote about the experience in a letter but never reported it during his lifetime.

On Christmas Eve of 1947, Black Elk was too infirm to accompany Brown and his family to Midnight Mass, so he remained home in bed. Upon Brown's return with the family from church, he observed that Black Elk was "extremely happy over something" (Brown 2007). When asked why he was so joyously animated, Black Elk told them that he had just returned from a visit with Father Gall in Belgium. Experiences like this one inspired the holy-man to remark that dreams were sometimes wiser than waking.

Shortly before he died, Black Elk called Lucy to his bedside and told her that his days were coming to an end. He assured her that he would be happy in the new life and no longer experience the constraints of illness and age. The holy-man told Lucy's husband to take care of Lucy as a father and mother would take care of her. He also asked that they drive to Hay Springs, Nebraska, where his son, Nick, Jr., was working. He wanted young Nick brought home for a last visit that never took place.

As he awaited death, Black Elk told his daughter that the best thing she could do for him when he was gone was to pray for him, a practice she had been taught during childhood. The custom of praying for the dead, or assisting them in some way, was a religious instruction that Black Elk had known since youth. If the custom were not observed, a deceased person could become a "wandering spirit" (Steltenkamp 1993, 130). By practicing the custom, one could help the deceased find his or her way to "heaven," or what the Lakota called "the land of many lodges." In addition to admonishing his daughter not to let a day pass without praying for him, Black Elk also told Lucy to attend Mass faithfully. She acknowledged that she complied with his request.

Black Elk's instruction to Lucy to stop at church often was rooted in a lifelong practice that bridged the old with the new. *The*

Sacred Pipe said that "keeping the soul" required the use of a "spirit house," where a lock of the deceased's hair was hung in the presence of a pipe. Parents taught their children to show reverence when visiting this sacred place of prayer. This was the same counsel they gave children later on when instructing them to visit church. Older Lakota like Black Elk compared a church to the *wanagi tipi* since it was there that tranquility prevailed and distraction was absent. Within both structures, one could pray for the living, the dead, and all the concerns that were part of life's ebb and flow.

One-time catechist Ben Marrowbone said that his people did not find it surprising to hear priests say that the sacred presence of the *wanikiye* was in each church's sanctuary tabernacle (mystically in the consecrated Communion wafers). Marrowbone said that for Black Elk's generation, visiting church was like visiting the spirit house. The church with its Communion and the *wanagi tipi* with its lock of hair both had a "real" spirit-presence (Steltenkamp 1993, 138).

Foretelling the Future

Black Elk's familiarity with the natural world perhaps included knowledge of a predictable meteor shower that took place at the time his life was ebbing. By seemingly foretelling the shower's appearance, he perhaps knew he would buoy the hope of those he left behind. Whether an indication of clairvoyance or simply the holy-man's knowledge of what astronomers call the Perseid meteor shower, prophetic words attributed to Black Elk near his death continue to evoke wonder over his legacy.

When he felt his life was slipping away, the holy-man told family and friends that all would be well if a celestial display occurred when he passed on: "I have a feeling that when I die, some sign will be seen," he said. "Maybe God will show something. He will be merciful to me and have something shown which will tell of his mercy" (Steltenkamp 1993, 131). Not surprising, Black Elk's reflection is consistent with the Lakota association of the firmament with eternal life. His comment eventually served to console his family and friends.

The holy-man's death was preceded by difficulty eating and holding down food. His paralysis also required that family members administer care. His granddaughter, Olivia, reported that toward the end, her brother, Henry, kept a nightly vigil with his grandfather. Then, one evening Henry called his parents and sisters to gather at Black Elk's bedside. There, held by his grandson, Black Elk quietly departed for the land of many lodges. The date was August 17, 1950.

Black Elk's Wake

For Black Elk's wake, Ben and Lucy thought their father should lie in repose wearing the black shirt he wore as a catechist. This plan was thwarted when they found that mice had made it threadbare; therefore, he was laid out in a suit and tie. Around his neck was a large crucifix that the early catechists wore, while his fingers were entwined with a large-beaded rosary. Years earlier, Black Elk had received it from a bishop he met in New York.

Since Lakota belief held that one's spirit parted the body at death and that the Milky Way served as a "spirit trail" leading to a new life, an occurrence at the wake stirred awe among those present when the sky seemed to confirm that the holy-man was walking a starlit road. It offered consolation that lent support to something Black Elk had confided to his daughter before he died. Awaiting death, he had given her the assurance that his "little angels" would be his "helpers" or "guides" (Steltenkamp 1993, 129). They would shepherd him down the spirit trail that would lead to "heaven." Lucy said that by "guides" he had meant the dying babies he baptized when he worked as a catechist.

Black Elk's pastoral experience and involvement over many years with infant baptisms gave him a special affection for the little ones. He told Brown that it was a sacred experience to look into the eyes of newborns. They had just come from Wakan Tanka, and their eyes could still reflect what they had seen. Similarly, he said elders should be reverenced, for their eyes would soon see again their creator. With the babies just coming from Wakan Tanka and

the aged about to return, he considered both to be special mani-
festations of the Sacred.

On the night of his wake, the evening sky became brightly lit
with stars, and Black Elk's old friend, John Lone Goose, thought
that the unusual firmament could be interpreted as "God sending
lights to shine on that beautiful man" (Steltenkamp 1993, 135).
Others were also mindful of something extraordinary taking place.
Although Brown was not present at the funeral, he later wrote that
Black Elk had once told him, "You will know when I am dying, because there will be a great display of some sort in the sky." Brown
thought that Black Elk's utterance was "true" because friends told
him "the sky was filled with falling stars" when Black Elk died.
Whatever people actually said, Brown's recollection of their account
was that "a very unusual display" took place the night of Black Elk's
wake (Brown 1979, 63).

Twenty-five years after the wake occurred, a Jesuit brother,
William Siehr, immediately remembered the night sky and vividly
referred to it as a "heavenly display" and "celestial presentation"
(Steltenkamp 1993, 132). Unaware of what Black Elk had pre-
dicted, Brother Siehr thought that the holy-man "had gone to his
reward and left some sort of sign to the rest of us." Moved by the
experience and the recollection, the aged Jesuit said that he thought
something of "real significance" had occurred at the wake that
night. Memory of the event made his voice trail off as he reflected,
"There was something there" (Steltenkamp 1993, 132–33).

Long after Black Elk died and shortly before his own passing,
John Lone Goose respectfully honored the memory of his old catechist friend. In a reverent tone that bespoke admiration, he recalled the bright lights the evening of the wake and said that they
made everything appear "miracle-like." With matter-of-fact simplicity, Lone Goose testified "I know God sent those beautiful objects to shine on that old missionary . . . the Holy Spirit shined upon
him because he was such a holy man" (Steltenkamp 1993,135).

In addition to the celestial lights, some people reported seeing
a circle and a figure eight in the sky, and this experience prompted
wonderment. As a kind of mystical signature to the event, the eight

could represent August, the eighth month of the year when Black Elk
died. Similarly, if viewed horizontally, a numeral eight is a symbol for
infinity (among the Lakota, however, this was not a traditional association). For Black Elk's people, the number would be more
meaningful when perceived as the conjunction of two circles—the
circle is a preeminent religious symbol within traditional Lakota culture (DeMallie 1984a, 80) that even Black Elk, fittingly, noted.

Embellishing what the holy-man said about the importance of
circles in Lakota culture, John Neihardt phrased the following reflection, which became an often-quoted passage:

> You have noticed that everything an Indian does is in a cir-
> cle, and that is because the Power of the World always
> works in circles, and everything tries to be round. . . . The
> sky is round, and I have heard that the earth is round like
> a ball, and so are all the stars. The wind, in its greatest
> power, whirls. Birds make their nests in circles. . . . The sun
> comes forth and goes down again in a circle. The moon
> does the same, and both are round. Even the seasons
> form a great circle in their changing, and always come back
> again to where they were. The life of a man is a circle from
> childhood to childhood. (DeMallie 1984a, 290–91)

Other literature reinforces this sense of the circle that Neihardt and
Black Elk described (Walker 1917, 60).

Elsewhere, the holy-man noted that the sun and moon, and all
stems that grow from out of the ground, are circular in form, as are
the holes made by diverse creatures for entranceways to their
homes. He said that his people's tipis were circular, and that the
Lakota sat in a circle for all ceremonial occasions. They did this because the circle symbolized Wakan Tanka who, like the circle, had
no beginning and no end, and all human enterprises should reflect
the Sacred that is their source (Brown 1953, 92). When life, therefore, was out of balance, it no longer fit this circular pattern. Black
Elk thus compared his people's plight to a nest of bird eggs, and
sadly reflected that his people were in a square nest, when only in
a round nest do birds hatch their young. Black Elk thought that

many of his people had lost a vision of the Sacred, and so lacked the spiritual energy to live as their creator intended.

The meaning of what people saw in the night sky at Black Elk's wake will remain open to interpretation. However, John Lone Goose probably best stated what those present powerfully felt. The assembled were a people of faith, and John's experience of the night was momentous enough that he could look back upon it and confidently affirm, "God was with us that time." Those who were present sensed a providential affirmation of Black Elk's life in what seemed to be a wondrous, heavenly sign (Steltenkamp 1993, 135).

However, people elsewhere beheld the same phenomena that were witnessed at Black Elk's wake, and they explained what they saw in scientific, not religious or poetic, language. The October 1950 issue of *Sky and Telescope* contained the account titled "August Auroral Displays Are Widely Observed." A magazine for astronomers, the report offered a secular perspective on what filled the skies the night of the wake. The article resonated with the account of mourners. While the holy-man might have been aware of the yearly Perseid shower, auroral displays referenced in the magazine are not so predictable. Representative sightings were as follows:

> Moline, Ill., reports . . . aurorae on two successive nights: August 18, . . . a very active display . . . lasted for four hours, and there was more activity observed . . . August 19th, when the entire sky was covered with rayed bands. . . . These met to form a corona . . . brilliant with rapid pulsations . . . the landscape as bright as with the moon. . . .
>
> From Toronto, Ontario, "The night of August 19–20 will be remembered for a long time. . . . A brilliant display of northern lights was seen from practically all regions of the province . . . the display was the best seen in many years." At times the whole sky was filled with the shimmering, darting forms.

Shakespeare wrote, "When beggars die, there are no comets seen; the heavens themselves blaze forth the death of princes."[6] His words were realized at the wake of one of America's most famous

Indians. In the role of catechist, Black Elk had taught many people
how to live as members of the St. Mary and St. Joseph Societies, as
Christians, or as sincere religious practitioners of other folds. At his
wake, the firmament seemed to affirm his faith and effort.

Life After Black Elk

When Black Elk was buried in a small community cemetery
outside Manderson about a half mile north of St. Agnes church,
there was no debate of issues that his biography would later raise.
Mourners were of one mind. They would miss the inspirational,
grandfatherly presence of a good man. Although the community's
first catechist was no longer in its midst, his memory was still vivid
for members of the parish. Some thought they actually saw Black
Elk at church after his death, but most people simply encouraged
one another to carry on as he had taught them to do. Nick, Jr.,
seemed to be following in his father's footsteps and regularly led
prayer at social gatherings or at funerals. He also preached when
not singing with the church choir. Tragically, he perished in a
house fire in 1959. As time passed, the simplicity of sentiment in
mourning the loss of Black Elk would be transformed in the years
following his death.

In 1973, American Indian Movement—or AIM—activists
occupied the settlement of Wounded Knee, South Dakota, for
seventy-one days. AIM was a diverse group of urban Indians from
around the country and Lakota from the region. Taking control of
several houses, churches, and businesses in the area, they held out
against the National Guard in protest of local and national issues
affecting Indian people.

Media personnel came to Wounded Knee from around the
world. They stirred global interest in occupation events that were or-
chestrated to a large extent by the extensive news coverage the media provided (Schultz 1973, 46–48, 53–56). AIM regarded its action
as an initiative on behalf of all Indian people. The activists' choice of
this site on the Pine Ridge Reservation was partly influenced by positive public relations generated by the books on Black Elk and the
popularity of *Bury My Heart At Wounded Knee* (1970).

Black Elk's grave north of Manderson. The stone marker
was donated by friends from Rapid City, South Dakota.
Photo by author.

One of AIM's spiritual advisers was named Black Elk, and this
lent credibility to the event that championed civil rights. "Wallace"
Black Elk was not related to the holy-man, but his name was enough
to garner sympathy among the public for AIM's action. The Black
Elk books were popular at the time, and it was natural to assume that
the late holy-man's blessing descended upon the occupation since
someone named "Black Elk" was involved with it. The battle at
Wounded Knee in 1890 had resulted from bureaucratic blundering,

military misjudgments, and social distress, and these same elements came together in 1973. The catechist's erroneous association with "Wounded Knee II" was added to the mix.

Black Elk's daughter, Lucy, was not sympathetic to AIM's invocation of the Black Elk name. She maintained that her father was not consumed by a vengeful memory of 1890 and did not identify with the anti-Christian rhetoric that was popular when the occupation occurred. Rather, Lucy recalled a father who once faithfully served the Wounded Knee church that occupiers seized (Steltenkamp 1993, 141).

Because of his role in establishing Catholicism within the Manderson community, which is located not far from Wounded Knee, the church meeting hall there was dedicated to Black Elk's memory. Many people even said they sensed his presence in the hall and the church. However, a quarter century after the holy-man died, the sign on the building that honored him was ripped from its mooring.

This vandalism occurred after the Wounded Knee occupation of 1973, perpetrated, presumably, by someone hostile to Black Elk's association with the parish. Most Pine Ridge residents under the age of thirty knew nothing of the holy-man, while many people off the reservation were only acquainted with his portrayal in *Black Elk Speaks* and *The Sacred Pipe*. These books had won a legion of admirers, but none of these people was familiar with what transpired in Black Elk's life after 1890. Someone apparently resented seeing what was, by then, an old dedication sign.

Off the reservation, Black Elk's reigning image became that of a Lakota elder who went to his death intolerant of invasive cultural or religious influences. It was in the service of this misrepresentation that the Catholic church at Wounded Knee was occupied and considerably damaged, along with its contents. Occupation supporters regarded its ruin as legitimate symbolic protest while Black Elk's daughter regarded this as the desecration of a sacred place that her father once served.[7] Twenty-five years later, a new sign replaced the one that was destroyed. Parishioners hoped that activists would not be intemperate but instead focus their efforts elsewhere and not remove the new memorial.

CHAPTER 17

Black Elk's Legacy

With Black Elk gone to the land of many lodges in 1950, people on the Pine Ridge Reservation born after that date would eventually know his name only from its appearance on a tombstone or meeting hall. As memory of him faded, "Black Elk" just became a reference, like many others, to an unknown ancestor. When Regina Looks Twice, Lucy's daughter, attended high school in the 1960s, she learned to her surprise that grandfather Black Elk was "famous."

As a cultural resurgence movement developed in Native North America, however, Black Elk eventually garnered a place at its heart as a standard-bearer for what it means to be Indian. Lakota author Vine Deloria said the holy-man's influence was particularly strong among young Indians who were "searching for roots" (V. Deloria 2000, xiii). Black Elk had been a beacon for others during life and continued being one after death.

It was Black Elk's nineteenth-century identity that also came to be associated with a growing environmental movement in the seventies. This partly occurred through an award-winning series of televised public announcements that invoked the holy-man's melancholic memory of an earlier America. The announcements showed actor Iron Eyes Cody (1904–99) dressed in Plains attire with a tear on his cheek. An inspired depiction for the period, the image of Cody became emblematic of ecologists and others who sought to imitate

Black Elk's nature-friendly way of life and thought. Seeing what had become of the American landscape, Indians like the holy-man would certainly be moved to weep. Cody and Black Elk represented a world that was free of the pollutants, civil strife, and cultural turmoil that defined America in the 1960s and 1970s.

Black Elk ratified the stereotype of Indians having a close relationship with animals, and this enabled the environmental movement to harvest quotations of the holy-man that became tenets of eco-spirituality, such as "the four-leggeds and the wings of the air and all green things . . . are children of one mother and their father is one Spirit" (J. Neihardt 1961, 1); and "all things are the works of the Great Spirit. We should know that he is within all things: the trees, the grasses, the rivers, the mountains, and all the four-legged animals, and the winged peoples" (Brown 1953, xx). Twentieth-century ecologists made these sentiments their own.

It was easy for readers to assume that Black Elk's worldview was not influenced by Western ways because his literary portrayal was culturally one-dimensional. That portrayal influenced films, which, in turn, reinforced notions of a golden age that many thought once existed for his people. The 1990 production *Dances with Wolves* provided moviegoers an especially compelling and sympathetic glimpse into Lakota life. Black Elk material helped inspire its perspective.

Black Elk within American Religious History

Black Elk prayed to a creator figure whose nondenominational status eventually came to seem more appealing to some people than many conventional representations of the sacred found across America. The holy-man was attuned to nature, and nature seemed more substantive than the synthetic world of a consumer culture. The idea of being "one with nature" in the spirit of Black Elk moved many people in the latter 1900s to walk through meadows, stroll beaches, swim rivers, and climb mountains. These were more satisfying experiences than trying to commune with a god they struggled to find in the stale air of impersonal churches.

This was the American ethos in which Black Elk's name became popular in the last decades of the twentieth century. People

were cobbling together elements from different religious traditions, and American Indian material was a significant part of the
mix. This eventually produced the many forms of behavior and
thought associated with New Age religion. An umbrella designation, it popularized non-Western terminology and practices that
previously were unknown to most people.

What began, then, as a sensitively told "life story" in 1932 became, in retrospect, a tremor that triggered an avalanche of books
that addressed some aspect of the Indian world. These works both
influenced and were influenced by New Age thought. Interspersed
with scholarly studies of Native life were pedestrian writings of un-
even quality. As a result, readers had to search for works that accurately represented the Indian world.

Literature in the Wake of Reprinted Black Elk Material

Black Elk Speaks and *The Sacred Pipe* stimulated religious
questing and a renewed interest in American Indian life in the
1960s. Inspired by these books, readers sought others, and many
could be found. However, the burgeoning number of Indian works
prompted one scholar to observe "the perceived authority of even
one falsely claiming to be Native American is almost absolute."[1]

The Education of Little Tree (1976) became a best-selling children's book while speakers naively invoked quotations related to the
environment from "Chief Seattle's speech" (Murray 1993). Few
consumers of these materials were aware that non-Indian writers
had authored them. Similarly, *The Memoirs of Chief Red Fox* (1971)
won many admirers by reporting the life story of a wise centenar-
ian who nostalgically remembered "the old ways." Its success,
however, was muted by charges that Red Fox was a fraud. Even
Iron Eyes Cody, the icon of the environmental movement for his
advertisements to keep America clean, was non-Indian.

Black Elk material fed the appetite of both Indians and non-
Indians of the late twentieth century. His religious practice seemed
more satisfying than institutional religion's perceived mantra of
"pray, pay, and obey." Alternative lifestyles emerged, and these often included religious "questing" that included the use of drugs for

"expanding consciousness." Carlos Castaneda (considered to be the "father of New Age" religion) contributed to this trend with *The Teachings of Don Juan* (1968).

Presented as the biography of a "Yaqui sorcerer," *Don Juan* (and its many spin-offs) generated courses and seminars. This material stoked curiosity about a realm within the Indian religious universe that Black Elk did not address. Although focusing on peoples south of the border, Castaneda's work led readers into "a separate reality" (the title for one of his books) of drug use. This topic dovetailed with the times. The Woodstock generation greeted Indian pharmacology as a kind of "mystic medicine" that altered perception and revealed the Sacred.

Another widely popular work was *Lame Deer, Seeker of Visions* (1972). A Lakota from the Rosebud Reservation, Lame Deer (1903–76) criticized the presence of Christian churches among his people. He found a sympathetic audience and even berated Black Elk's work as a catechist.

Unlike the Black Elk corpus, Lame Deer's material came across as more "down to earth," and so was accessible to a broad readership. Although both men were Lakota, their perspectives were simply different. Black Elk's mysticism attracted one audience, while Lame Deer's counsel spoke to a countercultural spirit of the period.

Lame Deer proposed that one should personally experience all that life offered, and that a "medicine man shouldn't be a saint" (Lame Deer 1972). Fifty years earlier, by contrast, Black Elk represented his fellow catechists in pledging that they would never commit a mortal sin (in Christian theology, a grievous offense against God). These contrasting perspectives were not the only ones for readers to contemplate.

Popular culture also brought attention to other Native elders who expanded the field of discourse. Appealing to some was *Rolling Thunder* (1974). This was the life story of a Shoshone man who served as a spiritual guide to The Grateful Dead, a band whose large following popularized the otherwise anonymous Indian religious leader. Rolling Thunder's teachings resonated with young people who felt constrained by conventional forms of religious involvement.

Black Elk's name reappeared with *Black Elk: The Sacred Ways of a Lakota Shaman* (1990). It was the biography of Wallace Black

Elk (1921–2004) who, like Lame Deer, resided on the Rosebud Reservation. This work's inspired title drew an instant audience probably because of its association with the senior holy-man. Although Wallace's co-author stated that the religious perspective of both Black Elks was similar, it is difficult to find a significant resemblance. Comparable to Lame Deer's narrative, Wallace echoed the criticism of Christian churches in Indian country and advocated the restoration of shamanic religion within Native communities.

Debate on Black Elk's Christian Identity

Brown had been critical of the Catholic Church's recruitment of catechists. He hoped that by establishing "the Order of the Pipe" he would motivate Lakota descendants to renew traditional rites. The new generation could fill the religious void that would be left when Christian elders (like Black Elk) died. This was, at least, the position Brown initially espoused when working with the holy-man.

Brown altered this position over the years and came to share Lucy's opinion that people were drawing erroneous conclusions about her father and the senior generation. He knew that Black Elk's Christianity was a significant part of his identity, and that this was difficult for some people to accept. Brown wrote: "I have felt it improper that this phase of his life was never presented either by Neihardt or indeed by myself. I suppose somehow it was thought this Christian participation compromised his 'Indian-ness,' but I do not see it this way and think it time that the record was set straight."[2] Brown had a change of heart, but time had entrenched the image of Black Elk that he and Neihardt created.

Celebrated Lakota author Vine Deloria tersely generalized that "Christianity has been the curse of all cultures into which it has intruded" (1995, 22). While not Black Elk's position, nor that of Fools Crow, Deloria's critique, for many, seemed applicable to Indian America. A conventional wisdom had begun to prevail that characterized Black Elk's generation as hostile to Christian teaching or that Christianity was hostile to it. Since nothing was known about the holy-man's transition from medicine man to missionary, it was easy to conclude that experiences within the religious sphere of cultural contact were just as horrific as those that occurred on the battlefield.

Late twentieth-century writers accorded compensatory respect for Native religious practice and thought, and this helped sustain the "noble savage" stereotype. A caricature of missionary presence outside Indian America also became a staple that reinforced a stereotype (celebrated author James Michener popularized the caricature in his book, and later movie, *Hawaii*). The missionary stereotype did not accurately describe the reality, but it nonetheless gained ascendance.

New Age religious practice borrowed from and contributed to Indian life and thought when *Don Juan* awakened audiences to what Castaneda portrayed as Native religious practice. He also claimed that there was good reason why so little was known about so much. Namely, the church was responsible for demeaning Native people: "Four centuries of Catholic repression in the name of faith and reason have reduced the old ways to a subculture, ridiculed and persecuted" (1968). Castaneda then revealed a pharmaceutical path that Native elders trod to enlightenment. Although later dismissed as fiction, his books drew an enormous following. They also inspired many readers to explore the mirages he conjured.

In his 1979 introduction to *Black Elk Speaks*, Deloria lauded Neihardt, and said that he produced a work that was "perhaps the only religious classic of this century." Deloria correctly evaluated the work in terms of its primacy among books related to the Indian world. However, its popular competition even within that world remained strong.

Removed from a living memory of Black Elk, readers were weaned on the fictitious Little Tree, a non-Christian Lame Deer, the botanical visions of Don Juan, and shamanic practices of Wallace, Rolling Thunder and New Age others. These works significantly influenced the ideas of what it meant to be Indian, or religious. Black Elk's misrepresentation was the wellspring for much of this literature.

Conversion of the Missionaries

When the twentieth century began, missionaries were seeking to replace traditional Indian religious forms with the varied practices of their different denominations. The close of the century, by contrast, saw many Christian ministers appreciating the spiritual succor that could be derived from Native ceremonialism. Changing times even saw Christian clergy assist in the revitalization of rituals traditionally honored in diverse Native communities (the 1969 publication of *Sweet Medicine* by Episcopalian Father Peter J. Powell is notable in this regard).

Black Elk material was in the forefront of this trend in the latter half of the twentieth century and was winning new readers who had no knowledge of the holy-man's fuller identity. Many writers reinforced the thesis that Christian theology did not appeal to Black Elk or other "traditional" Indians, so it was easy to assume that the holy-man had no contact with, or had rejected, Christian teachings. It seemed to be a tenet within the Indian world that Black Elk's generation would be honored if people forsook their association with Christian practice. Only later was it learned that this understanding was as much wrong as it was widespread.

Sectarianism had reigned earlier, but tolerance, dialogue, and ecumenical sharing later became commonplace. However, times had changed enough that some Indians imitated their clergy counterparts of the past. Some protested the use of Indian practices, symbols, and artifacts within Christian services (especially if employed by a non-Indian). They argued that the two traditions should be practiced separately. Although Black Elk probably would have lauded a merging, some offered rationales that restricted the use of Indian forms solely to Indians.[3]

The Pendulum of Post-mortem Analyses

With good reason, Brown was concerned about misconceptions that had arisen concerning Black Elk's religious identity. People seemed to think that any kind of religious assimilation detracted from one's identity as an Indian. Consequently, Black Elk's Christian participation had become a liability to his previously positive image. Some, perhaps, did not want any association of his wise words with a Western religious tradition.

Throughout Indian country, Christian churches retained membership, but social trends favored the equation of Indianness with non–church related practices. Even though DeMallie evaluated the literature on this topic as "political rhetoric rather than objective assessment" (1984a, 80), dwindling numbers within the denominations suggested that rhetoric (along with secularizing trends) was getting the upper hand. Black Elk had become better known than ever, but his nativist portrait was being popularly embraced at the expense of his real-life persona.

Neihardt considered it a "sacred obligation" to tell the holyman's life story, and his admission gave birth to a religious controversy that accompanied his book in the decades that followed. Julian Rice (*Black Elk's Story*) insisted that Black Elk was a "traditional" who made little compromise with modernity and none with Christianity (1992). In *Black Elk's Religion* (1995), Clyde Holler saw the holy-man as a traditionalist and innovator whose perspective was misrepresented by Neihardt.

Brian Holloway's *Interpreting the Legacy* (2003) paid homage to Neihardt and argued that his was an "emotionally powerful" rendering of the narrative Black Elk provided. After evaluating this lineage, DeMallie concluded that interest in Black Elk's worldview showed "no signs of receding in the twenty-first century" and that further scholarship should mirror Black Elk's vision (2006a, 596). In suggesting it go forth "in the world of true that doesn't judge," DeMallie could have chosen no better quote to reveal the holyman's spirit (601).

Ben and Lucy wanted to honor their father by producing a book that would tell of his work as a catechist, and this partly occurred when *The Sixth Grandfather* (1984) provided an overview of Black Elk's Christian practice. *Holy Man of the Oglala* (1993) then fulfilled their dream by treating the many years not addressed by Neihardt. Elders regarded this biography as an accurate account of Black Elk and his times, but this image of the holy-man stirred further speculation.

Did Black Elk *covertly* practice pre-Christian rites? Some Native people reported concealing their involvement in traditional practices lest they suffer social and economic sanctions. Perhaps Black Elk felt similar pressure from church and state officials who did not look kindly on people maintaining the old ways.

Maybe he was traditionalist or Christian depending upon which religion served his practical needs at a given moment. His work as a churchman could be explained away as a pragmatic (but insincere) adaptation to changing, stressful times. Since social disorientation arose from assimilation policies, his role as catechist was perhaps a kind of pathology.

This type of speculation was directed at Black Elk's experience and the experience of many patriarchs who identified with one or another Christian denomination. Although pressured to endorse these views, Lucy refused to do so. She was insistent that some Lakota from Black Elk's generation might have led a dual life but that this was not her father's experience.

Dissatisfied with stereotypes that defined missionaries as predators and Black Elk's generation as prey, Damian Costello presented *Black Elk: Colonialism and Lakota Catholicism*. He said the holy-man and others sincerely embraced Christianity as "a means for challenging the racism of colonial ideology" (2005, 49). Black Elk did not regard Christianity as "white culture" but rather as a set of teachings and way of life that helped protect his people from the worst of what was engulfing them. Black Elk saw his Christian practice build upon Lakota tradition, and this new life and commitment promised hope in a world controlled by non-Indians.

Learning about Christianity while in Europe, Black Elk came to understand its *wanikiye* during the ghost dance period as a liberator of the people and not a colonizing conqueror. Revelation of the wakan in Christian terms made navigable the waters of colonial secularism. Not every colonized convert may have held this position, but Costello evaluated Black Elk in these terms.

Black Elk's Literary Predecessor

When writing of his seventeenth-century travels in New France, Baron de Lahontan (1666–1715) introduced European readers to a Huron philosopher named Adario.[4] Ever since, this portrayal of Adario has been a prototype for other writers. Ready-made for critics of colonialism, the baron's articulate Native was depicted as astute as any European philosopher. Within the tradition

214 NICHOLAS BLACK ELK

of Rousseau's "noble savage," writers employed Adario figures to show that native peoples of America, Africa, India, or the South Pacific could teach much to those who came to transform their lifeways into European replicas. Black Elk's portrayal in J. Neihardt, Brown, and Costello comport with the Adario figure.

Neihardt and Brown portrayed a wise elder who resisted Western influence. For them, Black Elk was a Lakota Adario whose profound wisdom and spirituality were absent in the civilization that was suffocating his people. Uninfluenced by non-Indian ways, the holy-man was the noble Native whose traditionalist light shone upon the darkness of a contemporary world.

Costello's Adario, by contrast, was a Black Elk whose critique of the West came in the form of his identity as a catechist. This author's holy-man was like later Native peoples in Central and South America who associated themselves with "liberation theology." This movement emphasized biblical notions of social justice whereby the needs of the poor and marginalized demanded redress. For them, Jesus provided a new moral order that was a good ending to the bad story of colonial hegemony. For all three writers, Black Elk was a real-life Adario. For Costello, he was a liberation theologian, while for Neihardt and Brown he was a traditionalist wisdom keeper.

Hilda Neihardt's Contribution

John Neihardt's visit did not receive much scholarly coverage until fleshed out in *The Sixth Grandfather* and *Holy Man of the Oglala*. These works addressed Black Elk's life as a catechist and his interaction with the poet. Whereas Hilda Neihardt, the poet's daughter, had collaborated with DeMallie in editing her father's notes, she took issue with *Holy Man*. Hilda added her voice to the longstanding controversy over Black Elk's religious identity.

Since *Holy Man* showed that John Neihardt did not report the entirety of Black Elk's experience, Hilda's *Black Elk and Flaming Rainbow* (1995) challenged the book's portrayal (although without citing *Holy Man*'s title). Arguing that *Black Elk Speaks* faithfully reflected Black Elk's thought, Hilda implied that *Holy Man* was se-

Black Elk's daughter, Lucy Looks Twice, in 1977. Photo by author.

riously flawed. She added that her contact with Lucy revealed a different story than the one *Holy Man* told.

According to Hilda, Lucy regretted her contribution to *Holy Man* once she finally read *Black Elk Speaks* (in *Holy Man*, Lucy surprisingly admitted that she had never read the book). Saying that *Black Elk Speaks* "changed [Lucy's] life," Hilda further claimed that Lucy became a "pipe carrier" and repudiated her membership in what Hilda referred to as a "white church" (1995, 13). Hilda said that it was important the "truth" about Black Elk and his daughter be known (meaning that both were misrepresented in *Holy Man*).

Hilda also said that Ben's children told Lucy about a deathbed confession that Black Elk uttered (previously unbeknownst to Lucy). In it, he claimed adherence only to traditional Lakota practices and not the "new religion." Surfacing so long after Black Elk's death (and Lucy's), this testimony is difficult to evaluate. It does not resonate with what Black Elk's friends said of him, with Lucy's memory of her father, or her own quasi-deathbed confession.

Ten months before she died, Lucy was read a transcript of the interviews she provided for *Holy Man* and was satisfied with her account. Then, in a letter written four months before her death, she expressed the hope that her father's life as a catechist would reach print and be a successful book. She also hoped to be well enough to attend Christmas Midnight Mass at St. Agnes church and was eager to meet the visiting African priest who was to celebrate the service.

Apart from health concerns, her only expressed discouragement was that members of the St. Joseph and St. Mary Societies were dying off and that her children needed help. She prayed that they would "return to the sacraments" (i.e., that they would maintain an active church practice). As for being a "pipe carrier," she was respectful of her people's pipe tradition, but her spiritual regimen did not include its use.

Black Elk's Teachings

Lucy's interest in seeing *Holy Man* reach print was stoked in part because she was upset that people invoked her father's memory to affirm thoughts or behaviors she knew he would not endorse. For her, Black Elk's religious preferences were not a debatable matter. She saw him as a meek and loving father who was also a pious catechist.

Lucy was a devoted daughter who appreciatively recalled a man who was her famous "dad." He formed her religious perspective, and that of many others. Later generations might have found it difficult to fathom his emergence from medicine man to missionary, but that was a memory of her father that Lucy treasured, and insistently reported. As shown, she was not alone in providing this testimony. Others offered it, too.

The simplicity of religious instruction that Black Elk proffered contrasts with the sometimes-misleading philosophy that is periodically associated with him. For example, one attribution is that his vision foretold the rebirth of traditional Indian practices in the "fifth generation" (construed to be people in the 1970s).[5] However, the stenographic record ambiguously reported that the tree was to bloom in the sixth or seventh (not fifth) generation (DeMallie 1984a, 265).

Since the elusive tree symbolism can just as well refer to Black Elk's Christian practice, the vision's predictive value is questionable.

This is because the vision falls within a genre of experience (and literature) that opens itself to different understandings. Like the book of Revelation and Nostradamus's claims, it lends itself to an interpretation that expresses a reader's thought (eisegesis) instead of finding what is actually in the text (exegesis).

While there are problems with interpreting Black Elk's narratives, people's memories of him are clear. His daughter, for example, cited a down-to-earth, challenging counsel she received from him: "To live close to God is more enjoyable than to live easy—with all the pleasure and riches—because such things never will reach to heaven" (Steltenkamp 1993, 75). He also insisted that his children "do their duty" by attending Mass and receiving the sacraments. The accent on institutional forms of practice in this counsel might perplex some, but it was the legacy he bequeathed to his children.

When asked what she thought her father might tell young people, Black Elk's daughter said that he would call the people to religion: "teach your children prayers, see that they go to church—that's the only way—the Church and the family; to be children of God and soldiers for Christ—you must stand the ground and make the fight."[6] He admonished her to thank Wakan Tanka for the gift of life and for all the gifts of creation (when quoting her father, Lucy used the terms "Wakan Tanka," "Great Spirit," and "God" interchangeably). Like her father, Lucy could quote a number of Bible passages and said that his favorite was: "What does it profit a man if he gains the whole world and suffers the loss of his soul?"[7]

Lucy spoke of a loving father who cautioned her always to tell the truth, never to steal from anyone, to ask God for help with decisions, and to live with an awareness of God's presence. It was more important to conduct one's life in this manner than to seek pleasure and accumulate wealth. Lucy honored this memory by periodically mailing a dollar bill to Catholic relief efforts abroad, she said, "for people who are poor and in need of help."

Although she was on a low income, Lucy thought that others might need the assistance she could provide. Her form of generosity, though inspirational to some, had its critics. In 2002, a

Lakota journalist berated a priest's request of a Pine Ridge church congregation to send monetary aid to needy people overseas. The journalist contended that the nation's poorest population could use what few funds it had. However, this understanding was not shared by Black Elk and his daughter.

The Traditionalist Black Elk Reconsidered

Although Black Elk's niche as a "traditional" was secure for a long time as a result of John Neihardt and Brown's work, his status among the general public seemed to fade when people learned that he was more multidimensional than previously thought. They perhaps found his image as intransigent medicine man and Wounded Knee warrior more riveting than the work he had performed as a catechist. After his fuller identity was revealed, the holy-man who was once revered as a premier "wisdom keeper" seemed to be, for some, no longer as enchanting. This apparent shift elicited the claim that the holy-man did not enjoy particular prestige among his people. A new charge, it was without merit.

In the late twentieth century, a broad constituency regarded Frank Fools Crow as chief custodian of Lakota religious practice. Fools Crow, who died on November 27, 1989, at the age of ninety-nine, was the first Indian holy-man to pray at the United Nations. It was he, however, who said that "the renowned Black Elk has earned a place above all of the other Teton holy men. We all hold him the highest" (Mails and Chief Eagle 1979, 53). Fools Crow was echoing what Brown observed in 1947, that is, all "the leading holy men" regarded Black Elk "as their spiritual leader" (Brown 2007, 103).

Fools Crow resembled his uncle both in his being part of Buffalo Bill's show as a youth and in reconciling Christian participation with a "traditional" Lakota mind-set. This reconciliation was not the challenge for them that it was for some others. However, given the troubled history of contact and that not everyone thought alike, it was natural for different behaviors to prevail.

Marie Therese Archambault (a Lakota Franciscan nun from the Standing Rock Reservation) took readers to a contemplation

Black Elk's nephew and
holy-man, Frank Fools
Crow, in 1974. Photo by
Rev. Tony Dagelen, S.J.
Steltenkamp collection.

of the man's spiritual core. In her *A Retreat with Black Elk: Living in the Sacred Hoop* (1998), she gave substance to Deloria's preface in *Black Elk Speaks*. He observed that whatever analyses are set forth, or whatever labels are attached to Black Elk, the holy-man spoke "transcendent truth" that "encourages us to emphasize the best that dwells within us."

CHAPTER 18

Medicine Man, Missionary, Mystic

From earliest times, Black Elk's people confronted challenges within new landscapes that forced them to adapt lest they perish. Raised within this tradition, the holy-man and others adopted a "good" whenever it appeared and expanded their cultural inventory to include diverse additions. These ultimately ranged from basketball to Bible stories, coffee to Communion bread, and radios to rosary prayers.

As a young man, Black Elk was exposed to a larger world beyond the American frontier. This occurred when he toured with Buffalo Bill in Europe. There he was able to explore "the ways of the white men" (DeMallie 1984a, 245). His breadth of experience expanded when he visited cities throughout the country as a catechist, and when he performed for the Duhamels.

The reservation that became Black Elk's permanent address was a magnet for diverse people with different agendas. Coping with military personnel, the Lakota eventually had to deal with an array of transient entrepreneurs, bootleggers, and bureaucrats. Within the religious realm, interaction with missionaries in matters of the Sacred was, by comparison, easier than contending with people who represented secular self-interests.

Negatively viewed, of all the actors on this stage, missionaries were the least bothersome since they could be ignored or engaged.

Positively regarded, they regularly provided material relief to the many who were in need. Moreover, Lakota wisdom keepers shared common ground with their missionary counterparts. Both groups explored and debated the world of the *wakan*.

Religion and Cultural Contact

While people's religious practice is often affected when cultures come into contact, religion is just one aspect of that contact. Trade goods also usher in a massive change in lifeways, with people accepting or resisting each new item, whether it be a type of food or a blanket, coat, eyeglasses, hat, boots, etc. Black Elk's generation seems to have been as receptive to new religious teachings as it was to more mundane goods.

During the early reservation period, for instance, a ghost dance that included Christian themes attracted Black Elk and a great many Lakota. After Wounded Knee, Black Elk adopted a Catholic practice while others affiliated with different denominations. Still others joined a Native American Church that interwove the consumption of peyote with traditional religion and biblical teachings. Recall that Wounded Knee survivor Joseph Black Hair said that Big Foot's people "nearly all belonged to some church." People just did not walk lockstep with one another.

For Black Elk, the medium of the Christian message was an interpersonal relationship with missionaries like Lindebner, Westropp, Zimmerman, and Buechel. He did not experience this interaction as one of "oppressed" and "oppressor." Rather, he found Lindebner's considerate behavior very moving and could refer to him by a kin term. Black Elk's other priest friends appear to have been kindly men who brought a repertoire of ritual that was also a medium that spoke to the heart of the holy-man's religious upbringing. Their "sacraments" reminded him that Wakan Tanka still resided within the nation's hoop.

Metaphorically, Black Elk's religious biography is comparable to the blizzard experience of 1880 (described in chapter 4). On its surface, the story is just the report of an incident that occurred when Black Elk was with his father hunting buffalo. However, when recounting the memory later in life, he might have been expressing a deeper truth. Instead of simply narrating an event from the past, he might have been offering counsel for how life could be lived in the present.

The story recalled a time in which parents and children carried on as they always had. They successfully confronted the challenge of a buffalo hunt. However, the cold immediacy of death began to surround them, and members of a senior generation struggled to ensure that life continue for their young.

In the account, surviving the white onslaught of a wintry tempest, a father passes his child into safekeeping within a miraculously appearing tipi, whose occupants he can call friends. An old order passes away, entrusting its young to others who express their solidarity and ability to provide. These others somehow had found enough sustenance to gladly give support.

An honoring story that paid tribute to the senior generation, Black Elk's account-turned-parable captured the adversity faced by nineteenth-century Lakota peoples as a whole. The Black Elk family was able to carry on and endure storms while others, less fortunate, were barely able to survive. The tale reminded listeners that Black Elk's wisdom was of old, and that it could sustain them in the new order. Ever the catechist, Black Elk drew upon life experience and applied it to the teaching moment. In his story, the religious lodge he occupied was a life-giving shelter amidst the storm that engulfed his people. It miraculously provided nourishment to those who entered.

Adopting New Religious Practice

Once Black Elk's life as a catechist was fleshed out, debate arose regarding to what extent, if any, he (and others) internalized Christian doctrine. The issue often was reduced to an "either/or" proposition (i.e., he did or did not sincerely sustain a Christian identity). Even though there were other options, writers only seemed to address these two.[1]

Rice (1991), Hilda Neihardt (1995), Hoxie (1996), and McGaa (2005) concluded that Black Elk manipulated his colonizers for personal gain by feigning acceptance of Christian practice. However, people who actually knew the holy-man said that this was not the case at all. His Christian identity (and that of others from his generation) was transparent and sincere. Otherwise, it would be contradictory to understand Black Elk as being both duplicitous and praiseworthy. His life was not a charade.

As shown, the reality of conversion for Black Elk and the senior generation has been difficult for many to accept. The holy-man's pre-Christian image cast appeal, and it is this identity that invigorated a new nativism in the late twentieth century. Since the received wisdom concerning his experience is now understood to be flawed, an intriguing sociological study would be to examine why some heritage-minded Indians either ignore or repudiate the Christian identity that their revered ancestors assumed.

John Grim's study of shamanism showed that for "traditionals" like Black Elk, religion was more than just an "aspect" of culture. It was, rather, a bedrock of strength that helped them live each day as fully as possible. The holy-man represented a senior generation for whom "the Sacred [was] ... the deepest aspect of reality," and he dearly wanted younger people to share this same perspective (Grim 1983, 4). A fervent catechist until the end, Black Elk harbored no misgivings about his religious universe being fully Catholic and fully Lakota. Whatever sadness he experienced was because he witnessed so few people having any kind of religious practice at all.

Stated in other terms, Black Elk was a social critic whose worldview was rooted in a Lakota-Christian philosophy. From within this sphere, he challenged his people to renew themselves. For him, the ills that engulfed them could be remedied through adoption of a religious practice that he modeled and about which he preached.

Early on (1907), he knew that his task would be a daunting one. His March 15th letter in *Sinasapa Wocekiye Taeyanpaha*, the missionary newsletter, read: "I spoke mainly on Jesus—when he was on earth, the teachings and his sufferings. I, myself, do a lot of these things. I suffer, and I try to teach my people the things that I wanted them to learn, but it's never done. . . . [Y]ou know when one sheep is surrounded with wolves, it has no place to go. That's how we are. We are ready to be eaten up.[52]

The Sacred Pipe revealed a holy-man who invited readers to cultivate the same religious disposition that he had internalized. Although he was viewed as a mystic in retrospect, he understood his religious perspective differently. For him, the practice he maintained was not extraordinary, but was something that all people should own.

The Lakota were long accustomed to facing challenges and adjusting to new landscapes and new ways of living in their exodus from the woodlands to the plains. If something helped them survive in a new environment, all the better. Within their religious sphere, for example, Black Elk said that the sun dance and kin-making ceremonies were new practices they adopted.

This tradition of incremental change continued when nineteenth-century medicine men became twentieth-century catechists. Such adaptation had been a leitmotif of Lakota culture since time beyond memory. Religious conversion emerges, then, as one of many adjustments that people made to the new conditions they faced.

In light of this history, *The Sacred Pipe* can be seen as Black Elk's explanation of how his people acquired seven different ceremonies over time that presaged their acceptance of Christian practice. Eventually, as DeMallie points out, the "differences between traditional religion and Christianity began to blur" (1984a, 92). The holy-man thus came to embody a convergence of two religious traditions.

According to those who knew him, Black Elk's religious practice afforded him much satisfaction. However, the mystical niche he eventually occupied as a catechist–holy-man did not come to him easily. As a sickly youth, he endured a fever-induced vision-hallucination. A similar illness in Europe included his homesick dream of returning to his family. Later on, the harsh reality of Wounded Knee jolted him out of his ghost dancer's visionary trance, and he eventually came to learn about the "Two Roads Map." This colorfully illustrated, sacred narrative opened up for him a new vocational identity. As a catechist, he adopted conventional Catholic practice and, toward the end of his life, felt his spirit soar because of the joyous dream of visiting Father Gall in Europe.

Some readers might evaluate these life experiences as easily explainable and by no means unusual (i.e., very natural as opposed to *super*natural). By contrast, the holy-man saw as sacred revelation what others could dismiss as unextraordinary. Black Elk's perspective was that he had been graced with mystical moments wherein the wakan was palpably present.

Black Elk's Catholicism is not a matter of speculation. He sincerely embraced the Christianity he preached in earlier years, and he did so until the end. Despite some who assert otherwise, this was the vivid memory he bequeathed to most people who knew him (his daughter in particular). Ministers and medicine men might periodically argue or alienate one another, but Black Elk transcended conflicts that disrupted interpersonal relations. There was no room for discord to prevail within the religious realm. Such dissonance was not part of the Christianity he sought to see bloom within Lakota culture.

Black Elk came to regard the sun dance ceremony as a unique Plains Indian expression of Christian teaching and the pipe as a spiritual instrument able to convey religious meanings contained within the Gospels. He could pray with the pipe, and yet be remembered as always having a rosary in hand. "Inculturating" Christianity this way, or having Native forms uniquely express what the Christian faith teaches, the holy-man was in the vanguard of a Catholic practice and mission theology that unfolded in this direction at the close of the twentieth century.

Early in his visit with Black Elk, Brown wrote Father Gall and articulated a "Metaphysics of the Pipe" that revealed his own synthesis of the two religious traditions. He wrote: "Essentially to smoke the Pipe is the same as taking the Holy Christian communion. The form of the pipe is the same as the Xian [i.e., Christian] Cathedral, & it too represents the Universe, with God at the Center" (Brown 1947c). Given Brown's understanding, and given Black Elk's innate tendency to see sacred connectedness everywhere, the two men no doubt helped one another find parallels where others might not.

This photograph used in mission literature of the 1940s shows Black Elk teaching a young child how to pray the rosary (a decades-earlier promotional photo showed him similarly teaching daughter Lucy). Courtesy of Marquette University Catholic Indian Mission Archives.

The Gospel of the Pipe

As ghost dancers awaited the *wanikiye* to save them from distress, missionaries of the Native American Church addressed this same longing. They formatted biblical religion to a Lakota cultural configuration that included the consumption of peyote. Less known is how the pipe's origin story came to be regarded as a precursor to, or forerunner of, the arrival of the gospel story among the Lakota.

This occurred when many pre-reservation Lakota compared the sacred maiden's bringing of the pipe to the sacred maiden who brought her son, Jesus. Buffalo Cow Woman was described as carrying what appeared to be her "child" (the sacred calf pipe), so it was not difficult for many people to equate these sacred women. Lucy claimed that her father and Father Buechel shared this understanding (that it was Mary who also brought the pipe).

Elders wondered if, in some mysterious, wakan way, the mother of Jesus came to the Lakota twice. Father Craft reported in 1890 that a well-known oral tradition stated that it was she who brought the sacred pipe (Craft 1890). Some told him that the sacred pipe maiden was dressed in a blue gown (blue a color traditionally associated with Mary). Even if people did not equate the two women, they did not find it surprising that another sacred woman's child (Jesus), like the pipe, was said to join heaven with earth.

Speculation of this nature occurred earlier with the Aztecs when they linked their sacred maiden, Tonanzin, with what came to be known as Mexico's Virgin of Guadalupe. As did the Aztecs, the Lakota associated a traditional belief with a later one. Their religious world was never set in stone but expanded to include new revelations.

Paul Steinmetz was a priest for many years at Pine Ridge, and he presided at the funeral of Ben Black Elk. On that occasion, he told of speaking with Ben and concluding with him that the coming of Jesus was what the pipe foretold. Lucy echoed this theme when she said: "We were like the Israelites, the Jews, waiting for Christ. And some Jews didn't want to accept Jesus as God. . . . They knew, somehow, that in the future our Lord Jesus Christ would come one day to his people. Well, actually they didn't see him but he did come. And the missionaries brought the teachings of Our Lord. They knew, somehow, in the future they would learn this" (Steltenkamp 1993, 102). Theologizing of this nature has its critics, but Lucy's statement gives some insight into the experience of people like Black Elk.

The apocalyptic savior sought by ghost dancers became a *wanikiye* who the people later accepted in more sober terms. Instead of ending the world, he provided direction through life and to the land of many lodges. Buffalo Cow Woman's pipe-child helped the people down life's road, and maiden Mary's child led the way by example. For some, this might be the stacking of one fiction upon another. For people like Black Elk, however, this was not the case. His generation (and later ones) saw the stories reveal how the Sacred revealed itself and remained accessible over time.

Black Elk found it natural to speculate in this vein and to discuss with priests (and anyone) the similarities and differences within Christian and Lakota traditions. Commonalities of thought were not what solely made new "ways of prayer" acceptable, but they at times probably helped elicit affirmation (recall that denominations were, like the sun dance, referred to as "ways of prayer"). However, correspondence with the old was by no means necessary. The Arikara brought the "making of relatives" ceremony to the Lakota, and it was totally new, as was the sun dance. Why *not* adopt these ceremonies (or Christian practices and teachings) if they were worthwhile?

Black Elk survived a turbulent period of Lakota history. In order to better understand how he did this, insight can be drawn from the formative period of his youth, when his worldview took shape. Tapping this period makes it easier to appreciate how the child became the man.

In childhood, Black Elk learned about creation and his place within it. What he learned reveals to some extent how he understood the ways of the Wakan. Like his peers, he was taught to look for the Sacred wherever, and however, it might appear. He believed that if one looked, it could be found, and if one listened, it could be heard. The Sacred was not restricted to one vision, one cultural tradition, one conversion experience, or one insight, but was cumulative.

Star Boy

Black Elk took to heart the lessons he learned at his mother's knee. One story she told her attentive child was about a young man named Star Boy. The version recounted here is what Black Elk's mother told Lucy—and so, presumably, what she also told her son. It reported strange and sacred happenings, and conveyed a wisdom that Black Elk carried into manhood.

Black Elk narrated for Neihardt a longer version of this Star Boy tale in 1944, and it concluded their visit. Black Elk offered no analysis, and just let the narrative stand by itself. In hindsight, it might have been part of the "addition" he wanted to provide for *Black Elk Speaks*. After all, why did the holy-man conclude their visit with this one, peculiar tale when he was the repository of many, many others? Beneath the tale's simple plot is a glimpse into the holy-man's religious worldview:

> Long ago there were two mothers who really kept a careful watch over their daughters. These girls just lay outside their tipis every day talking to one another. Then it happened that one of them looked up and saw a very shiny star in the sky. It was a pretty blue, but had other colors, too.
>
> Gazing at the beauty of this star, the girl said: "I really love that star." However, the other girl said: "Oh no, I like that one over there better. It has a beautiful red color to it." So the two girls lay there staring into the sky at the stars they loved.
>
> While the girls were talking about their stars, two boys came down from that vast region above. These boys, however, did not appear to be any different from human boys. They just came and started to talk to the girls.
>
> The girls thought these boys were really handsome, and so they respectfully stood up and began to speak with

them. They knew very well that their mothers would not object to their having a conversation with the boys (at least, this is what they told themselves). They could not get over how these boys were so handsome and engaging. Words and smiles came easily to the girls, and their visitors were ever so friendly.

Pretty soon, the girls seemed to be in a trance. The boys told them to close their eyes, and they obeyed. The next thing the girls knew, they both were transported to the stars they liked. One landed on one, and one landed on the other—high above the earth.

They married the boys, and were told not to wander far from their camp on the star. One of the girls went to dig turnips quite a distance away from home, and she found lots of them—the kind she missed, Indian turnips. But in her eagerness to get them, she dug too deeply and, leaning over too much, lost her balance and fell headfirst into the hole. Instead of finding herself at the bottom of a hole, the girl fell to earth. Falling this great distance killed her.

The girl had been expecting a baby, but the baby did not die in the fall. It probably survived because it was a child from the heavens. [At this point in the telling, Lucy said: "I think people who come from the stars are pretty strong. But when you hear a story like this, you are not supposed to ask why that child did not also die in the fall. Just listen to the story."]³

Near where the girl fell, two meadowlarks lived, a female and a male. They saw what had happened to the girl and the baby, so they took the baby back to their nest and raised it. How they could take care of a child like this was difficult for them, but they somehow did.

The male meadowlark said some kind of a prayer over the baby, and then threw it. It came back crawling to their home. Then he threw it out again, and it came back to them walking. He threw it out a third time, and it came back a little older, as a teenager, talking. They kept him, but pretty soon he did not want to stay with them, so he took off one night and went to his mother's people.

Everyone was amazed at how intelligent he was. He was also an exceptional hunter. He helped the people learn new ways to hunt the buffalo.

During this time, the crow was a white bird. He would see the Star-boy sneaking up on the bison, and holler to them in an animal way. Because he was an animal, this crow did not want the buffalo or deer to get hurt. That is why he would warn them. He would alert them that the hunters were coming to kill them, so the herd would all run away.

One day, the Star-boy told the people that he would catch the white crow so it would not warn the buffalo of their approach ever again. What he did was kill a young buffalo, butcher it, and make himself a disguise out of the hide so that he would look just like a buffalo. He put that covering on, and went in among the herd—a big herd. They did not even know he was there.

He was lying there making believe that he was a dead buffalo when all of a sudden that white crow landed nearby. The crow said: "You look like that falling star." Getting no response, he hopped on top of Star-boy's head, pecked at his eyes and nose, but got no response. Star-boy just lay there. The crow said: "You sure look like that falling star. You certainly look like that tricky person."

The crow no sooner had said this when Star-boy got hold of him by the leg. That crow was hollering and flapping its wings, but Star-boy held on tight and brought him back to the camp. There he told some people to build a fire.

Star-boy hung the crow above that fire so that the smoke turned the white crow to black. Then, he released him. After this, there were times when the crow would try to warn the herd about approaching hunters, but they would not listen to him because he was now black. The buffalo did not recognize him anymore. Ever since Star-boy did that to this bird, all crows have been black.

Black Elk was raised within a storytelling tradition that not only entertained listeners, but that also educated them. A story like that of Star Boy moved listeners to look beyond appearances and appreciate the mysteriously sacred nature of reality. This type of literature is often referred to as a "folktale," but that term suggests the story is fictional. Lakota listeners regarded such a tale's content otherwise. Outsiders tend to evaluate these tales as mythological, and do not regard a plot's miraculous happenings in quite the same way as would a person who was raised within a storytelling milieu. For Black Elk, however, these tales told of truths that were important to ponder.

Black Elk's experience of listening to stories like these was comparable to that of people within scriptural traditions. Within both Lakota culture and others possessing some type of sacred writ, people know they might have to look beyond a story's extraordinary details. Its teachings, or "truths," exist beyond the literal level.

A Star Boy Variant

Black Elk listened just as attentively to other sacred stories he learned in Europe, to what was taught during the ghost dance period, and to the priests when he conversed with them. He did not find it surprising to learn in biblical literature of another *wakan* child (i.e., Jesus) who was born to a human mother and heavenly father. This child was like other supernatural but real heroes his people had told of, who were born in a long-ago, different land. This Jesus was a special kind of "Star-boy" revelation.

Although he had come from the heavens, this new Star Boy was also a member of the human family, and his life mission (according to Christian theology) was to teach that "all are relatives." If the Lakota formerly regarded any nations that spoke a different language as enemies, this Star Boy's teaching was dramatically new. The now-common Lakota ceremonial utterance "all my relatives" is also sometimes stated as "all *are* relatives" (the universality of this latter rendering perhaps having its roots in the gospel story-revelation).

The Star Boy tale was a prelude to the gospel story among the Lakota. People like Black Elk could hear the Christian tale and integrate it into an already-established tradition of sacred stories. Both accounts told of how miraculous occurrences took place long ago that had significance for later generations.

The holy-man did not consider the Christian Star Boy as the founder of a new religion. Rather, the Christian figure added new revelation to what the people already believed. The ghost dance *wanikiye* would not displace but, rather, restore the fine ways of Lakota tradition. Buffalo Cow Woman carried the pipe as if carrying a child, and the sacred maiden, Mary, brought a child.

Black Elk and others of his generation learned from Christian missionaries that a kind of Star Boy was killed for teaching that all people are relatives. In hearing about this heroic figure, they found his example praiseworthy. The ghost dance version of Jesus as a Star Boy did not end at the tragedy of Wounded Knee.

When he first started working as a catechist, Black Elk often dealt with people who were schooled in ghost dance teachings. They would say they "knew" that "white people" killed Jesus long ago. Lucy said that her father found these people easy to instruct and prepare for baptism. Already accepting this "Son of God" as a needed *wanikiye,* they agreed that his was the path they wanted to walk. Many in Black Elk's generation looked at the Two Roads Map and appreciated the story it told. To walk its good red road seemed wise, and the holy-man accepted this teaching. In doing so, he neither felt the need to repudiate all of his pre-contact religious practice, nor did he cling to everything within that earlier practice. Rather, he simply broadened his religious worldview to include the conventional Catholic practice of his era.

Photographs of Black Elk throughout his life reveal the aging process at work on a man who stood less than six feet in height but who died a religious giant. While his thought, like his appearance, may have changed over time, Nicholas Black Elk remained very much the same, devout person throughout life as medicine man, missionary, and mystic holy-man of the Oglala. His memory continues to be honored each time one says "*mitak oyasin,*" or acknowledges that "all are relatives."

Chronology of Events Related to Nicholas William Black Elk

ca. 1865   Born to (Mary) Leggings Down and Black Elk the year "four Crows were killed" in the "month when chokecherries are ripe" on Little Powder River (in what is now present-day Wyoming); an Oglala Lakota in Big Road's Band; one brother, five sisters

ca. 1875   Boyhood vision

1876   Battle of the Greasy Grass (i.e., Little Bighorn)

1877   Under leadership of Big Road, flees to Canada after Crazy Horse's death

1880   Under the spiritual direction of Black Road

1881   Recognized as a medicine man

1886   Tours with Buffalo Bill's Wild West Show

1888   Leaves show to drift in England, Germany, and France, and works for "Mexican Joe" Shelley's Wild West Show

1889   Buffalo Bill pays for Black Elk's return to Pine Ridge
Black Elk's father dies
He serves as a store clerk

1890   Wounded Knee

1892   Marries Katie War Bonnet

1893   Son Never Showed Off (baptized "William") born

1895   Son Good Voice Star (baptized "John") born
"William" Never Showed Off dies

1899   Son Benjamin ("Ben") born
1901   Black Elk's wife, Katie, dies
1904   Baptized "Nicholas William Black Elk" on December 6
1905   Marries Anna Brings White (Brings White Horses), a
         widow with two daughters, Agatha and Mary
         Waterman
1907   Daughter, Lucy, born
1908   Catechist among the Arapaho
1909   Catechist among the Winnebago; son John Good Voice
         Star dies
1910   Catechist among Yankton
         Son Henry born (dies in infancy)
         Agatha and Mary also die
1912   Treated for tuberculosis at Hot Springs
1913   Catechist at Yankton reservation
1914   Son Nicholas, Jr., born
1915   Black Elk's mother dies
1916   Tubercular condition limits his activity to Pine Ridge
1921   Catechist at Oglala
1922   Chosen to declare on behalf of all catechists their
         corporate resolve never to commit a mortal sin
1931   John Neihardt's three-week visit with Black Elk
1932   Publication of *Black Elk Speaks*
1933   Injured in wagon accident
1936–45 Summer work with Duhamel pageant near Rapid City
1941   Wife Anna dies
1944   Interviewed again by John Neihardt
1947–48 Joseph Epes Brown visits
1948   Disabled by a broken hip
1950   Death of Nicholas Black Elk, August 17
1953   Publication of *The Sacred Pipe*
1959   Son Nicholas, Jr., dies
1961   *Black Elk Speaks* reprinted
1970   Countercultural interest in Black Elk's life
1971   *The Sacred Pipe* reprinted
1973   Son Benjamin dies
1978   Daughter, Lucy, dies

1980   Congress sets aside the "Black Elk Wilderness," an area of 13,426 acres within the Black Hills National Forest

1984   *The Sixth Grandfather* published

1993   *Black Elk: Holy Man of the Oglala* published

2000   *The Black Elk Reader* published

2008   The publishing contract for *Black Elk Speaks* is transferred from the University of Nebraska Press to SUNY Press

2009   *Nicholas Black Elk: Medicine Man, Missionary, Mystic* published

Notes

Chapter 1: Cultural Background

1. "Sioux" is the abbreviation of a longer Ottawa word that literally meant "little snakes." It also could have the more general meaning of "enemy." A less popular etymology is the word for a French coin "sous" (a coin of minimal worth).

2. Misconceptions related to "Sioux" social organization are addressed and clarified by DeMallie (2006b).

3. No longer a staple of Lakota cuisine, dog is at times served within the context of traditional religious rituals.

4. The magpie also won the race, so was given the right to go where it pleased year-round. The bird also received a rainbow-like color on its tail.

Chapter 2: Childhood

1. This naming of months was not unique to the Lakota but was, rather, widespread in Native North America. Compare Black Elk's Lakota month names with the Anishnabé system: January, moon of the big spirit; February, sucker or carp moon; March, moon of crust on snow; April, snowshoe breaking moon; May, moon of flowers; June, moon of strawberries; July, moon of raspberries; August, little huckleberry moon; September, big huckleberry moon; October, moon of trout; November, moon of whitefish; and December, little spirit moon.

2. *When People Lived Legends: American Indian Myths.* VHS. William Free Productions and Mythology Ltd. 1989.

3. According to Catholic bishop Martin Marty, Sitting Bull said that "DeSmet was . . . the only friend of the Indian" (Kreis 2007, 149).

4. A Lakota childhood included endurance tests that made little boys want to "be classed as a man." Reflecting on that distant period, Black Elk remarked, "The older boys taught us lots of endurances" (DeMallie

1984a, 149). While his observation no doubt characterizes the growing-up years for many children everywhere, bearing pain with courage (fortitude) was a Lakota virtue.

5. Literary references to Black Elk's boyhood vision are numerous. Philosopher John Neafsey drew a quote from it for the title of his book *A Sacred Voice Is Calling: Personal Vocation and Social Conscience* (2006).

6. Walter Holden Capps (1976) dedicated his collection of essays to Black Elk's vision while Eagle Walking Turtle's book is wholly indebted to it, viz., *Keepers of the Fire: Journey to the Tree of Life Based on Black Elk's Vision*. Time-Life books featured the vision in a special series of works dealing with mysticism and the occult (1989).

7. *The Sixth Grandfather* contains the transcript of Neihardt's stenographic notes, which served as the basis for the holy-man's biography. Because they most approximate Black Elk's testimony, these notes are most quoted throughout this text.

Chapter 4: Little Bighorn

1. A week earlier (June 17), General Crook had been in pursuit of these people and failed to position sentries around his camp. As a result, the Indians did to him what Custer later did to them—they attacked an unsuspecting foe. Both sides lost more than thirty combatants in this battle of the Rosebud.

2. Iron Hail was about eighteen years of age in 1876. Recalling how many people were in camp that day, he said: "Never before or since that time did my people gather in such great numbers. Our camp on the Greasy Grass . . . stretched four miles along the river—six great camp circles, each a half mile across, with thousands of Lakota fighting men and their families. In that long-ago time, none of my people knew more than a thousand numbers. . . . There was my own tribe, the Miniconjou. There were our cousins, the Hunkpapa, the Sans Arc, the Two Kettles, the Sihasapa . . . the Brulé, and the Oglala—all our Seven Council Fires. There were many of our eastern relatives, too—the Yankton and the Santee. And our kinsmen from the north were there—the Yanktonai and the Assiniboin. Our friends and allies the Cheyenne were there in force, and with them were smaller bands of Arapaho and Gros Ventre" (Miller 1971).

3. On November 4, 1791, the Miami (under Little Turtle) and Shawnee (under Blue Jacket) defeated Gen. Arthur St. Clair at the battle of the Wabash. The loss on this occasion of 623 soldiers represents the largest toll suffered by the American military in one engagement with Indian opponents. This conflict never won the popular or scholarly attention that Little Bighorn did.

4. The U.S. Army medical report is at odds with a purported Cheyenne oral tradition that claimed one of their people pierced Custer's eardrum with a sewing awl. This tradition received considerable attention in Evan Connell's book (1984) and later television movie (1991) *Son of the Morning Star*. The matter involves a disputed report that Custer fathered at least one child with a Cheyenne woman named Monahsetah (the ear piercing

via the awl related to Cheyenne wanting him to "hear better" in the next life, and to not behave as he did in this one).

5. Eli Ricker's interview of William Garnett stated that when Crazy Horse was scuffling, Lakota scouts raised their revolvers "to fire at Crazy Horse" but were restrained from doing so by the officer of the day (Jensen 2005, 70). Ricker also noted that some Lakota observers thought the bayoneting was intentional while others thought it clearly was not.

6. The U.S. Postal Service honored the memory of Crazy Horse by depicting a likeness of him on the thirteen-cent stamp, and Hollywood portrayed his life in two biographical films. Tourists can also visit the Crazy Horse Memorial, a stone monument in the Black Hills that is larger than Mount Rushmore.

Chapter 5: Medicine Man

1. Brown (2007, 102) said that Black Elk told him that at least 550 herbs were used in Lakota medicinal practice. He also mentioned that "parts of the bear" were "mixed in."

2. Similarities can be found here and elsewhere between Black Elk's real-life and vision experiences. John Neihardt's portrayal of Black Elk suggested the latter were prophetic of the former, but a less mystifying interpretation is that the inventory of Lakota ritual elements was limited. Similarly, similarities might also be the result of Black Elk retrospectively making a connection between the two.

3. Matthew 22:14.

4. The show's main features were a reenactment of Little Bighorn, attacks on stagecoaches, and cowboys showing their skills. Twenty-eight thousand people were in attendance opening night.

5. "All slicked up" was a colloquial expression for Ben and John Neihardt but not for Black Elk.

Chapter 6: Ghost Dance

1. "The Messiah Craze Spreading," *New York Times,* November 26,1890.

2. Just as Little Bighorn is better known than the battle of the Wabash, so Wounded Knee eclipses the little known yet intentional slaughter of nearly one hundred Delaware men, women, and children at Gnadenhutten, Ohio, in 1782. There, too, a mass grave marks the site of their interment.

3. This information is accessible in "Letters Received by the Commissioner of Indian Affairs," Ghost Dance Special Case 188, Doc. No. 1890–37076, Record Group 75, National Archives and Records Service.

4. John Slocum's "Shaker religion," founded in the 1880s around Puget Sound, is considered by its members also to represent Indian Christianity. With roots in traditional Northwest Coast religious practices, the group's rituals resemble Christian Pentecostalism's emphasis on being "slain in the Spirit." Indian Shakers will fall onto the floor quivering, in a

trance-like state, and sing. Healings, likewise, figure prominently within this practice.

5. This passage echoes the concluding lines of the Gospel of Matthew (28:18) wherein Jesus informs his followers that all power has been given to him by the Father.

6. Translations vary from one source to the next, but all say substantially the same thing.

7. This quotation is from a documentary, The Alcan Highway, aired by The History Channel Television Network's Modern Marvels series (New York: A&E Television Networks, 2003).

Chapter 7: Wounded Knee Legacy

1. Neihardt identifies this priest as Craft, but it is probably a composite of him and Father Jutz (who brokered peace with Two Strike and who led perhaps a thousand from the Stronghold to the agency). Jutz met with these people on December 3 and 5 while Craft did not arrive at Rosebud until December 10, and then only saw his first ghost dance on the 14th.

2. Craft's positive evaluation of the ghost dance appeared in Jesuit Father Emil Perrig's diary entry of December 15, 1890 (on file at Marquette University's Catholic Indian Archives).

3. Letter to the editor of Chicago Daily Inter-Ocean, signed "A Frontiersman," reprinted in New York Freeman's Journal, February 7, 1891.

4. Baum's solution of "the Indian problem" by way of extermination appears twice in the Aberdeen Saturday Pioneer. On December 20, 1890, in an editorial titled "Sitting Bull," he addressed the death of the Lakota leader, and on January 3, 1891, in a piece headlined "Wounded Knee," he commented on the event. Journalism of this period fomented fears that helped bring about military intervention, so Baum's writings could be read as proposals for a genocidal solution to Indian affairs. An alternative reading is that his remarks represent a satirical condemnation of the government's recurrent inability to negotiate a peaceful settlement. This latter interpretation seems fitting in light of a satirical comment he made that was pro-Indian (and which has become a cliché among historians of the American West). Claiming to quote "an eastern contemporary," Baum wrote that "when the whites win a fight, it is a victory, and when the Indians win it, it is a massacre" (January 3, 1891).

Chapter 8: Conversion

1. In The Sacred Pipe, Black Elk states that the sweat lodge door is oriented toward the east and not, as is also a Lakota custom, toward the west. Stolzman (1986) was told that Black Elk's placement of a door in the east reflected his heyoka background (i.e., saying or doing things that are contrary to the norm—which for many would be placing the door in the west). However, since the holy-man most often is quoted as beginning the pipe ritual in the west (which is customary), since The Sacred Pipe was intended as a primer on mainstream Lakota tradition, and since neither he nor his

translator-son made reference to this matter, his placement of a door in the east is not remarkable.

2. For Lindebner's obituary, a Jesuit wrote: "Towards the very end, he seemed to have forgotten every language but that of his apostolic labors and he spoke and prayed only in Lakota Sioux" (Weisenhorn 1923).

3. Personal communication.

Chapter 9: Catechist

1. Eugene Buechel came to the United States from Germany in 1900 and began work on the Rosebud Reservation in 1902. He served among the Lakota at Rosebud and the Pine Ridge Reservation until his death in 1954. Buechel took copious notes and numerous photographs (his ethnographic legacy on file in the archives of Marquette University). His presence on the reservations yielded a Lakota grammar, dictionary, and a collection of artifacts displayed in a museum on the Rosebud Reservation. Black Elk's generation was particularly fond of this priest who, according to a Pine Ridge elder, was "the only one who spoke the [Lakota] language perfect" (Steltenkamp 1993, 64).

2. An 1894 government survey stated that medicine men wielded much influence—especially at Pine Ridge.

3. Catholicism's religious nomenclature, along with Christianity's basic theme of humanity being "God's children," struck a resonant chord with the Lakota because the cultural tradition placed great importance on kin relations. This same tradition maintained the custom of killing people whose language was not Lakota! At the expense of one custom (killing enemies), Christianity's "new way of prayer" expanded the meaning of another custom, i.e., the value of creating kin relations.

4. Hinman noted that Red Feather "attends mass three times a week at the Holy Rosary Mission" (Hinman 1930, 4).

5. Brown's criticism of missionary presence is not unique to him. Perception and reality also came into conflict in the 1970s. An exposé of Boys Town revealed that the charity had amassed a fortune via its successful fund drives. Because of this revelation, benefactors of Holy Rosary Mission began to dwindle (as occurred with other charitable causes nationwide since people were led to believe that *all* charities were doing well). Indian activists accused the Jesuits of acquiring vast funds via donations to their Pine Ridge Indian school and then using the money to subsidize projects elsewhere. Jesuits responded that Holy Rosary struggled to remain in operation, that the order funded the school (and not vice versa), that all mission funds were used for maintenance of the mission alone, and that its coffers bore no resemblance to Boys Town's. Nonetheless, the spirit of critique was alive two decades later in a television series in which the lead actor struck the pose of a reflective sage and said that the only thing missionaries ever did was get rich off Indians.

6. Bishop Martin Marty's first assignment was to Standing Rock. In recalling his relationship with Sitting Bull, Marty wrote: "The principles of the Christian revelation as once explained to him by Fr. DeSmet, and later

by me, appealed to him . . . and during my last conversation [with him] he . . . requested that I build a church and a school there. I believe that, at the time, it was his intention to become a Christian himself, as had been the case with Spotted Tail. A premature death prevented both from executing their plans" (Kreis 2007, 149).

Chapter 10: The Two Roads Map

1. It is possible that Black Elk had some kind of exposure (if only by word of mouth) to a "two roads map" as a child since Father DeSmet devised one that became popular among missionaries in the mid-1800s (DeSmet 1843, 245–53; Hanley 1993, 94–96).

Chapter 11: Holy Humor

1. Black Elk's dog at the time of Neihardt's visit was named "Bob"— the holy-man apparently having a predilection for the names of domestic animals that begin with the letter *b*.
2. Black Elk's fellow heyoka, Kills Enemy, was sometimes called "One Side." Iktomi was sometimes depicted as wearing a hat tilted to one side—a behavior that Kills Enemy imitated.

Chapter 12: Neihardt's Visit

1. In *Black Elk Speaks*, this agent is referred to as "W. B." Courtright, while DeMallie cites the man's initials as "B.G." (DeMallie 1984a, 58).

Chapter 13: Sanctity

1. Shannon County in South Dakota (the Pine Ridge Reservation) has long held the unwanted distinction of being one of the poorest counties in the United States.
2. The sculptor's full name was John Gutzon de la Mothe Borglum.
3. Becoming "blood brothers" as described by Duhamel was folklore within mainstream America, but the ceremony he reported as "tribal adoption" does not exist.

Chapter 14: Sacred Pipes

1. Black Elk told Neihardt, "The moment I see anybody I want to get along with him and I always do get along with him" (DeMallie 1984a).
2. The posthumous publication of Brown's letters in 2007 shed light on the philosophy that guided his effort.
3. For the artist's account of Indian perspectives related to the pipestone area, see M. Mooney (1975).
4. Controlling weather is also part of the shamanic vocation among the Anishnabé (Landes 1971, 134).

5. For a fuller discussion of color words and culture, see Brent Berlin and Paul Kay (1969).

Chapter 15: Sacred Rites

1. Clipping a lock of hair from the deceased was also a custom outside Lakota culture during the Victorian period.

2. The 1970 film *A Man Called Horse* was the first in a trilogy of films that contributed to the real-life Indian revitalization movement. A box office success, it featured the romantic depiction of a sweat lodge ceremony and the realistic portrayal of a sun dance tradition. It was followed in 1976 by *Return of a Man Called Horse* and then in 1982 with *Triumphs of a Man Called Horse*.

3. Lucy's husband was for years a key official charged with acquiring the ceremonial cottonwood used for the tribal sun dance.

4. Reemergence of the sun dance ceremony in the late twentieth century did not take place in a vacuum. It was abetted by an American culture that introduced body piercing as a fashion that gained acceptance by the public at large.

5. When one prays in English, "all are relatives" or "all my relatives" might be heard.

Chapter 16: The Land of Many Lodges

1. For a description of Little Warrior's yuwipi ceremony, see Brown (2007, 120).

2. Powers reported that yuwipi practitioners do not permit the presence of "holy pictures" or rosaries within their ceremony: "No one wearing a (Catholic) medal would be permitted to stay in the meeting. One man had a rosary in his pocket but was afraid to say so. Soon something in the darkness picked him up and threw him out the window" (1982, 54).

3. One of Ben's daughters contributed to *Black Elk Lives* what she described as a childhood memory. On the book's dust jacket is her account of Black Elk and Father Sialm throwing one another's religious objects on the ground (and then reconciling after their debate).

4. Lucy's memory of the priest was a positive one. Reflecting on the loss of six children during their infancy, Lucy said, "I felt bad for a long time, but Father Zimmerman was right there to comfort me" (Steltenkamp 1993, 188n13).

5. Lucy was disheartened when hearing stories that some people told about Black Elk. She said that some people claim to speak with authority about her father, but they are not to be trusted. That the holy-man fathered children in Europe is one such story that her side of the family insisted was not true.

6. *Julius Caesar*, act 2, scene 2.

7. The Wounded Knee church later burned down, presumably by arson, but was rebuilt at a nearby site.

Chapter 17: Black Elk's Legacy

1. Sam Gill (personal communication).

2. Personal communication.

3. "Ethno-gnosticism" refers to the philosophy that claims only a given ethnic group (e.g., Indians) should conduct rituals associated with the group's culture or use implements (e.g., the pipe, sacred herbs, etc.) associated with its religion.

4. An example of Adario's purported wisdom was cited in McLuhan (1971, 50), a popular work of the 1970s that romanticized Native life. It was drawn from de Lahontan (1905, 533).

5. The length of a "generation" is more arbitrary than precise. While twenty years might be the conventional figure associated with a generation, the documentary on Wounded Knee (Kifaru Productions, *Wiping the Tears of Seven Generations*, 1992) quoted a Lakota teenager as saying it is "the time it takes for a girl to reach child-bearing age." Given the range between these figures, matching references in Black Elk's vision to a future "generation" is problematic. This is especially true if Black Elk material is misquoted—as was done in the film documentary titled *The New Indians* (The National Geographic Society, 1977). While he should have said "sixth," the film's narrator said that "now" was the era of "the fifth generation," and that this generation would bring about a rebirth of the nation (DeMallie 1984a, 265)! Assigning twelve or twenty years as the length of a generation, the fifth or sixth from Black Elk's birth could refer to people born in the 1920s, 1930s, 1960s, or 1980s! Since Neihardt's notes are ambiguous, reference might also be to the seventh generation. This disparity indicates that interpreting a vision is not an exact science.

6. Lucy Looks Twice (personal communication).

7. Matthew 16:26.

Chapter 18: Medicine Man, Missionary, Mystic

1. For a discussion of the various forms that conversion can take, see Starkloff (2002) and Boff (1985).

2. This newsletter, along with material from all the Catholic Indian missions in Native North America, is available at the archive library of Marquette University. This and translations of Black Elk's letters appear in appendix E of Steltenkamp 1987 (249–58). They are also on file at Marquette University's Catholic Indian Mission archives.

3. Lucy Looks Twice (personal communication). At this very same point in the tale, Black Elk also interrupted his narration to Neihardt, and said something different. Perhaps his meaning was the same but translated and transcribed inadequately (since his meaning is unclear). Neihardt's 1944 notes had him saying: "At this point usually in olden times when they are telling stories, the listeners are interested and say, 'That will be me!' So I had to say that" (DeMallie 1984a, 397).

Note on Sources

This biography is drawn from the primary works related to Black Elk. For Black Elk's perspective on his life, in his own words, see Raymond J. DeMallie's *The Sixth Grandfather* (1984). In this work, DeMallie provides transcripts of and extensive commentary on the holy-man's interviews with John Neihardt, which were the basis of Neihardt's *Black Elk Speaks* (Lincoln: University of Nebraska Press, 1961).

The works of Joseph Epes Brown, *The Sacred Pipe* (Norman: University of Oklahoma Press, 1953), and Michael F. Steltenkamp, *Black Elk: Holy Man of the Oglala* (1993), are the principal resources from which other Black Elk material lineally descends. Fuller coverage of what is addressed in this biography can be found in these works. An extensive bibliography is cited in Raymond A. Bucko's chapter titled "Sources and Suggestions for Further Study of Black Elk and Lakota Culture" in Clyde Holler's *The Black Elk Reader* (2000). *The Black Elk Reader* is a collection of fifteen articles related to the holy-man and his world. Additional coverage can be gleaned from previously unpublished letters written by Brown when he lived with Black Elk. These are available in the commemorative edition of Brown's *The Spiritual Legacy of the American Indian* (2007), at Scourmont Abbey in France, and in the article "Frithjof Schuon and the American Indian Spirit: Interview with Michael Fitzgerald" (Religioperennis.org, *Vincit Omnia*

Veritas III, no. 2, 2007, http://www.religioperennis.org/documents/
Fitzgerald/Indian.pdf).

Useful information on Lakota culture is available in DeMallie's
editing of James Walker's fieldwork. See Walker's *Lakota Belief and
Ritual* (1980), *Lakota Society* (1982), and *Lakota Myth* (1983).
Bucko's *The Lakota Ritual of the Sweat Lodge* (1998) is also key.
Supplemental to these works are William K. Powers's *Oglala Reli-
gion* (1975) and *Yuwipi* (1982). Articles found in the *Handbook of
North American Indians,* Vol. 13, *Plains* (2001) provide rich ethno-
graphic coverage of the Lakota.

Marquette University's Catholic Indian Mission Archives contains the diaries of missionaries such as Father Buechel, their
notes, and additional resources. The definitive lexicon for the language is Buechel's *Lakota-English Dictionary* (Pine Ridge, S.Dak.:
Holy Rosary Mission, 1970). Jesuit Paul Steinmetz blended years
of priestly experience at Pine Ridge with scholarly reflection in *Pipe,
Bible and Peyote among the Oglala Lakota* (Syracuse: Syracuse University Press, 1990) and *The Sacred Pipe: An Archetypal Theology*
(1998). A historical overview of pipes and their use can be found
in Jordan D. Paper's "The Sacred Pipe: The Historical Context of
Contemporary Pan-Indian Religion" (1998). Carl Starkloff's *A
Theology of the In-Between* (2002) addresses the process whereby a
dominated people resists or absorbs religious practice and thought.
See also Leonardo Boff's *Church: Charism and Power—Liberation
Theology and the Institutional Church* (1985).

For insight into contemporaries of the holy-man and his family, notable biographies of other Lakota leaders include Robert Larson's *Red Cloud: Warrior-Statesman of the Lakota Sioux* (1997),
Kingsley M. Bray's *Crazy Horse: A Lakota Life* (Norman: University of Oklahoma Press, 2006), and Mari Sandoz's *Crazy Horse: The
Strange Man of the Oglalas* (1961). Lakota historian Joseph Marshall's ethnohistory drawn from late twentieth-century interviews
is *The Journey of Crazy Horse: A Lakota History* (2004), while
Robert Utley's *The Lance and the Shield: The Life and Times of Sitting Bull* (1993) provides the authoritative text on this epic figure
of the late nineteenth century. The twentieth-century holy-man
Frank Fools Crow recounted his life story to Thomas E. Mails and

Dallas Chief Eagle, which they wrote in *Fools Crow* (1979) and Mails in *Fools Crow: Wisdom and Power* (1991).

General Lakota history, leading up to and including the time of Black Elk, is well-reported in George Hyde's *Red Cloud's Folk* (1937) and *A Sioux Chronicle* (1961); James C. Olson's *Red Cloud and the Sioux Problem* (1965); Catherine Price's *Oglala People 1841– 1879: A Political History* (1996); Robert Utley's *The Indian Frontier of the American West 1846–1890* (1985); Stanley Vestal's works *New Sources of Indian History, 1850–1891* (1934), *Warpath and Council Fire* (1948), and *Warpath: The True Story of the Fighting Sioux Told in a Biography of Chief White Bull* (1984); and Charles Allen's *From Fort Laramie to Wounded Knee: The West That Was* (1997). Appreciating the Lakota plight in confronting immense odds is Jeffrey Ostler's *The Plains Sioux and U.S. Colonialism from Lewis and Clark to Wounded Knee* (2002).

Moving to specific events in Lakota history covered in this work, controversial opinions reign in the numerous books and articles related to Custer and Little Bighorn. A primer on this vast material is Thom Hatch's *Custer and the Battle of the Little Bighorn: An Encyclopedia* (1997). A pictographic perspective from the viewpoint of Indians is available in Sandra L. Brizee-Brown's *For All to See: The Little Bighorn Battle in Plains Indian Art* (2003). As with writings on Wounded Knee, magazine articles from the period are often unreliable. The best official governmental sources can be found in J. D. Cameron's *Report of the Secretary of War; Being Part of the Message and Documents Communicated to the Two Houses of Congress at the Beginning of the Second Session of the Forty-Fourth Congress* (1876) and Robert Utley's works *The Reno Court of Inquiry: The Chicago Times Account* (Fort Collins, Colo.: Old Army Press, 1972) and *Cavalier in Buckskin* (Norman: University of Oklahoma Press, 1988).

For additional information on the specifics of the battle, an accessible evaluation of the archaeological evidence combined with Indian accounts can be found in Gregory F. Michno's *Lakota Noon: The Indian Narrative of Custer's Defeat* (1997). More technical material is available in Douglas D. Scott, Richard A. Fox, Jr., Melissa A. Connor, and Dick Harmon's *Archaeological Perspectives on the Battle of the Little Bighorn* (1989) and Richard Allan Fox, Jr.'s *Archaeology, History, and Custer's Last Battle* (1993). Popular topical studies include a medical examination of battle casualties in William Boyes's *Surgeon's Diary with the Custer Relief Column* (1974), a scout's insights into the battle and its participants in John S. Gray's *Custer's Last Campaign: Mitch Boyer and the Little Bighorn Reconstructed* (1991), and Custer's battle strategy in Larry Sklenar's *To Hell with Honor: Custer and the Little Bighorn* (2000).

Even more controversial than sources on Little Bighorn are the materials on Wounded Knee since much of the literature tends to blame either a vengeful U.S. Army or fanatical Indians for the violence. Anecdotal reports support one or the other contention, and novice readers may find it easy to adopt whatever position a given work argues. Testimony before Congress in 1976 was similar to the often-quoted condemnation of the army in James McGregor's *The Wounded Knee Massacre from the Viewpoint of the Sioux* (1940). For an opposing view, see Brig. Gen. E. D. Scott's "Wounded Knee, A Look at the Records" (1939). Scott vindicates the army, as does material in "Foreigners in Action at Wounded Knee," edited by Christer Lindberg (1990). An excellent discussion of who was present at Wounded Knee and the difficulty of establishing the number of casualties can be found in Richard E. Jensen's "Big Foot's Followers at Wounded Knee" (1990). A succinct summary of the varied interpretations is presented by Merrill J. Mattes in "The Enigma of Wounded Knee" (1960). Susan Forsyth relies on Lakota sources for making a case against the army in *Representing the Massacre of American Indians at Wounded Knee, 1890–2000* (Ceredigion, U.K.: Edwin Mellen Press, 2003).

General Miles spent many years protesting the U.S. Army's tactical blunders at Wounded Knee but later defended the Medal of Honor bestowals. See Peter R. DeMontravel's "General Nelson A. Miles and the Wounded Knee Controversy" (1986) and Carrie Kilman's article "Wounded Knee: A Campaign to Rescind Medals" (Tolerance.Org, A Web Project of the Southern Poverty Law Center, Feb. 3, 2005, http://www.tolerance.org/news/article_tol.jsp?id= 1355). As readable as Dee Brown's *Bury My Heart at Wounded Knee* (1970) is Rex Alan Smith's *Moon of Popping Trees* (1975). The government defends its actions in the *Sixtieth Annual Report of the Commissioner of Indian Affairs to the Secretary of the Interior, 1891* (1891). A centennial Lakota response to other histories of the event is the film *Wiping the Tears of Seven Generations* (1992).

The reprinted classic on the topic of Wounded Knee is James Mooney's *The Ghost-Dance Religion and the Sioux Outbreak of 1890* (1896). Robert Utley, *The Last Days of the Sioux Nation* (1963), drew upon correspondence in the National Archives (Record Group 48 of the Bureau of Indian Affairs; RG 48 of the Secretary of the Interior; RG 107 of the Secretary of War; RG 94 of the Adjutant General's Office; and RG 98 of the U.S. Army Commands). Marla and William Powers, in *Testimony to Wounded Knee: A Comprehensive Bibliography* (1994), expand on Utley with their annotated bibliography for the many evaluations of this tragic incident. A look at Father Francis M. Craft, the larger-than-life, controversial priest at Wounded Knee, sheds light on that event and other aspects of early reservation life in Thomas Foley's works *Father Francis M. Craft: Missionary to the Sioux* (2002) and *Hovering Eagle: The Standing Rock Journals and Wounded Knee Papers of Father Francis M. Craft, 1888–1890* (2009).

Survivors of Wounded Knee were interviewed some years after the event, and this material appears in "The Wounded Knee Interviews of Eli S. Ricker" (1981). An annotated version of this material is more readily available in Richard Jensen's *The Indian Interviews of Eli S. Ricker, 1903–1919* (2005), in which Lakota witnesses recall events of the late nineteenth century.

The occupation of Wounded Knee in 1973 received extensive news coverage that was addressed provocatively by Terri Schultz in "Bamboozle Me Not at Wounded Knee" (1973). Different perspectives on the event are available in Bill Zimmerman's *Airlift to Wounded Knee* (1975) and Stanley Lyman's *Wounded Knee, 1973: A Personal Account* (1991). Reliable scholarly reportage can be found in Jay Furlong's University of Oklahoma master's thesis, *The Occupation of Wounded Knee, 1973* (1980).

A bibliographical sampling of Black Elk material outside the scope of this text includes biblical scholar Norman Perrin. He drew upon Black Elk for purposes of cross-cultural comparison vis-à-vis New Testament writers (1974). William Willoya and Vinson Brown cited Neihardt's holy-man as an example of universal religious thought (Healdsburg, Calif.: Naturegraph Company, 1962). Sculptor Marshall M. Fredericks honored Black Elk with a bronze monument.

Artists F. W. Thomsen and Paul Goble did the same as Leanin' Tree and Sunrise Publications. All produced greeting cards, sold nationwide, featuring quotations from Black Elk. Poet Donna Duesel de la Torriente produced *Bay Is the Land (To Black Elk)* (1982), a work claiming to be "an astounding proclamation made by a white American about the long-awaited dream of Black Elk."

Psychologist Carl Jung cited Black Elk when addressing a theory of archetypes in *Mysterium Coniunctionis* (1970, 206), while novelist Thomas Berger's *Little Big Man* (1964) featured the character Old Lodge Skins, whose name is a pseudonym for Black Elk. Christopher Sergel's 1979 play was titled *Black Elk Speaks*, and David Humphreys Miller's two books, *Custer's Fall* (1957) and *Ghost Dance* (1959), cited Black Elk as an important consultant. William Least Heat-Moon's 1982 best seller *Blue Highways* noted Neihardt's *Black Elk Speaks* as an inspirational touchstone for the author.

Reference List

Akwesasne Notes. 1974. *Voices from Wounded Knee: The People Are Standing Up.* Via Rooseveltown, N.Y.: Mohawk Nation, Akwesasne Notes.

Allen, Charles. 1997. *From Fort Laramie to Wounded Knee: The West That Was.* Lincoln: University of Nebraska Press.

Ames, C. W. 1933. "Winners of the West." *Official Bulletin National Indian War Veterans U.S.A.* (St. Joseph Missouri) 10 (3).

Anderson, Gary Clayton. 1984. *Kinsmen of Another Kind: Dakota-White Relations in the Upper Mississippi Valley, 1650–1862.* Lincoln: University of Nebraska Press.

Archambault, Marie Therese. 1998. *A Retreat With Black Elk: Living in the Sacred Hoop.* Cincinnati: St. Anthony Messenger Press.

Archambault, Marie Therese, Mark G. Thiel, and Christopher Vecsey, eds. 2003. *The Crossing of Two Roads: Being Catholic and Native in the United States.* Maryknoll, N.Y.: Orbis.

Arnold, Philip P. 1999. "Black Elk and Book Culture." In *Journal of the American Academy of Religion* 67 (1). Cary, N.C.: Oxford University Press.

Baraga, R. R. Bishop. 1973. *A Dictionary of the Otchipwe Language.* Minneapolis: Ross and Haines.

Bataille, Gretchen M. 1984. "Black Elk—New World Prophet." In *A Sender of Words: Essays in Memory of John G. Neihardt,* ed. Vine Deloria, Jr. Salt Lake City: Howe Brothers.

Berger, Thomas. 1964. *Little Big Man.* New York: Dial Press.

Berkhofer, Robert F. 1978. *The White Man's Indian: Images of the American Indian from Columbus to the Present.* New York: Alfred A. Knopf.

Berlin, Brent and Paul Kay. 1969. *Basic Color Terms: Their Universality and Evolution.* Berkeley: University of California Press.

Black Elk DeSersa, Esther; Olivia Black Elk Pourier; Aaron DeSersa, Jr.; Hilda Neihardt Petri; and Lori Utecht. 2000. *Black Elk Lives: Conversations with the Black Elk Family.* Lincoln: University of Nebraska Press.

Boff, Leonardo. 1985. *Church: Charism and Power—Liberation Theology and the Institutional Church.* New York: Crossroad.

Boyes, William, ed. 1974. *Surgeon's Diary with the Custer Relief Column.* Washington, D.C.: South Capitol Press.

Brizee-Brown, Sandra. 2003. *For All to See: The Little Bighorn Battle in Plains Indian Art.* Spokane, Wash.: Arthur H. Clark.

Brown, Dee. 1970. *Bury My Heart at Wounded Knee: An Indian History of the American West.* New York: Holt, Rinehart and Winston.

Brown, Joseph Epes. 1947a. Letter to Father Gall. September 4. Scourmont Abbey, France.

———. 1947b. Letter to Father Gall. October 1. Scourmont Abbey, France.

———. 1947c. Letter to Father Gall. November 12. Scourmont Abbey, France.

———. 1953/1971/1989. *The Sacred Pipe: Black Elk's Account of the Seven Rites of the Oglala Sioux.* Repr. Baltimore: Penguin Books.

———. 1979. "The Wisdom of the Contrary." *Parabola* 4 (1): 54–65.

———. 2007. *The Spiritual Legacy of the American Indian.* Bloomington, Indiana: World Wisdom.

Bucko, Raymond A. 1998. *The Lakota Ritual of the Sweat Lodge.* Lincoln: University of Nebraska Press.

———. 2006. "Night Thoughts and Night Sweats, Ethnohistory and Ethnohumor: The Quaker Shaker Meets the Lakota Sweat Lodge." In *New Perspectives on Native North America: Cultures, Histories, and Representations,* eds. P. Turner Strong and S. A. Kan, 162–84. Lincoln: University of Nebraska Press.

Buechel, Eugene. Diary and notes. Marquette University Catholic Indian Mission Archives.

———. 1970. *A Dictionary of the Teton Dakota Sioux Language.* Ed. Paul Manhart. Pine Ridge, S.Dak.: Red Cloud Indian School.

Cameron, J. D. (Secretary of War). 1876. *Report of the Secretary of War; Being Part of the Message and Documents Communicated to the Two Houses of Congress at the Beginning of the Second Session of the Forty-Fourth Congress.* Washington, D.C.: Government Printing Office.

Capps, Walter Holden, ed. 1976. *Seeing with a Native Eye: Essays on Native American Religion.* New York: Harper Forum Books.

Castaneda, Carlos. 1968. *The Teachings of Don Juan: A Yaqui Way of Knowledge.* New York: Ballantine Books.

Chittenden, Hiram M. and Alfred T. Richardson. 1905. *Life, Letters, and Travels of Father Pierre Jean DeSmet, S.J.* 4 vols. New York: Burrows.

Clark, R. A. 1976. *The Killing of Chief Crazy Horse.* Lincoln: University of Nebraska.

Collier, John. 1947. *Indians of the Americas.* New York: Mentor Books.

Costello, Damien. 2005. *Black Elk: Colonialism and Lakota Catholicism.* Maryknoll, N.Y.: Orbis.

Craft, Francis M. 1890. "Catholic Indian Missions in America (Written for *The Irish World* by a Catholic Indian Missionary)." *The Irish World and American Industrial Liberator,* August 16, 1890.

Dary, David A. 1974. *The Buffalo Book.* New York: Avon.

De Lahontan, Baron. 1703. *Old Canada: New Voyages to North America.* Introduction, notes, and index by Reuben Gold Thwaites. Chicago: A. C. McClurg.

Deloria, Ella. n.d. "Teton Myths." Franz Boas Collections. American Philosophical Society, Philadelphia.

———. 1944. *Speaking of Indians.* New York: Friendship Press.

Deloria, Vine. 1969. *Custer Died for Your Sins.* New York: Macmillan.

———. 1973. *God Is Red.* New York: Grosset and Dunlap.

———, ed. 1984. *A Sender of Words: Essays in Memory of John G. Neihardt.* Salt Lake City: Howe Brothers.

———. 1995. *Red Earth, White Lies: Native Americans and the Myth of Scientific Fact.* New York: Scribner.

———. 2000. Foreword to *Black Elk Speaks,* by John Neihardt. Lincoln: University of Nebraska Press.

———. 2002. *Evolution, Creationism, and Other Modern Myths: A Critical Inquiry.* Golden, Colo.: Fulcrum.

DeMallie, Raymond J. 1978. "Pine Ridge Economy: Cultural and Historical Perspectives," in *American Indian Economic Development,* ed. Sam Stanley, 237–312. The Hague: Mouton.

———. 1979. "Change in American Indian Kinship Systems, The Dakota," in *Currents in Anthropology: Essays in Honor of Sol Tax,* ed. Robert Hinshaw, The Hague: Mouton.

———. 1984a. *The Sixth Grandfather: Black Elk's Teachings Given to John G. Neihardt.* Lincoln: University of Nebraska Press.

———. 1984b. "John G. Neihardt's Lakota Legacy," in *A Sender of Words.* Salt Lake City: Howe Brothers.

———. 2001. *Plains.* Vol 13 of *The Handbook of North American Indians.* Washington, D.C.: Smithsonian Institution.

———. 2006a. Review Essay: "Black Elk in the Twenty-First Century." *Ethnohistory* 53 (3): 595–601.

———. 2006b. "The Sioux at the Time of European Contact: An Ethnohistorical Problem." In *New Perspectives on Native North America: Cultures, Histories, and Representations,* eds. Sergei Kan and Pauline Turner Strong, 239–60. Lincoln: University of Nebraska.

DeMontravel, Peter R. 1986. "General Nelson A. Miles and the Wounded Knee Controversy." *Arizona and the West* 28 (Spring): 23–44.

DeSmet, Pierre-Jean. 1843. *Letters and Sketches: with a Narrative of a Year's Residence among the Indian Tribes of the Rocky Mountains.* Philadelphia: M. Fithian.

Dombrowski, Daniel A. 1987. "Black Elk's Platonism." *North Dakota Quarterly* 55 (1): 56–64.

Dorsey, James Owens. 1894. "A Study of Siouan Cults." 11th Annual Report of the Bureau of American Ethnology, 351–544.

———. 1897. "Siouan Sociology." 15th Annual Report of the Bureau of American Ethnology, 205–44.

Duesel de la Torriente, Donna. 1982. *Bay Is the Land (To Black Elk).* Reseda, Calif.: Mojave Books.

Dunsmore, Roger. 1977. "Nickolaus Black Elk: Holy Man in History." *Kuksu: Journal of Backcountry Writing*, no. 6:4–29.

Duratschek, Sister Mary Claudia. 1947. *Crusading Along Sioux Trails: A History of the Catholic Indian Missions of South Dakota*. Yankton, S.Dak.: Grail.

Eggan, Fred R. 1966. *The American Indian: Perspectives for the Study of Social Change*. Chicago: Aldine Press.

Erdoes, Richard and John (Fire) Lame Deer. 1972. *Lame Deer Seeker of Visions: The Life of a Sioux Medicine Man*. New York: Simon and Schuster.

Faulkner, Virginia and Frederick C. Luebke, eds. 1982. *Vision and Refuge: Essays on the Literature of the Great Plains*. Lincoln: University of Nebraska Press.

Feraca, Stephen E. 1961. "The Yuwipi Cult of the Oglala and Sicangu Teton Sioux." *Plains Anthropologist* 6:155–63.

Foley, Thomas. 2002. *Father Francis M. Craft: Missionary to The Sioux*. Lincoln: University of Nebraska Press.

———. 2009. *Hovering Eagle: The Standing Rock Journals and Wounded Knee Papers of Father Francis M. Craft, 1888–1890*. Norman: University of Oklahoma Press.

Forsyth, Susan. 2003. *Representing the Massacre of American Indians at Wounded Knee, 1890–2000*. Lewiston, N.Y.: Edwin Mellen Press.

Fox, Jr., Richard Allan. 1993. *Archaeology, History, and Custer's Last Battle*. Norman: University of Oklahoma Press.

Furlong, Jay. 1980. "The Occupation of Wounded Knee." Master's thesis, University of Oklahoma.

Gallagher, H. D. 1890. *Report of the Commissioner of Indian Affairs*. Washington, D.C.: Government Printing Office.

Gessner, Robert. 1931. *Massacre*. New York: Cape and Smith.

Gill, Sam D. 1982. *Native American Religions: An Introduction*. Belmont, Calif.: Wadsworth.

Goddard, Ives. 1984. "The Study of Native North American Ethnonym." In *Native American Naming Systems*, ed. Elizabeth Tooker. New York: American Ethnological Society Proceedings 1980.

Goll, Louis J. 1940. *Jesuit Missions Among the Sioux*. St. Francis, S.Dak.: St. Francis Mission.

Gray, John S. 1976. *Centennial Campaign: The Sioux War of 1876*. Fort Collins, Colo.: Old Army Press.

———. 1991. *Custer's Last Campaign: Mitch Boyer and the Little Bighorn Reconstructed*. Lincoln: University of Nebraska Press.

Greene, Carol. 1990. *Black Elk: A Man with a Vision*. Chicago: Children's Press.

Grim, John A. 1983. *The Shaman*. Norman: University of Oklahoma Press.

Grimes, Richard S. "The Making of a Sioux Legend: The Historiography of Crazy Horse." *South Dakota History* 30 (Fall 2000): 277–302.

Grobsmith, Elizabeth S. 1981. *Lakota of the Rosebud: A Contemporary Ethnography.* New York: Holt, Rinehart and Winston.

Hanley, Philip M. 1993. *History of the Catholic Ladder.* Fairfield, Wash.: Ye Galleon.

Hassrick, Royal B. 1964. *The Sioux: Life and Customs of a Warrior Society.* Norman: University of Oklahoma Press.

Hatch, Thom, ed. 1997. *Custer and the Battle of the Little Bighorn: An Encyclopedia.* Jefferson, N.C.: McFarland.

Hebard, Grace Raymond, and E. A. Brininstool. 1922. *The Bozeman Trail: Historical Accounts of the Blazing of the Overland Route into the Northwest, and the Fights with Red Cloud's Warriors.* 2 vols. Cleveland: Arthur H. Clark.

Hill, Ruth Beebe. 1979. *Hanta Yo.* New York: Doubleday.

Hinman, Eleanor. 1930. "Oglala Sources on the Life of Crazy Horse." *Nebraska History* 57, no. 1 (Spring 1976).

Holler, Clyde. 1984. "Black Elk's Relationship to Christianity." *American Indian Quarterly* Winter:37–49.

———. 1995. *Black Elk's Religion: The Sun Dance and Lakota Catholicism.* Syracuse: Syracuse University Press.

———, ed. 2000. *The Black Elk Reader.* Syracuse: Syracuse University Press.

Holloway, Brian. 2003. *Interpreting the Legacy: John Neihardt and Black Elk Speaks.* Boulder: University Press of Colorado.

Hoxie, Frederick, ed. 1996. *Encyclopedia of North American Indians.* New York: Houghton Mifflin.

Hyde, George E. 1937. *Red Cloud's Folk: A History of the Oglala Sioux Indians.* Norman: University of Oklahoma Press.

———. 1961. *Spotted Tail's Folk: A History of the Brulé Sioux.* Norman: University of Oklahoma Press.

———. 1961. *A Sioux Chronicle.* Norman: University of Oklahoma Press.

Indian Sentinel. 1923–50. Washington, D.C.: Bureau of Catholic Indian Missions.

Jaschik, Scott. 2008. "Fight over a Beloved (and Lucrative) Book." *Daily News Update,* Insidehighered.com. July 15.

Jeltz, Patsy. 1991. "Elder Pete Catches Shares Wisdom." *Lakota Times,* July 24, sec. B1, 11(4).

Jensen, Richard E. 1990. "Big Foot's Followers at Wounded Knee." *Nebraska History* 71 (4): 194–212.

———, ed. 2005. *The Indian Interviews of Eli S. Ricker, 1903–1919.* Lincoln: University of Nebraska Press.

Jesuit Fathers of St. Francis Mission. 1927. *Lakota Wocekiye na Olowan Wowapi (Sioux Indian Prayer and Hymn Book).* St. Louis: Central Bureau of the Catholic Central Verein of America.

Johnson, Willard. 1988. "Contemporary Native American Prophecy in Historical Perspective." *Journal of the American Academy of Religion* LXIV (3): 575–612.

Jung, C. G. 1970. *Mysterium Conjunctionis*. Princeton, N.J.: Princeton University Press.

Kelley, William Fitch. 1971. *Pine Ridge 1890: An Eyewitness Account of the Events Surrounding the Fighting at Wounded Knee*. San Francisco: Pierre Bovis.

Kemnitzer, Luis. 1969. "Yuwipi." *Pine Ridge Research Bulletin* 10:26–33.

———. 1970. "Cultural Provenience of Objects Used in Yuwipi: A Modern Teton Dakota Healing Ritual." *Ethnos* 35:40–75.

Kifaru Productions. 1992. *Wiping the Tears of Seven Generations*. VHS. Directed by Fidel Moreno and Gary Rhine. Los Angeles: Kifaru Productions.

Killoren, John. 1994. *"Come Blackrobe": DeSmet and the Indian Tragedy*. Norman: University of Oklahoma Press.

Kreis, Karl Markus, ed. 2007 *Lakotas, Black Robes, and Holy Women: German Reports from the Indian Missions in South Dakota, 1886–1900*. Lincoln: University of Nebraska Press.

Krupat, Arnold. 1981. "The Indian Autobiography: Origins, Type and Function." *American Literature* 53 (1): 22–42.

Lame Deer, John. 1972. *Lame Deer, Seeker of Visions*. New York: Simon and Schuster.

Landes, Ruth. 1971. *The Ojibwa Woman*. New York: W. W. Norton.

Larson, Robert W. 1997. *Red Cloud: Warrior-Statesman of the Lakota Sioux*. Norman: University of Oklahoma Press.

Lehmer, Donald J. 1977. *Selected Writings of Donald J. Lehmer*. Reprints in Anthropology, vol. 3. Lincoln, Neb.: J and L Reprint Company.

Lewis, Dale. 1993. *Duhamel: From Ox Cart to Television*. Chamberlain, S.Dak.: Register-Lakota Printing.

Lewis, Thomas. 1970. "Notes on the Heyoka: The Teton Dakota 'Contrary' Cult." *Pine Ridge Research Bulletin*, no. 11:7–19.

Lincoln, Kenneth. 1983. "Native American Literatures." In *Smoothing the Ground: Essays on Native American Oral Literature*, ed. Brian Swann. Berkeley: University of California Press.

Lindberg, Christer, ed. 1990. "Foreigners in Action at Wounded Knee." *Nebraska History* 71 (4): 170–81.

Linton, Ralph. 1943. "Nativistic Movements." *American Anthropologist* XLV:230–40.

Lowie, Robert. 1948. *Social Organization*. New York: Rinehart.

———. 1963. *Indians of the Plains*. Garden City, N.Y.: The Natural History Press.

Lyman, Stanley. 1991. *Wounded Knee, 1973: A Personal Account*. Lincoln: University of Nebraska Press.

Lyon, William, and Wallace Black Elk. 1990. *Black Elk*. New York: Harper and Row.

MacGregor, Gordon. 1946. *Warriors Without Weapons: A Study of the Society and Personality Development of the Pine Ridge Sioux*. Chicago: University of Chicago Press.

Mails, Thomas E., and Dallas Chief Eagle. 1979. *Fools Crow*. Garden City, N.Y.: Doubleday.

———. 1991. *Fools Crow: Wisdom and Power*. Tulsa, Okla.: Council Oak Books.

Marshall, Joseph. 2004. *The Journey of Crazy Horse: A Lakota History*. New York: Viking Press.

Martin, Joel W. 2005. "Before and Beyond the Sioux Ghost Dance: Native American Prophetic Movements and the Study of Religion." In *War in Heaven / Heaven on Earth: Theories of the Apocalyptic*, ed. Stephen D. O'Leary and Glen S. McGhee, 95–118. Millennium and Society Series, vol. 2. London: Equinox Publishing.

Mattes, Merrill J. 1960. "The Enigma of Wounded Knee." *Plains Anthropologist* 5:1–11.

McCluskey, Sally. 1972. "Black Elk Speaks and So Does John Neihardt." *Western American Literature* 6:231–42.

McGaa, Ed. 2005. *Crazy Horse and Chief Red Cloud*. Minneapolis: Four Directions.

McGregor, James H. 1940. *The Wounded Knee Massacre from the Viewpoint of the Sioux*. Baltimore: Wirth Brothers.

McLuhan, T. C. 1971. *Touch the Earth: A Self-Portrait of Indian Existence*. New York: Promontory Press.

Means, Russell. 1995. *Where White Men Fear to Tread*. New York: St. Martin's Press.

Mekeel, Scudder. 1935. *The Economy of a Modern Teton Dakota Community*. New Haven, Conn.: Yale University Press.

Michno, Gregory F. 1997. *Lakota Noon: The Indian Narrative of Custer's Defeat*. Missoula, Mont.: Mountain Press.

Miller, David Humphreys. 1957. *Custer's Fall*. New York: Bantam.

———. 1959. *Ghost Dance*. New York: Duell, Sloan, and Pearce.

———. 1971. "Echoes of the Little Bighorn." *American Heritage Magazine* 22 (4).

Milligan, Edward A. 1973. *Wounded Knee 1973 and The Fort Laramie Treaty of 1868*. Bottineau, N.Dak.: Bottineau Courant Print.

Mirsky, Jeannette. 1966. "The Dakota." In *Cooperation and Competition Among Primitive Peoples*, ed. Margaret Mead, 382–427. Revised edition. Boston: Beacon.

Momaday, N. Scott. 1984. "To Save a Great Vision." In *A Sender of Words*, 30–38. Salt Lake City: Howe Brothers.

Moon, William Least Heat. 1982. *Blue Highways: A Journey Into America*. New York: Fawcett Crest.

Mooney, James. 1896. *The Ghost-Dance Religion and the Sioux Outbreak of 1890*. 14th Annual Report of the Bureau of American Ethnology, pt. 2. Washington, D.C.: Smithsonian Institution.

Mooney, Michael Macdonald, ed. 1975. *George Catlin Letters and Notes on the North American Indians*. New York: Clarkson N. Potter.

Murray, Mary. 1993. "The Little Green Lie: How a Hoax Becomes a Best-Selling Book When It Serves a Special Cause." *Reader's Digest* 43, no. 855 (July): 100–104.

Neafsey, John. 2006. *A Sacred Voice Is Calling: Personal Vocation and Social Conscience*. Maryknoll, N.Y.: Orbis.

Neihardt, Hilda. 1995. *Black Elk and Flaming Rainbow: Personal Memories of the Lakota Holy Man and John Neihardt*. Lincoln: University of Nebraska Press.

Neihardt, Hilda and Lori Utrecht, eds. 2000. *Black Elk Lives: Conversations with the Black Elk Family*. Lincoln: University of Nebraska Press.

Neihardt, John G. 1932/1961/1972. *Black Elk Speaks: Being the Life Story of a Holy Man of the Oglala Sioux*. Repr. New York: Pocket.

———. 1972. "The Book That Would Not Die." *Western American Literature* 7 (Winter): 227–30.

———. 2008. *Black Elk Speaks: Being the Life Story of a Holy Man of the Oglala Sioux*. Ed. Raymond J. DeMallie. Albany: State University of New York Press.

Newcomb, W. W. 1950. "A Re-Examination of the Causes of Plains Warfare." *American Anthropologist* 52 (July-September): 317–30.

Nichols, William. 1983. "Black Elk's Truth." In *Smoothing the Ground: Essays on Native American Oral Literature*, ed. Brian Swann, 334–43. Berkeley: University of California Press.

Nurge, Ethel, ed. 1970. *The Modern Sioux: Social Systems and Reservation Culture*. Lincoln: University of Nebraska Press.

Obrian, Lynn Woods. 1973. *Plains Indian Autobiographies*. Boise State College Western Writers Series 10. Boise, Idaho: Boise State College.

Oliver, Symmes C. 1962. *Ecology and Cultural Continuity as Contributing Factors in the Social Organization of the Plains Indians*. University of California Publications in American Archeology and Ethnology, vol. 48, no. 1. Berkeley: University of Califonia Press.

Olson, James C. 1965. *Red Cloud and the Sioux Problem*. Lincoln: University of Nebraska Press.

Ostler, Jeffrey. 2002. *The Plains Sioux and U. S. Colonialism from Lewis and Clark to Wounded Knee*. Cambridge: Cambridge University Press.

Overholt, Thomas W. 1978. "Short Bull, Black Elk, Sword, and the 'Meaning' of the Ghost Dance." *Religion*: 171–95.

Paper, Jordan D. 1998. "The Sacred Pipe: The Historical Context of Contemporary Pan-Indian Religion." *Journal of the American Academy of Religion* LVI (4): 643–65.

Paul, R. Eli, ed. 1998. *The Nebraska Indian Wars Reader 1865–1867*. Lincoln: University of Nebraska Press.

Perrig, Emil. n.d. *Diary*. Marquette University Catholic Indian Mission Archives.

Perrin, Norman. 1974. *The New Testament: An Introduction*. New York: Harcourt Brace Jovanovich.

Perry, Ted. 1991. *Brother Eagle, Sister Sky: A Message from Chief Seattle*. New York: Dial Books.

Pipes, Nellie B. 1936. "The Protestant Ladder." *Oregon Historical Quarterly* 37 (September): 237–40.

Powell, Peter. 1969. *Sweet Medicine*. Norman: University of Oklahoma Press.

Powers, Marla and William Powers. 1994. *Testimony to Wounded Knee: A Comprehensive Bibliography*. Kendall Park, N.J.: Lakota Books.

Powers, William K. 1975. *Oglala Religion*. Lincoln: University of Nebraska Press.

———. 1982. *Yuwipi: Vision and Experience in Oglala Ritual*. Lincoln: University of Nebraska Press.

———. 1990. "When Black Elk Speaks, Everybody Listens." In *Religion in Native North America*, ed. C. Vecsey. Moscow: University of Idaho Press.

Price, Catherine. 1996. *Oglala People, 1841–1879: A Political History*. Lincoln: University of Nebraska Press.

Prucha, Francis Paul. 1988. "Two Roads to Conversion: Protestant and Catholic Missionaries in the Pacific Northwest." *Pacific Northwest Quarterly* 79 (4): 130–37.

Radin, Paul. 1971. *The Trickster: A Study in American Indian Mythology*. New York: Schocken Books.

Rice, Julian. 1991. *Black Elk's Story: Distinguishing Its Lakota Purpose*. Albuquerque: University of New Mexico Press.

Ricker, Eli. 1981. "The Wounded Knee Interviews of Eli S. Ricker." *Nebraska History* 62, No. 2.

Riggs, Stephen. 1893/1977. *Dakota Grammar, Texts and Ethnography*. Repr. Marvin, S. Dak: Blue Cloud Abbey.

Riley, Paul D., ed. 1976. "Oglala Sources on the Life of Crazy Horse: Interviews given to Eleanor H. Hinman." *Nebraska History* 57, no. 1 (Spring 1976): 1–51.

Rothenberg, David. 1996. "Will the Real Chief Seattle Please Speak Up? An Interview with Ted Perry." *Terra Nova: Nature & Culture* 1, no. 1.

Ruby, Robert H. 1970. "Yuwipi, Ancient Rite of the Sioux." *Pine Ridge Research Bulletin* 11: 20–30.

Sandoz, Mari. 1942. *Crazy Horse: The Strange Man of the Oglalas, A Biography*. Lincoln: University of Nebraska Press.

———. 1942/1961. *Crazy Horse: The Strange Man of the Oglalas*. Repr. Lincoln: University of Nebraska Press.

Santino, Jack. 1982. "Sucking Doctor." *The Journal of American Folklore* 95, no. 378 (October-December): 501–504.

Schultz, Terri. 1973. "Bamboozle Me Not at Wounded Knee." *Harper's* 246, no. 1477 (June): 46–48, 53–56.

Schwarz, O. Douglas. 1981. *Plains Indian Theology: As Expressed in Myth and Ritual and in the Ethics of the Culture*. Ann Arbor, Mich.: University Microfilms International.

Scott, Brig. Gen. E. D., Ret. 1939. "Wounded Knee: A Look at the Records." In *Winners of the West* vol. 16, no. 5. St. Joseph, Mo.: May 1939.

Scott, Douglas D.; Richard A. Fox, Jr.; Melissa A. Connor; and Dick Harmon. 1989. *Archaeological Perspectives on the Battle of the Little Bighorn*. Norman: University of Oklahoma Press.

Shaw, Dennis E. 1981. *Wounded Knee: Myth Versus Reality*. Coral Gables, Fla.: University of Miami.

Sialm, Placidus. 1923. *Indian Sentinel* 3:85.

Sklenar, Larry. 2000. *To Hell with Honor: Custer and the Little Bighorn*. Norman: University of Oklahoma Press.

Smith, Rex Alan. 1975. *Moon of Popping Trees.* New York: Reader's Digest.

Spier, Leslie. 1921. "The Sun Dance of the Plains Indians: Its Develop-ment and Diffusion." *Anthropological Papers of the American Museum of Natural History* 16:451–527.

Starkloff, Carl. 2002. *A Theology of the In-Between.* Milwaukee: Marquette University Press.

Stedman, Raymond William. 1982. *Shadows of the Indian: Stereotypes in American Culture.* Norman: University of Oklahoma Press.

Steinmetz, Paul B. 1990. *Pipe, Bible and Peyote among the Oglala Lakota.* Knoxville: University of Tennessee Press.

———. 1998. *The Sacred Pipe: An Archetypal Theology.* Syracuse: Syracuse University Press.

Steltenkamp, Michael F. 1987. *No More Screech Owl: Lakota Adaptation to Change as Profiled in the Life of Black Elk.* Dissertation, Michigan State University.

———. 1993. *Black Elk: Holy Man of the Oglala.* Norman: University of Oklahoma Press.

———. 2003. "Black Elk and Ecology." In *Encyclopedia of World Environmental History.* Great Barrington, Mass.: Berkshire Publishing Group.

———. 2005. "American Indian Religion." In *Encyclopedia of Anthropology.* Thousand Oaks, Calif.: Sage Publications.

Stolzman, William. 1986. *The Pipe and Christ.* Chamberlain, S.Dak.: St. Joseph's Indian School.

Sullivan, Lawrence E. 1994. "Song and Dance: Native American Religions and American History," In *Religion and American Culture* 4 (Summer): 255–73.

Tedlock, Dennis, and Barbara Tedlock. 1975. *Teachings from the American Earth: Indian Religion and Philosophy.* New York: Liveright.

Terrell, John Upton. 1979. *The Arrow and the Cross: A History of the American Indian and the Missionaries.* Santa Barbara, Calif.: Capra Press.

Thiel, Mark. 1998. "Catholic Sodalities among the Sioux, 1882–1910." *U.S. Catholic Historian* 16 (2): 56–77.

U.S. Dept. of Interior. 1891. *Sixtieth Annual Report of the Commissioner of Indian Affairs to the Secretary of the Interior.* Washington, D.C.: GPO.

Utley, Robert M. 1963. *The Last Days of the Sioux Nation.* New Haven, Conn.: Yale University Press.

———. 1985. *The Indian Frontier of the American West 1846–1890.* Albuquerque: University of New Mexico Press.

———. 1988/2001. *Cavalier in Buckskin.* Revised edition. Norman: University of Oklahoma Press.

———. 1993. *The Lance and the Shield: The Life and Times of Sitting Bull.* New York: Henry Holt.

——— and Kenneth Hammer. 1972. *The Reno Court of Inquiry: The Chicago Times Account,* Vol. 1, and *Men with Custer: Biographies of the 7th Calvary, 25 June, 1876.* Fort Collins, Colo.: Old Army Press.

Vestal, Stanley. 1932. *Sitting Bull: Champion of the Sioux.* Boston: Houghton Mifflin.

————. 1934. *New Sources of Indian History, 1850–1891*. Norman: University of Oklahoma Press.

————. 1948. *Warpath and Council Fire*. New York: Random House.

————. 1984. *Warpath: The True Story of the Fighting Sioux Told in a Biography of Chief White Bull*. Ed. Raymond J. DeMallie. Lincoln: University of Nebraska Press

Walker, James R. 1917. "The Sun Dance and Other Ceremonies of the Oglala Division of the Teton Dakota." In *Anthropological Papers* 16, pt. 2, 50–221. New York: American Museum of Natural History.

————. 1980. *Lakota Belief and Ritual*. Eds. Raymond J. DeMallie and Elaine A. Jahner. Lincoln: University of Nebraska Press.

————. 1982. *Lakota Society*. Edited by Raymond J. DeMallie. Lincoln: University of Nebraska Press.

————. 1983. *Lakota Myth*. Ed. Elaine A. Jahner. Lincoln: University of Nebraska Press.

Walking Turtle, Eagle. 1989. *Keepers of the Fire: Journey to the Tree of Life Based on Black Elk's Vision*. Santa Fe, N.M.: Bear and Company.

Wallace, Anthony F. C. 1969. *The Death and Rebirth of the Seneca*. New York: Knopf.

Warren, Louis S. 2005. *Buffalo Bill's America: William Cody and the Wild West Show*. New York: Knopf.

Waters, Frank. 1984. "Neihardt and the Vision of Black Elk." In *A Sender of Words: Essays in Memory of John G. Neihardt*, ed. Vine Deloria, Jr. Salt Lake City: Howe Brothers.

Weisenhorn, C. M. 1923. "Obituary for Revered Joseph Lindebner." *The Indian Sentinel*, 84–86. Marquette University Catholic Indian Mission Archive.

West, G. A. 1934. "Tobacco, Pipes, and Smoking Customs of the American Indians." *Public Museum of the City of Milwaukee*, bulletin 17.

Westropp, Henry. n.d.(a). *Missionary Life among the Sioux*. Marquette University Catholic Indian Mission Archives.

————. n.d.(b). *In the Land of the Wigwam*. Marquette University Catholic Indian Mission Archives.

Willoya, William, and Vinson Brown. 1962. *Warriors of the Rainbow: Strange and Prophetic Dreams of the Indian Peoples*. Healdsburg, Calif.: Naturegraph Company.

Wilson, Roy I. 1996. *The Catholic Ladder and Native American Legends—A Comparative Study*. Bremerton, Wash.: Roy I. Wilson.

Wissler, Clark. 1912. "Societies and Ceremonial Associations in the Oglala Division of the Teton-Dakota." In *Anthropological Papers* II, pt. I, 1–99. New York: American Museum of Natural History.

Zimmerly, David. 1969. "On Being an Ascetic: Personal Document of a Sioux Medicine Man." *Pine Ridge Research Bulletin*, no. 10:46–69.

Zimmerman, Bill. 1975. *Airlift to Wounded Knee*. Chicago: Swallow Press.

Index

Lone Goose, John, 93, 102, *125*, 158, 199, 201
Looking Horse, Arvol, 82, 84, 169, 171
Looking Horse, Stanley, 6, 84
Looks Twice, George, 6, 108, 152, 154, 174, 176
Looks Twice, Lucy, 124, *215*, 246
Looks Twice, Regina, 205
Lowanpi, 51–52

Mackenzie, Col. Ranald S., 39
Manderson, S.Dak., 90, 93, 97, 102, 151, *193,* 195; Black Elk as catechist in, 97, 204; Black Elk's daily life in, 110, 156, 158; Black Elk's grave near, 202, *203*; Joseph Epes Brown's visit to, 161
Martinez, Richard Black Elk, Jr., 83
McGaa, Ed, 62, 93–94
Mdewakantonwan, 6
Mechling, Henry, 37
Miniconju, 6
Monahsetah, 240n4
Monotheism, 11

Navajo. *See* Diné
Neihardt, Enid, 23, 118, 122, 140, 144
Neihardt, Hilda, 140–45, 214–15, 221
Neihardt, John, 3, 45, 57, 73, 97, 138, 144, 146, 177, 200, 214, 218, 236, 241n2 (chap. 5), 247
Never Showed Off, 83, 90, 235

Oglala, S.Dak., 66, 108, *150*, 156, *157*, 236
Oglala (Sioux), 6, 17, 39–40, 45, 50, 65, 165, 233, 235, 240n2

Oneiromancy (divination via dreams or visions), 85
One Side. *See* Kills Enemy
Oohenunpa, 6
Order of the Pipe, 162, 172, 209
Ornithomancy (divination via birds), 85

Pawnee, 19, 22, 24, 165
Pejuta wichasha (medicine man), 45
Petroglyphs, 85
Pictographs, 14
Pikes Peak, 31
Pine Ridge, S.Dak., *66*, 70
Pine Ridge Indian school, 243n5
Pine Ridge Reservation, 6, 18, 39–40, *42*, 54, *66*, 138, 169, 243n2 (chap. 9); Black Elk and, 15–16, 50, 58, 204–205, 235–36; Jesuits' activities on, 61, 70, 83, 92, 94, 103–104, 109, 112–13, 115, *143*, 227, 243n1, 248; life on, 18, 57, 59, 62, 80, 83, 129, 148, 218, 244n1 (chap. 13). *See also* Ghost dance; Sun dance; Wounded Knee, S.Dak.
Pipe, 46, *48*, *101*, 152, 162–64, 166–68, 215–16, 246n3 (chap. 17), 248; Black Elk and, 3, 26–27, 46, 85–86, 110, 151, 160–61, 195, 225, 242n1 (chap. 8); Christianity and, 192, 225, 227–28, 233; keeper of, 82, 84, 169, 171; ritual and prayer use of, 51, 165–68, 174–75, 179, 182, *193*, 197; stories about, 111, 163–64, 166, 169, 171. *See also* Order of the Pipe
Pipestone, 167, 171, 244n3 (chap. 14)